The 20th Maine—
To Little Round Top and Beyond

The 20th Maine—
To Little Round Top and Beyond
A Personal Account & History of a Famous Union Regiment in the American Civil War

Army Life: A Private's Reminiscences of the Civil War

Theodore Gerrish

With a Brief History of the 20th Maine Regiment in the American Civil War

H. S Melcher

The 20th Maine—
To Little Round Top and Beyond
A Personal Account & History of a Famous Union Regiment in the American Civil War
Army Life: A Private's Reminiscences of the Civil War
by Theodore Gerrish
With a Brief History of the 20th Maine Regiment in the American Civil War
by H. S. Melcher

FIRST EDITION

Leonaur is an imprint of Oakpast Ltd
Copyright in this form © 2018 Oakpast Ltd

ISBN: 978-1-78282-718-4 (hardcover)
ISBN: 978-1-78282-719-1 (softcover)

http://www.leonaur.com

Publisher's Notes

The views expressed in this book are not necessarily those of the publisher.

Contents

Preface	7
Introduction	9
The Battle of Antietam	21
From Antietam to Fredericksburgh	33
Three Visits to Fredericksburgh	47
Hooker's Campaign—Chancellorsville	55
Gettysburgh	64
From Gettysburgh to Rappahannock Station	77
Rappahannock Station	86
The Wilderness Campaign Opened	99
The Battle of Spottsylvania	110
North Anna to the James	119
In Front of Petersburgh	127
The Weldon Railroad	135
Five Forks	143
The Surrender	157
Appomattox to Richmond	170
Marching through Richmond	182
"The Great Review"	188

Homeward Bound	193
Hospital Life	198
Pen Pictures of Union Generals	206
A Review	223
A Brief History of the 20th Maine Regiment in the American Civil War	239

Preface

Many volumes have been published in regard to the late Civil War in America. By these the nation is made familiar with the movements of our armies, and the results of those great military campaigns. These volumes have been written by civilians and officers of high rank, and consequently the story of the private soldier's life has never been told.

That life was made up of events and surrounded by circumstances of the most interesting character. Not interesting to the soldier alone, but of interest to his friends, and all who enjoy the fruits of victory purchased by his sacrifices and patriotism.

It was to supply, to a limited extent, this want so universally felt that the writer consented to furnish "The Sketches of Army Life" for the *Republican Journal*, of Belfast, Maine. The officers had spoken, but this was a voice from the ranks.

Through the kindness of its editors, the *Republican Journal* bore the utterances of that voice to thousands of American homes. Other papers generally assisted in the movement, and gave the "Army Sketches" a circulation that the writer never dared to hope they would obtain. From the homes thus reached, there has come forth such a demand to have the Sketches preserved in permanent book form, that the writer has consented (by thoroughly revising the articles already published, and adding much new material), to make the book of which this is a preface.

It is the author's design to give a truthful representation of the marches, skirmishes, battles, associations, and camp-life of the private soldier.

While the narration of events here recorded will furnish a complete history of the Twentieth Maine Regiment, it will also be a volume designed to interest all classes of readers.

Hoping that its contents will inspire each reader to an intense loyalty for the country, and a greater affection for its defenders, this book is submitted to the public.

T. G.

Bucksport, Mr., April, 1882.

Introduction

The story of "The War" has been often told, but such were the magnitude and immense extent of the operations that every successive account of it adds much of interest that had been left untold. But while this book is no exception to the rule just stated, it has one peculiarity not found in any of its predecessors. Hitherto the story has been told only by officers, or parties not actually engaged in the military operations, but, so far as I know, this work of Mr. Gerrish is the first from the standpoint of a private.

Considering the vast number represented by the author, it is quite remarkable that, within the *twenty-one* years since the war began, (as at 1882), no one has, heretofore, attempted to tell the experiences, sufferings, and noble exploits of the men who enabled their officers to gain an undying fame, and whose patient endurance, unwavering patriotism, and unsurpassed heroism, saved the union of the States, demonstrated that the United States is a Nation, and not a mere Confederation, and rescued from its sorest peril the Republican form of government.

Those of us who were in active life during the war, by personal communication with the soldiers themselves, learned much of what came within their own experience and observation; but the generation which is coming upon the stage, and those which shall succeed it, must depend upon what has been or shall hereafter be, written. But the time within which these reminiscences can be written by those actually engaged in the war, is rapidly passing away; and the day will soon come when all which has not been made a matter of record, will be found only in the domain of uncertain and unreliable tradition.

The number, too, of those who knew the events of the war, as they transpired, is already less than that of those who must learn those events from history. We, who have the daily bulletins of that terrible struggle indelibly stamped upon our memory, can scarcely realise that even now more than one-half of the community have learned the details of the contest, as we learned those of the War for Independence.

While, therefore, all will find much that is new, and very interesting in this book, it is an acquisition exceedingly valuable to those who must look to such a source in order to learn the routine of a private soldier's life in the War for the Union.

Of the manner in which the author has performed his undertaking, it is not necessary to speak, for, whoever begins to read this work, will certainly not be content to lay it aside until the last page has been completed. But one circumstance connected with its preparation should not be overlooked. It was first mainly published as newspaper articles, and read by hundreds who participated in the events of which Mr. Gerrish has written. If there were any material errors in his statements, they would have been challenged at once by those properly jealous of their own reputation, and that of their officers; so that the author has really had the advantage of the criticism and indorsement of very many, equally as familiar with the facts as himself, and, on that account, his history may be taken as unusually reliable.

In another respect, for the purposes of this work, the author is fortunate. His regiment participated in so many of the great and decisive battles of the war that his field of experience was quite exceptionally broad.

I most earnestly commend this book to all who love their country, and have faith in a government by the people. While we will not detract one iota from the credit due to the great heroes of the war, who led our forces to final victory, we must not allow the brightness of their glory to eclipse that of our soldiers, who were ready to follow wherever they were ready to lead. That we have a country, and a government by the people, is due to both officers and soldiers. Let each have their meed of honour , and let their glorious deeds, without discrimination, be kept alive in the memory of their countrymen.

J. H. D.

CHAPTER 1

From Portland to Antietam

On the second day of September, 1862, a regiment of uniformed, but unarmed men, marched from Camp Mason, near Portland, Maine, to the railroad depot, from whence it proceeded by rail to the city of Boston. The regiment numbered "a thousand strong"; and as we marched through the streets of Boston, the sidewalks were covered with people who were eagerly looking at us.

"Where are you from?" bawled an old salt, who stood leaning his back against a lamp-post.

"From the land of spruce gum and buckwheat cakes," loudly responded a brawny backwoodsman fresh from the forests of his native state.

A loud laugh rang out from the crowd. One gentleman swung his hat, and proposed "three cheers for the old pine tree state." *Hip, Hip, Hip*, and a rousing volley of cheers ran along the street for many blocks.

We soon reached the wharf, where we embarked on board the United States transport *Merrimac*, a huge steamer of some three thousand tons burden.

We quickly proceeded to our new quarters "between decks," but had barely time to stow our knapsacks away in the rough berths, before we heard the sound of music and loud cheering upon the wharf, and the 36th Massachusetts regiment, a gallant body of men, twelve hundred in number, marched on board the *Merrimac*, and shared our quarters with us. The two regiments numbered some twenty-two hundred men, and occupied every square foot of space that the steamer afforded.

Preparations for departure were rapidly made, and soon the plank was pulled in, the lines were cast off, the great engine began to throb with a fiery life, and we glided down the harbour,—I knew not where.

With moist eyes and heart strangely throbbing, I stood in the midst of the crowd pressed against the steamer's rail, and looked toward the city, now fast receding from view, but I saw not the countless domes and spires of the great town. I did not notice the great business blocks, and heard not the rush and hum of traffic that fell upon my ear like the music of a distant waterfall. I was thinking of home, and seemed to see, like a picture on the distant sky, a great forest, a small clearing on the hillside, a little cottage home, and a circle of dear friends as they stood with tearful eyes to say goodbye, as I thus took my departure from home.

A sickly sensation came creeping over my heart, a great lump gathered in my throat, but just at that moment a sergeant, who sat on a huge pile of baggage, began to read a paper just purchased in the city: it contained the condensed telegrams of the preceding week—telegrams that had sent mourning and consternation all through the loyal North. "McClellan's retreat from the peninsula." "Major General John Pope assumes command of the Army." "His headquarters are to be in the saddle." "A terrible battle has been fought on the old battlefield of Bull Run, in which the union forces have been disastrously defeated." "A terrific encounter between the right of Pope's army and Stonewall Jackson at Chantilly, twenty miles from Washington, in which the Unionists are defeated." "General Stevens and brave Phil Kearney are among the slain." "Lee still advancing." "Washington is in danger." "The war to be transferred to Northern soil."

It would be difficult to describe the emotions of the listeners as the news was read. Each man comprehended the fearful situation of the army we were hastening to reinforce, but not a cheek grew pale at the thought of coming danger. A son of the old Bay State, from the hills of Berkshire, climbed up in the rigging of the steamer, and proposed three cheers for "Old Abe," and at least a thousand voices responded to the call. Three more were given for "Little Mac," and then three times three for the "red, white and blue." Men cheered until they were hoarse, the air was filled with flying caps, and the good steamer *Merrimac* shook from truck to keel.

Thus, began my first voyage on the ocean. Everything was new and exciting to my boyish vision. The steamer's space between the decks had been filled with rude bunks, and in these we were stowed until every square foot of space was occupied, and then hundreds of men were obliged to remain on deck.

The first night was one of unnecessary alarm. Several rumours were flying. "The lower hold was said to be filled with powder and munitions of war." "And one of the Confederate privateers had been seen cruising in the vicinity within a short time. If we came in contact with her, we would be all captured, or blown to the stars, by their firing a shell into the magazine under our feet." "Some wondered what we should do if the steamer should strike a rock and go down." And thus, the hours pass. The steamer rolls in the swells of the ocean. There is the sickening and monotonous roar of the machinery, and the tramp of feet overhead.

The atmosphere grows thick and foul; sleep refuses to come to my relief. At last all is still save the rumble of machinery, and the ceaseless lapping of the waves against the sides of the steamer. All are sleeping; suddenly there is a fearful crash. Fifty voices shout, "She has struck a rock." Fifteen hundred men spring from their bunks, and with a mighty surge rush for the gangway. The panic is terrible. Men push, swear, crowd, strike, and rush on, but to our horror the hatch is fastened down, and there is no escape. Then someone for the first time discovers the cause of the alarm. The boat has not struck a rock, but a long tier of bunks insecurely fastened had fallen upon the tiers below, and all had gone down together.

A general laugh followed this discovery, all declaring they had not been frightened in the least, and we returned to our bunks wiser, and I trust, braver men.

Thus, days and nights passed; the weather was beautiful, and the ocean like a sea of glass.

Through the days, we studied the ever-changing sea, dotted here and there with snowy sails. We watched the flight of birds, and the playing of the fish. At night we would dream of home and friends, or of the scenes of carnage toward which we were hastening.

On the morning of September 7th our steamer drew up to a wharf at the city of Alexandria, Virginia, seven miles below Washington. At this point the Potomac River is a mile in width, and in the harbour of Alexandria the largest vessels can find anchorage.

The landing was made; our regiment disembarked, and stood for the first time upon the "sacred soil of Virginia."

Alexandria was a city of some twelve thousand inhabitants at the breaking out of the rebellion, and was of considerable commercial importance. At this time, it was occupied by a small Union force, and the "stars and stripes" were flying from the public buildings.

We were to remain for a short time, and went forth to make our first visit in a southern town. Darkies, dirt, and demoralization met the eye in every direction. There were but few places of interest to visit, and the most important of these was the "Marshall House," from which Colonel E. E. Ellsworth removed the secession flag, on the 24th of May, 1861. We climbed to the roof from which the flag had been torn, and stood on the stairs where the blood of the brave patriotic colonel had mingled with that of the disloyal Jackson.

As we stood on the stairs, and cut small pieces of wood from them, to bear away as relics, we seemed to draw an inspiration from the memory of the brilliant soldier who there gave his life to his country.

At night we encamped near the city. Our blankets were unrolled, and we lay down to rest. The air was balmy and scented with southern mint. We were weary with the excitement of the past week. God's stars twinkled overhead as if to assure us of his protection and care. Amidst the falling shower of mist and dew we passed our first night on southern soil. At sunrise the reveille awakens us. Breakfast is eaten, and we embark on board a small steamer for Washington.

The capital of our country in 1862 but little resembled the capital of today.

It was the Sabbath day when we entered the city. At home it had been a day of quiet rest, or delightful worship. How strange the surroundings seemed to us as we marched along the streets of Washington. Everyone was excited over the recent defeats suffered by the Union army, and the rapid advance of General Lee.

The demoralisation of war was visible on every hand. Regiments of soldiers filled the squares, squadrons of cavalry were dashing along the streets, batteries of artillery, long lines of baggage wagons and ambulances were seen in every direction. We marched to the United States Arsenal, and here everything reminded us of war. Great piles of dismounted cannon looked grimly upon us, stacks of shot and shells surrounded them, the building itself was packed with fire-arms of every design, from the old flintlock musket of continental times to the rifle of most modern make. Our regiment was equipped and armed with Enfield rifles, and there was dealt out to each man forty rounds of ammunition. We now supposed we were model soldiers, and marched proudly away. That night we encamped near the arsenal grounds.

On the 8th we were assigned to Butterfield's famous "Light Brigade," "Morrell's Division," "Porter's Corps," and late in the afternoon of that day, by the way of the long bridge, we marched to Fort Craig, on Arlington heights, to join our brigade.

It was a most ludicrous march. We had never been drilled, and we felt that our reputation was at stake. An untrained drum corps furnished us with music; each musician kept different time, and each man in the regiment took a different step. Old soldiers sneered; the people laughed and cheered; we marched, ran, walked, galloped, and stood still, in our vain endeavours to keep step. We reached our destination, joined the brigade, stacked our arms, and encamped for the night. We were now a part of the Army of the Potomac.

The brigade which we joined was composed of the Twelfth, Seventeenth, and Forty-Fourth New York regiments, Eighty-Third Pennsylvania, and Sixteenth Michigan. The army was greatly excited over the grave situation of affairs, and the soldiers were loudly rejoicing over the fact that General McClellan had again assumed command of the army.

We remained on Arlington heights until the 12th of September. The situation daily grew more serious and alarming. General Lee had advanced with great rapidity, and with a large army had crossed the Potomac River, and invaded Maryland, while another portion of his army, under the irresistible "Stonewall Jackson," was reported as moving swiftly toward Harper's Ferry, intending to crush and capture the Union forces of Colonel Miles, and then rejoin the main rebel army under General Lee.

On the 11th we received marching orders. A large portion of the army had already entered Maryland, and were in hot pursuit of the rebels.

Through the entire night we could hear the steady tramp of infantry, the rattle of cavalry, and the heavy rumble of passing artillery.

Early on the morning of the 12th our brigade was in line; it was a novel scene upon which we looked; long lines of blue-clad men were moving down over the slopes of Arlington, and crossing the Potomac River to Maryland. Bands were playing, bugles blowing, drums beating, and orderlies were dashing to and fro. Division and brigade commanders, surrounded by their staff officers, were moving rapidly to the front. Our brigade soon formed a part of the moving column, and we thus entered upon a forced march through "Maryland, my Maryland."

At first the novelty of our situation made marching very easy work, but this was soon worn off, and we began to learn the hardships of a forced march.

No pen can describe the sufferings and physical exhaustion of an army of infantry marching thirty miles a day, and no one but a person who has looked upon such a scene can form an opinion of the true situation.

My readers have all read the brilliant description given by army correspondents, of soldiers upon a march, and you have looked upon pictures portraying the same, and have admired the well-dressed lines and solid columns. Each man perfectly erect, and measuring just so many inches of space at each step, his gun carried in just such a position, his knapsack and all equipments in perfect order; and you have wondered how drill and discipline could transform men into machines in so short a space of time. These things look well on paper, but they only exist in the brilliant imaginations of the correspondents.

Let us for a brief time review a passing column of the "old Army of the Potomac."

On the crest of this hill we will have an excellent outlook, and obtain a fine view of the situation. The sun is swiftly rolling down the western skies, mantled in fleecy clouds of gold. The vision can extend for miles in almost any direction, far out over broad acres of meadow land, up over rich, fertile hillsides, over great farms, magnificent orchards, bending low under their burden of golden fruit, and far in the distance you see Frederick City, said to be in possession of the enemy, and beyond are the heights of South Mountain, where he is intrenched.

The advanced lines of the two armies are now near each other, and there must soon be a battle.

Now we will look at these passing troops: first comes a few squadrons of cavalry, brave, sunburned fellows, covered with dust. Each man sits so naturally upon his horse that we almost imagine them to be one. The distinctive colour of the cavalry is yellow. You will notice yellow stripes and straps upon the uniforms of officers and men.

Each man is armed with a sabre, a breech-loading carbine, and a huge navy revolver. Men and horses are worn and jaded by long marches, but are dashing at a rapid pace to the front. They are followed by a battery of artillery. The artillery colour is red, red straps and chevrons upon uniforms of dark blue. There are six twelve-pound guns in this battery. Each gun is drawn by three pairs of horses, and after each gun follows a caisson, or ammunition wagon, also drawn by six horses. Each pair of horses, upon both guns and caissons, have a single rider.

All battery officers, both commissioned and non-commissioned, are mounted on horses, while the men ride on guns and caissons as best they can. The commands of the commanding officer are all given to a bugler by his side, who repeats them in bugle calls. Each man and horse understands the orders thus given. When a battery goes into action, it advances at a sharp gallop, as nearly as possible to the position it wishes to occupy. The horses are then detached, and sent a short distance to the rear. The men seize the guns, and run them into position. Each caisson is stationed directly in rear of its respective gun. Every man has his position, and knows what work he has to do.

They are so well trained that in the most terrible battle there is no confusion, and everything moves like clockwork.

Closely following the artillery is a column of infantry, winding like a great serpent along the dusty road.

I will tell you something of the organisation of the Army of the Potomac, and how you can easily distinguish one portion from another. The army is divided into what is known as "Army corps," each corps being numbered, and having a peculiar mark or badge by which it can be recognised from either of the others.

The badge worn by the First corps was a globe. This badge was placed upon the corps flags, and also upon the uniforms of the men. The badge of the Second corps was a clover leaf, or club, that of the Third corps, a diamond, that of the Fifth corps, a Maltese cross, that of the Sixth, a Roman cross, and that of the Eleventh, a crescent. Each corps was divided into three divisions. These are distinguished from each other by the colour of the corps badges just referred to. The first division is always red, the second white, and the third blue.

Each division is usually divided into three brigades, and these are distinguished from each other by the colour of their corps badge and the border of the brigade flag. The latter is a small triangular flag. The corps badge with division colour will be in the centre. If it is the first brigade, one side of the flag will have a heavy border of opposite colour from the flag; if the second brigade, two sides will be thus distinguished; if the third, then the border will extend around the entire flag. Each brigade is composed of an indefinite number of regiments, depending much upon their size.

Look at that passing brigade; it has a small white, triangular flag, a dark blue border extending around the entire field, and a red Maltese cross in the centre. It is the Third brigade, First division, Fifth Army corps; in the army it is known as "Butterfield's Light Brigade," so called in honour of its late gallant Commander General Daniel Butterfield, who at this time is filling another position.

That short, thick, gray-haired man in a colonel's uniform, at the head of the brigade, is Colonel Stockton, of the Sixteenth Michigan regiment, now in command of the brigade.

That first regiment in *Zouave* uniform is the Forty-Fourth New York, or the "Ellsworth Avengers," as they are called. The next is the Twelfth and the Seventeenth New York regiments, and then the Eighty-Third Pennsylvania, followed by the Sixteenth Michigan.

These regiments were all mustered in 1861, and are fresh from the Peninsula Campaign, and the more recent battlefields of Bull Run and Chantilly, where they have displayed great bravery. The last regiment in the brigade is clad in a new uniform, and has nearly as many men as the rest of the brigade. It is a new regiment, and this is their first march. The colonel is every inch a soldier. He is well mounted, and his eyes flash as brightly as the silver eagles upon his shoulders. That is Colonel Adelbert Ames, a graduate of West Point, and a soldier of the regular army. He was severely wounded at the first battle of Bull Run, is a native of Rockland, Maine, and one of the bravest officers in the army. That tall, scholarly officer, riding by his side, is Lieut.-Colonel Chamberlain, late a professor in Bowdoin College: he has made an excellent record in the field of letters, and will undoubtedly distinguish himself upon the field of battle. The regiment is the Twentieth Maine, and the same whose movements I traced in the beginning of this chapter.

But look at the men of which the brigade is composed, and they are only a sample of the entire army. It is "rout-step and arms-at-will." The ranks are in disorder, and nearly every file is broken. Every man is for himself; many have fallen out from the ranks; others are footsore and exhausted,—see them limp and reel and stagger as they endeavour to keep up with their regiments. These men were doubtless acquainted with fatigue before they entered the army, but this fearful strain in marching so many miles, in heavy marching order, for successive days, is too much for them. Brave, strong men fall fainting by the wayside, and will never see their regiment again. They had hoped to defend the old flag on the battlefield, but that is denied them; and far back in the rear of regiments and brigades, is a legion of stragglers, sick, lame, discouraged, cowardly, all grades mixed in hopeless confusion. Some are there from choice; they enlisted only to secure the pay and bounty, and are determined to "play out" as quickly as possible; others, brave and ambitious, are mortified because they are not able to keep up with their regiments.

The first class will crawl into the barns and out buildings to sleep and escape the "Provost Guard." The others will tramp painfully on all night long, and perhaps overtake their comrades in season to begin with them tomorrow's march. It is a sad spectacle upon which we look, and all caused by the sinfulness of men.

But still the steel-crowned column surges on like the links of an endless chain.

Our line of march lay through the beautiful town of Frederick City, that nestled like a gem amidst the great green hills of Maryland. Its inhabitants had passed through a strange experience that week, as the two hostile armies had passed back and forth through its streets.

"Stonewall Jackson," fresh from the siege of Harper's Ferry, was reported to have been in command of the forces that held the town for several days. The larger portion of its inhabitants, like so many of the people of Maryland, were undoubtedly in active sympathy with the rebels, and rejoiced in all the successes they had gained. They had given the rebels a warm reception, but when we passed through in pursuit, they met us with frowns and angry words. A few were loyal to the union, and among these was old "Barbara Frietchie," whose Spartan-like devotion to the old flag has been immortalised in the poem of Whittier.

There was intense excitement in the town, as we passed through; our troops had driven the enemy from his intrenched position at South Mountain, after a desperate struggle, and had followed him through Sharpsburg to Antietam Creek. The houses and yards were filled with the wounded soldiers who had been brought back from the field of battle. We were pushed rapidly forward, and soon began to see signs of the late conflict. A large squad of prisoners were being brought to the rear—the first live "Johnnies" our regiment ever saw; they were tall, lank, slouchy looking fellows, clad in dirty gray uniforms. We soon came to where the earth had been torn up by exploding shells, buildings were riddled through and through with shot, and trees were torn and twisted by flying missiles. We marched over the field and up the hillside where our troops had fought. Every house and barn was filled with the wounded; fresh mounds on the hillsides told where our dead had been buried.

Surgeons with sleeves rolled to their shoulders were busily at work around the rough tables they had hastily constructed. Legs and arms were being amputated by dozens, and the poor groaning victims upon the tables were objects of pity. Squads of men were at work caring for the wounded and burying the amputated limbs. It all looked cruel and bloody to us who were unused to such scenes.

I climbed the stone wall and rude breastwork where the enemy had made their final stand, and from which our men had driven them. There had not been time to bury the rebel dead. They lay, as they had fallen, in groups of half-a-dozen each, and single bodies scattered here and there, all through the scattering oak growth that crowned the crest of the hill. They were of all ages, and looked grim and ghastly. Old men with silvered hair, strong men in the prime of manhood, beardless boys, whose smooth, youthful, upturned faces looked strangely innocent, although sealed in a bloody death. With a hushed voice and careful tread, I passed over them, wondering if the time would come in the varying fortunes of war, when the enemy would thus pass over the bodies of our own regiment, lying lifeless and cold upon some bloody field.

Ominous sounds were coming from the front. Clouds of dust hung thick and heavy over the moving columns of both armies, the roaring of artillery and bursts of musketry were frequently heard, showing that the advanced lines of the army had come in contact, and that each was endeavouring to obtain the "vantage ground." Darkness came on and we camped. We now learned that the enemy's line of battle was in our immediate front, that General Burnside was in command of our left wing, that extended to Antietam Creek, that "Fighting Joe Hooker" commanded our right, and had already gained an important advantage, and with his usual audacity had pushed his troops across Antietam Creek, close up to the enemy's front. Everything was now in readiness, and the great battle was to be fought on the morrow.

The rattle of musketry died slowly away. All was as quiet as the grave, save a scattering firing occasionally heard from the right. The blankets were unrolled, and the tired soldiers, both blue and gray, lay down to sleep and rest. The Antietam Creek rolled on its sullen course, breaking the silence of night with its murmuring waters. Thick clouds of solemn vapor seemed to hang over the sleeping combatants. The stars twinkled down sorrowfully through the gloom, and the mists came in gentle showers from the skies, as if the angels were weeping over those who were to be slain upon the morrow.

CHAPTER 2

The Battle of Antietam

Daylight dawned upon anxious hearts, on the eventful day of September 17, 1862. At an early hour the troops were in line. The battle began on our right flank, where Hooker opened a terrible fire of artillery and musketry upon the enemy.

Our division was ordered forward, as we supposed, to take a place in the line of battle, but after marching a short distance we halted under the protection of a long ridge of land, a short distance in rear of our line of battle.

We were in Fitz John Porter's corps, and it is well known that his corps was held in reserve at Antietam.

Up to this time all had been quiet in our immediate front, which was near the centre of our line of battle, but suddenly a twelve-pound gun, planted upon the opposite side of the hill from us, sent a shell screaming across Antietam Creek, and far within the rebel lines. The enemy quickly responded, battery after battery joined in the combat, and in every direction, we could hear the hissing, screaming shells, and see the puffs of white smoke where they exploded. Two of us obtained permission to leave the ranks for a short time, and ascended the hill in front of our regiment, hoping that from its top we could obtain a good view of the battlefield.

Slowly we ascended the elevation of land. A wounded soldier who had just come over the hill, sat upon the ground in our front, and was vainly endeavouring to remove the boot from his wounded foot. Before we could reach him to lend our assistance, he was relieved from all further difficulty. A solid shot from a rebel gun came bouncing like a football over the hill, struck the poor fellow upon the shoulders, crushed them to a jelly, bounded over our regiment, dashed and rolled down the road, sending confusion among a squadron of passing cavalry, as it rattled among the feet of their horses.

From the crest of the hill we obtained a fine view of the conflict. The rebel line, we judged from the rising clouds of smoke, was some four miles in length, his right reaching to within a mile of the Potomac River, and rested upon the Antietam Creek, at what was known as the Stone bridge. Their entire line was on the western bank of this creek, and occupied a very strong position on the ridges of land and among the trees.

The rebels, undoubtedly, had brilliant expectations that morning. The delay of our commanding general, on the day before, in not pressing the battle, had enabled the rebel divisions under Lawton and Jackson, fresh from the victory of Harper's Ferry, to join the main army. General Lee, the most brilliant commander of the Confederacy, now commanded an army of one hundred thousand men; his left wing was commanded by Jackson, his right by Longstreet, and his centre by Hill. To reach them, our men must cross the deep Antietam Creek, and storm the heights beyond, and these were covered with rebel troops, and crowned with flaming batteries.

The only visible means of crossing the creek was upon three bridges, one on our right, at the Hagerstown road, one near the centre, and the Stone bridge upon our left; and on the day before, when Lee arranged his line of battle, he so massed his infantry, and planted his field-pieces in such a manner, that he considered it impossible for our troops to carry them by assault. The rebel officers congratulated themselves that they held the key to an easy and most important victory.

Their soldiers were highly elated. A victory for them at Antietam, and the North lay defenceless and hopeless at their feet.

The battle was raging desperately on our right. Yesterday afternoon, when Hooker made his advance, he carried the upper bridge on the Hagerstown road—a most important advantage. During the night his men slept upon their arms to hold the position, and in the night the commands of Sumner and Mansfield had been pushed over to support him.

It was evident from our point of observation that Hooker was advancing; we could catch glimpses of moving columns and waving banners through the smoke and mists. Two batteries of union guns, supported by strong lines of infantry, advanced from the woods, where for a brief time our men had been concealed, into an open cornfield.

The rebels evidently did not see the infantry; they only saw the much-coveted guns, and upon them they charged with a savage yell.

The guns were prepared to receive them. Bursting shells, grape shot and canister, with fearful precision, went tearing through the densely massed lines of the enemy.

Our infantry joined in the bloody reception. Back and forth the lines advanced and receded; first one and then the other was victor. We watched with suspended breath. We had never seen war before. Whole lines melted away in that terrible carnage.

For a full hour the conflict raged, and then the rebel lines began to fall back, and their fire to slacken. A cheer of triumph arose from the Union victors.

"Stonewall Jackson" has found his match in desperate daring today. Joe Hooker's tall, erect form on his gray horse, has been dashing for that hour through the thickest of the fight, inspiring his men by the cool and reckless exposure of his own person. General Meade, with his Pennsylvania Reserves, was then ordered to follow up the advantage gained. They charge across the cornfield ploughed with bursting shells and made slippery with blood, to reach the woods in which the rebels have disappeared. We looked. Great God, what a reception! The forest seemed to yawn and vomit forth upon them a volcano of leaden fire; it checked their advance. They endeavoured to return the fire; they reeled and staggered like drunken men under that fearful tempest. Brigades were reduced to regiments in a moment's time; and soon the small remnant of that noble division retreated back across the cornfield to the woods from which they came. The enemy had been reinforced, and now from the forest once more they charge to follow up the repulse of Meade.

It was a critical moment: unless that advance is checked, all is lost. Hooker sat on his horse amidst the flying lead, as the broken brigades of Meade were hurled past him. He saw the coming lines of the foe; there was no time to lose.

A staff officer dashed away from Hooker to Doubleday, with the command: "Send me your best brigade instantly," and Hartsuff's brigade, composed largely of Massachusetts troops, double-quicked through the woods, out into the cornfield, past Hooker, and charged upon the enemy. We saw the wild, reckless manner in which they made the assault. They struck the rebel line with terrible force, and the latter, although fivefold the stronger, recoiled before the shock.

Hartsuff's men threw themselves flat upon the ground, along a low ridge of land, and opened a fire upon the staggering lines of the foe, and for thirty minutes the conflict raged. Hartsuff was wounded; his men have exhausted their ammunition; no reinforcements have arrived, and he must not retreat.

The shattered line sprang to its feet, mantled in sheets of flame, and again charged upon the enemy. Like a line of withering fire, they rolled on. The enemy could not withstand the shock, and once more fell back to the woods. It is now ten o'clock. The battle has been raging for four hours, and neither side has gained any decided advantage. The carnage on both sides must have been fearful.

With anxious hearts we scanned the distant field, for we knew that some movement would soon be made by blue or gray. We soon saw that Hooker's entire command was advancing. It was a desperate movement, but a grand spectacle to be hold. Our view was broken by clumps of trees and distant hilltops, but at many points we could see the advance. Regiments, brigades, divisions, were swinging and wheeling into line, and all at a double-quick; banners waved, bayonets gleamed, officers shouted, and the men cheered. Hooker in person led the charging column. The hillsides flamed with fire. There was a fearful roar, and all were concealed by clouds of smoke. The hills shook as if with agony and fear. Anxiously we asked each other: "What will be the result?"

"Joe Hooker is wounded and carried from the field," we heard a courier exclaim as he dashed down the road near where we were standing. The enemy received reinforcements from their centre; men and officers fell thick and fast. General Sumner assumed the command when Hooker was wounded, and bravely rode to the thickest of the fight, and led on the advance. Our men began to waver; they fell back a short distance and halted, and once more the cornfield was in the possession of the enemy.

It was now past noon, and as we watched the falling back of the Union lines, our hearts sank. But our artillery fire prevented the enemy from following our men a great distance. Sumner's command must be badly shattered. We understood enough of war to know that those broken lines could not without reinforcements make another successful charge that day. If they held their position they would do well. At this the most gloomy hour in the history of that battle, we saw a body of men marching down the Hagerstown road, cross the bridge, and form on the left of Sumner's command.

"Reinforcements!" we gladly cried, "and it must be General Franklin's corps."

Closely we watched the developments. We saw a brigade, which we afterward learned was General Smith's, and which was composed of troops from Maine and Vermont, charge and once more retake the cornfield, and they halted not until they had swept through the woods beyond, and sent the rebels flying back in wild disorder.

The musketry on the right died gradually away, and only the growling of artillery was heard. But while we had been so intently watching the struggle on our right, the battle had been raging from our centre to the left. The artillery planted along the side of the hill upon which we stood, had been thundering at the rebels, all the forenoon, and the ground had trembled and throbbed under the fearful roar.

Down upon the left, General Burnside had been doing noble work. The Ninth corps under the command of Burnside had slept on the night of the 16th, upon a ridge of land near the Stone bridge. And there, General Lee had massed his troops to prevent our crossing. His artillery was planted upon the ridge that stretched along the western bank of the Antietam Creek, and raked the bridge from every point, while in three lines of rude earthworks built on the hillside was the rebel infantry. At nine o'clock in the morning Burnside led his men to storm the bridge. It was a fearful undertaking. Nowhere in the campaigns of Napoleon can we find raw troops making a more brilliant assault than was made by Burnside's men at the Stone bridge.

A single regiment dashed out as skirmishers, a brigade followed, and then divisions. They reach the bridge; five hundred bursting shells fall among their closely massed ranks; twenty thousand muskets are pouring their leaden rain upon the assaulting column. They cross the bridge, deployed right and left; a battle line is formed. They dash up the hill and are hurled back. Reinforcements that have crossed the creek at a ford below, now arrive; they charge again; back and forth they surge. It is a hand-to-hand conflict with the advantages all on the side of the enemy. The first line of works is carried at the point of the bayonet. There is another struggle, and a terrific yell rolls up the line, to tell us that our men have won. The clouds of smoke and dust showed clearly that Burnside held the hill, and that the rebels were falling back.

It is now late in the afternoon; whatever is done today must be done quickly. The losses on both sides have been great. The enemy having had the advantage of position, our losses are probably the greater.

Our brigade bugle calls, "*fall in, fall in*" There is a fearful roar of musketry on the right, where all has been so quiet for an hour. Forward at a double-quick we move, to reinforce the right; we march a mile or two, then halt; the firing has ceased, and the emergency has passed. As we halt, a mournful procession passes us, bearing the remains of brave General Mansfield, who has just been killed at the front.

In a few moments we return to our former position. The rebels have been driven back on both flanks, and are forming a new line near Sharpsburg. We listened; the battle is still raging on our left; Burnside is evidently advancing; those terrible volleys of musketry, the ceaseless din of artillery, the clouds of smoky dust, were rolling back toward Sharpsburg, where rested the rebel centre. Burnside is pushing their right flank back, doubling it upon their centre. If that movement succeeds the fate of the rebel army is sealed. Great interests are at stake, and with breathless interest we awaited the result.

Burnside's men are exhausted; their ranks are sadly thinned; each regiment is but a shattered wreck. If his command could only be inspired with reinforcements! A cloud of dust is seen rolling from the rebel centre to their right. Lee has seen his danger, and A. P. Hill is hastening down to reinforce Longstreet, to check and crush Burnside. And look, up the dusty highway, his horse covered with foam, dashes a staff officer from Burnside to McClellan! "Burnside says, send him men and guns, and he will sweep all before him, but without reinforcements he cannot hold the position he has gained." Will McClellan grant his request? Fifteen thousand fresh troops are in the valley at his feet, each man impatient for a part in the day's work, and a share in the glory of victory.

Fifteen thousand reinforcements for Burnside mean the overthrow of both Longstreet and Hill. They will be hurled back upon the centre, and the rebel army will be enclosed between the forces of Burnside and Sumner. The fords of the Potomac will be in our possession, and Antietam will be the deathbed of the Confederacy.

Oh, for one hour of Grant, or dashing Phil Sheridan! For a moment McClellan hesitates; he is loyal, but too timid and slow for a great commander.

> Tell Burnside to hold on; it is the greatest battle of the war; I will send him a battery; I have no infantry to send; if he is driven back, he must hold the bridge, for if we lose that we lose all.

The fatal mistake has been made. Burnside is overpowered, and slowly relinquishes the ground he has gained; but the rebels have been so roughly handled they do not press him far. They halt, the firing ceases, Burnside holds the bridge, and darkness conceals the situation from our view. The enemy are beaten at every point. We have Porter's corps of troops, who have not been in the battle at all. The waters of the Potomac River are swollen to a flood tide; the fords are few and dangerous; they afford General Lee his only avenue of escape. It is not too late to redeem the blunder of the afternoon, but no advance of our troops was ordered. General Lee understands that he must regain by his own cunning what he has failed to gain upon the field of battle, and the defeated general proposes an armistice to bury his dead, and to the mortification and disgust of the army, it was granted. And under this false pretence, Lee recrossed the river, and escaped, leaving his wounded and dead to be cared for and buried by the victors before whom he was fleeing.

The men in the ranks were all indignant that the substantial fruits of their dearly bought victory should thus slip through their fingers, through the stupidity of their dearly beloved commanding officer.

Many opinions have been given as to General McClellan's conduct at Antietam, and many serious charges have been made against him, but I think the surviving members of the rank and file of the old Army of the Potomac will with me agree that he was a loyal, brave, skilful officer, that as an engineer he has no superiors, but he was sadly lacking in the elements of energy, decision and reckless courage that qualifies a man to command armies in an active campaign. But notwithstanding the escape of the rebel army, the victory at Antietam was of vast importance. It prevented an invasion of the North, and rolled the tide of war back upon the soil of Virginia.

On the 19th of September, two days after this battle was fought, there was great excitement in our regiment, as we were ordered to cross the Potomac, and follow up the retreat of General Lee. This was to be a new experience to us. Up to this time we had not been in the advance. We had seen our comrades fight and go down in the smoke of battle, but now we were to experience that which hitherto we had only seen.

The regiment quickly obeyed the order to "fall in." Then the command "by the right flank, march," was given, and away we went. We soon reached the Potomac River, and crossed at the Shepherdstown fords. The river was wide, the water deep, the current swift, and the ledges upon which we walked were so narrow that our crossing was necessarily very slow; but we finally reached the Virginia shore.

Not a gun had been fired, and not an enemy had been seen. Our regimental line was formed upon the bank of the river, and we began to climb the steep bluff that rose some two hundred feet above the water. Before the ascent was completed, we heard heavy firing up the river on our right, showing that those who crossed the river above us had encountered the enemy. With a desperate resolution to crush the rebellion, we scrambled to the top, and our line was quickly formed upon its crest. A dense forest was in our immediate front, the firing on our right had increased, and the roar of regular volleys of musketry came rolling down the river.

Gray forms were seen flitting among the trees before us, puffs of white smoke suddenly burst out from the forest, and the uncomfortable "*zip, zip*" of leaden messengers over our heads warned us that the enemy meant business. We returned the fire, and sent our first greetings to the Southern Confederacy, in the form of minie bullets, that went singing and cracking through the forest in our front; and we made a target of every gray form we could see.

Our regiment was about to make a charge upon them, when the order came for us to get down over the bluff, and recross the river as rapidly as possible, and down through the rocks and trees we ran. We reached the river, and began to make a most masterly advance upon Maryland. The enemy followed us to the top of the bluff, and would have punished us severely as we were recrossing the river, but one of our batteries went into position on the Maryland side, threw shells over our heads, and drove the rebels back. Several of the regiments on our right had sustained great losses; one of them, the 118th Pennsylvania, had been almost annihilated. Upon reaching the Maryland shore, we took possession of the Chesapeake and Ohio Canal, and there formed the advanced line of the army.

One very amusing incident occurred in our retreat. In Company H was a man by the name of Tommy Welch, an Irishman about forty years of age, a brave, generous-hearted fellow. He was an old bachelor, and one of those funny, neat, particular men we occasionally meet. He always looked as if he had emerged from a bandbox; and the boys used to say that he would rather sacrifice the whole Army of the Potomac, than to have a spot of rust upon his rifle, or dust upon his uniform. He was always making the most laughable blunders, and was usually behind all others in obeying any command. When our regiment went tumbling down over the side of the bluff, to reach the river, the men all got down before Tommy understood what they were doing.

Then very slowly he descended, picking his path carefully among the trees and rocks, and did not reach the river until the rear of the regiment was nearly one-half of the way across. The officer who commanded our regiment on that day rode a magnificent horse, and as the regiment recrossed, he sat coolly upon his horse near the Virginia shore, amidst the shots of the enemy, speaking very pleasantly to the men as they passed him. He evidently determined to be the last man of the regiment to leave the post of danger.

He saw Uncle Tommy, and although the danger was very great, he kindly waited for him to cross. When the latter reached the water, with great deliberation he sat down upon a rock, and removed his shoes and stockings, and slowly packed them away in his blanket. Then his pant legs must be rolled up, so that they would not come in contact with the water; and all the time the rebels were coming nearer, and the bullets were flying more thickly.

At last he was ready for an advance movement, but just as he reached the water, the luckless pant legs slipped down over his knees, and he very quietly retraced his steps to the shore, to roll them up again. This was too much for even the courtesy of the commanding officer, who becoming impatient at the protracted delay, and not relishing the sound of the lead whistling over his head, cried out in a sharp voice: "*Come, come, my man, hurry up, hurry up, or we will both be shot.*"

Tommy looked up with that bewildered, *serio*-comic gravity of expression for which the Emerald Isle is so noted, and answered in the broadest brogue: "The divil a bit, sur. It is no mark of a gintleman to be in a hurry." The officer waited no longer, but putting spurs to his horse, he dashed across the river, while Tommy, carrying his rifle in one hand, and holding up his pant legs in the other, followed after, the bullets flying thickly around him.

Poor Tommy Welch, brave, blundering and kind, was a favourite in his company, and his comrades all mourned when he was shot down in the Wilderness. He was there taken prisoner, and carried to Andersonville prison, where he died of starvation.

On forming our line at the canal, we soon found that we were in an uncomfortable position. The rebels were concealed on the side of the bluff, across the river, by trees and underbrush, so that we could not see them, but the moment that one of our men would step from the muddy canal to the bank, the air around him would be filled with bullets. Quite a number of our men were thus wounded. We soon learned to watch for the white puff of smoke, and the moment it was detected, we would send a hundred bullets at it. Thus, through the day and night that followed our retreat, a constant picket firing was kept up.

On the second day the rebels seemed to grow weary of this, and almost ceased firing; but there was another and more dangerous annoyance. Down by the side of the river were the brick walls of an old mill, and in the night a company of rebel sharpshooters took possession of it, and if a soldier made his appearance anywhere on the Maryland shore, within range of their famous rifles, there would instantly be seen the little cloud of smoke, and the peculiar singing sound of the bullet would be heard, and the victim, unconscious of danger, would fall. We peppered away at the walls with our rifles, but of course with no effect.

On the afternoon of the second day a battery of artillery galloped down near where we were stationed. The bullets flew thick and fast from the brick walls. Men and horses fell. The guns were quickly unlimbered, and returned the compliment with twelve-pound shells. *Whiz—bang—Crash,* they went into the old mill; the air was filled with pieces of bricks and mortar; whole sections of the walls went tumbling down; a thousand rifles opened upon the ruins, and the rebel sharpshooters, or the few who survived, made a dash from the ruins, amidst the wild cheering of our men, up over the steep bluff, and troubled us no more.

One of the most difficult things in the world for a genuine Yankee to do, was to settle down, and become accustomed to the experience of a soldier's life. He was naturally inquisitive, and wanted to know all the reasons why an order was given, before he could obey it. Accustomed to be independent, the words *go* and *come* grated harshly upon his ear. At home he had considered himself as good as any other person, and in the army, he failed to understand why a couple of gilt straps upon the shoulders of one who at home was far beneath him, should there make him so much his superior.

The Yankee is usually a practical sort of a man, and in all his work shows a great deal of good common sense, and when, in his loyal love for the old flag, he went South to help crush the rebellion, he expected to use the same practical common sense that he had used at home, to fight the rebels in as practical a manner as he had planted potatoes or felled the forest trees, and consequently all the red tape of army life was very distasteful to him. He could not understand how dress parades, guard mounting, reviews and grand rounds could ever crush the rebellion, and they were all regarded in supreme contempt.

While we were in the front line at the Potomac River, our picket line was extended for a considerable distance along its banks. The ground was in many places very rough, and after dark it was difficult to find the posts upon which some of the men were stationed.

One dark and stormy night, a member of our regiment was placed upon one of these posts. His relief was to stand from eleven to one o'clock, but in the darkness and storm, the corporal in charge of the next relief failed to find him, and consequently he was not relieved.

The moments passed slowly. He knew that something was wrong, but disdaining to call the corporal, an officer for whose rank he had a great contempt, he stood and growled, and stamped his feet in the cold storm, and as he reviewed all these petty annoyances that I have named, his anger was kindled to a greater degree.

At last he heard the tramp of men and horses approaching him. As they came down the line, with a stentorian voice he yelled—"*Who comes there?*" and the mincing voice of a newly-fledged colonel commanding a New York regiment, who was that day in charge of the picket line, was—"The grand rounds, sir."

Imagine his surprise when the exasperated son of Maine yelled back in reply—"To h—ll with your grand rounds. I want the corporal of the second relief." Perhaps under the great provocation the profanity was excusable.

During the five weeks of inactivity in the Army of the Potomac that followed the Battle of Antietam, one of the most disastrous features of the gloomy situation was the terrible sickness of the soldiers, and this was especially true in the new regiments. The men were unused to the climate, the exposure, and the food, so that the whole experience was in direct contrast to their life at home. Many were sick and discouraged; strong men grew weak with disease; no sanitary measures were enforced in camp; the buildings used as hospitals were but illy adapted to such a purpose, being very imperfect in ventilation, cleanliness, and general convenience. It was a sad spectacle to walk through the hospitals, and see the helpless men.

Our regiment was encamped near the old "Antietam Iron Works." The weather became very cold, and the bleak, penetrating winds swept with terrible force down the hillsides and through the valleys of Maryland. We had no tents, and for a number of weeks were without overcoats. With shivering bodies and chattering teeth, we used to sit around the camp-fires, along the picket lines, and endeavoured to make ourselves believe that a soldier's life was a very pleasant one. One of the most painful duties that we performed was to visit the hospitals, and care for our sick comrades—men who had left their homes but a few weeks before, strong, robust, hearty and hopeful, now weak, sick, hopeless and dying. The strong men of middle age, from whom so much was expected, were the first to yield, while the mere boys, of whom no account had been made, seemed to more easily adapt themselves to the situation.

It was a sad mission, to sit by the dying in the midst of all the dirt and disorder with which they were surrounded, to gather up little trinkets to send as priceless keepsakes to distant friends, to write the last goodbyes and messages of love whispered from dying lips, and to hold their thin, hollow hands as the spirit floated away from its earthen casket. Then would follow the soldiers' burial, the corporal's guard with reversed arms keeping step to the mournful beat of the muffled drum. That was a hard, bitter experience; and the surviving members of our regiment have not forgotten the hillsides of Maryland, where we laid the bodies of the first victims that death called from our ranks.

It has been urged as a defence for this delay on the part of General McClellan, that he disliked to sacrifice his men, and that a special regard for their welfare caused him to move so slowly. If this be true, it was a mistaken policy, for experience taught us that lead was a much less cruel butcher than disease, and that if soldiers must die to preserve the government, they prefer to die upon the battlefield. There is some inspiration to die in the shock of conflict, amidst the crash of contending hosts, to pass away in a whirlwind of fire; but there is no satisfaction in struggling with disease, and to grow weak and shadowy under its touch, and to know from the beginning that death is the only relief. It is a sad comment upon this hesitating policy, that when our regiment marched from that camping ground, and advanced into Virginia, three hundred of our members were sent to the hospitals as invalids, many of whom never saw the regiment again.

CHAPTER 3

From Antietam to Fredericksburgh

On the 30th of October we marched from Antietam, in the direction of Harper's Ferry, and on the following day we crossed the Potomac River, passed through the village named above, and then crossed the Shenandoah River. There was much around Harper's Ferry to interest us. The scenery is among the most magnificent on the continent. The two great rivers here break in resistless force through the Blue Ridge, while the mountain looks down upon the rushing waters, from its bold bluffs, which rise perpendicularly hundreds of feet in the air. Thomas Jefferson declared that the passage of the Potomac through the Blue Ridge was one of the most stupendous scenes in nature, and well worth a voyage across the Atlantic to witness.

We saw the ruins of the old United States Arsenal, and remembered that it was this arsenal that John Brown had seized when he made his raid into Virginia in October, 1859.

In the first years of the civil war the village often changed hands, as the armies advanced and retreated, and now it looked poor and dilapidated. A great pile of gun barrels burned, bent and twisted, told where the arsenal had formerly stood.

Our line of march was around the base of Louden Heights, and through the valley of the same name. While we were marching along this valley, the enemy on the other side of the Blue Ridge was marching in the same direction through the Shenandoah valley.

Louden valley is one of the most fertile sections of Virginia, and in 1862 it had not been desolated with war, as many other sections of the state had been; and the boys will all remember that there was grand foraging on that march. Cattle, sheep, pigs, and all kinds of vegetables, were plenty, and we made many requisitions upon the "Secesh" plantations as we passed them.

Foraging soon becomes a science in the soldiers' life. We had just entered the army, and did not understand it as well as did those who had been longer in the service, but we applied ourselves closely to the work, and soon became quite expert. We must always remember that customs in the army vary from those in civil life, and things which in the latter would not be tolerated for a moment, would be commendable in the former. Many laughable incidents occurred, which, if written, would fill volumes. While marching through Louden valley, our regiment encamped one night at a small village called "Snickersville," and the following day we remained in camp. A small squad of us sallied forth in the afternoon, without permission, "to seek whom we might devour."

Some few miles from camp, in an outbuilding on a large plantation, we found a very large hive of bees which appeared to be well filled with honey. Now honey and hard tack together make a most desirable diet, and we knew that we had found a prize; but, as I have already intimated, foraging was new business to us, and we were a little timid, and consequently concluded that the better way for us to pursue, was to return to camp, and then come out after dark and secure it. We returned to camp highly elated at the prospect of securing the coveted prize. Of course, our comrades were to know nothing about it. We held a small council of war, and arranged our plans.

Late in the evening we passed through the guard unnoticed by the sentinels, and quickly tramped over fences and across fields until we reached the plantation, and to our joy found the hive of honey as we had left it in the afternoon. It was a huge, old-fashioned affair, some four feet in height, by two and a half square. It was so heavy that it required our united strength to carry it. We soon found that "the way of the transgressor is hard." We had just passed from the building to the open yard, when a smothered exclamation from Joe, which was half way between an oath and a yell, attracted our attention; we hurriedly dropped the hive, and Joe began to make the most lively antics around the yard.

We soon learned the cause; there was a small opening in the side of the hive, through which the bees had been accustomed to pass in and out. Joe had, unfortunately, placed his hand near this opening, the occupants of the hive had been aroused by their removal, and a large cluster of them had passed up under his sleeve, and intrenched themselves upon his arm. It was the first wound that he had received in the war of the rebellion.

"Confound them!" muttered Joe, "I will fix them," and taking off his overcoat, a new one that he had just drawn, he proceeded to wrap it around the hive in such a manner that the opening was covered. We then lifted our burden and tugged away. We passed out beyond the barn, and reached a narrow lane enclosed on either side by a very high fence, when to our horror we heard a party of men approaching.

"Here they are," cried one, leaping upon the fence.

"*Surrender, surrender,*" cried the newcomers.

"The provost guard," we all exclaimed together.

Now if there is a thing in the world that a new soldier is afraid of, it is the provost guard. Guns rattled, we dropped the hive, overcoat and all, and sprang over the high fence and ran; our pursuers crying out that if we did not stop they would fire. At a break-neck rate we went across the broad field; a deep, wide ditch was in our way; with a most desperate leap we cleared this obstacle, and rushed on to our camp. When we arrived there, we lay down together to talk over our narrow escape. We were highly elated to think that we had eluded the grasp of the much dreaded "provost guard."

If we had made a charge upon the enemy, and covered ourselves with honour, we would not have felt better than at that time. We were so much excited that we could not sleep. In about an hour we heard a commotion in the street of the adjoining company. Some men seemed to be carrying a heavy burden, while others were convulsed with laughter, which they were endeavouring vainly to suppress.

We listened; they were talking. Their whole company seemed to be gathered around them. As we listened we became disgusted. They had got our honey. They had overheard us in the afternoon as we made our plans. A squad of them had followed to make us believe they were the provost guard, and they had succeeded. We endeavoured to induce Joe to ask them about his coat, but he declared that he would freeze to death like a man before he would take such a step.

The affair soon leaked out, and for six months, if any of the boys wished to silence either of us, they only had to speak the one word "*honey.*"

November 9th, we reached Warrenton, where we encamped until the 17th. While here, General McClellan was relieved of his command, and bade farewell to the army, and General Burnside assumed its command. The old Army of the Potomac was once more on the advance. We were marching from Warrenton toward the city of Fredericksburgh, where the army of General Lee was awaiting us. It had been a long, weary march. The mud was thick and deep. We halted in a large field on a hillside, just as the sun was sinking from view at the close of a November's day. The little shelter tent was soon spread over its frame work of small poles, and the work for the night was quickly divided among our tent's company of three. William was to get the water, Charley was to act as cook, and I was to secure rails for firewood.

It was not an extensive "bill of fare" in those days—coffee, hard tack and salt pork. The supper was eaten with a keen relish. I arose to my feet, but to my surprise everything around me seemed to be changing its position; my head whirled, and I fell to the ground. Then for a time all was indistinct. The surgeons were summoned, and decided that it was an attack of typhoid fever.

In the evening it began to rain in torrents, and for thirty-six hours the army did not move.

I can indistinctly remember how the rain poured upon the thin cotton above my face, and how the tiny streams of water were running upon the ground on which I was lying. William and Charley exposed themselves to that fearful storm to protect me. With their bayonets they dug trenches around the tent, to prevent the water from pouring in; they piled their blankets and overcoats upon me to keep me warm and dry; they carried wood from a great distance, through the darkness, and kept a great fire burning at the tent door.

Kind, noble-hearted fellows! As I look back over the nineteen years that have passed, and recall those incidents, I find that time and changing circumstances have not changed or chilled my gratitude to them for their kindness in that season of suffering. It was at an early hour in the morning I was awakened from a troubled sleep. The rain had ceased to fall, but the air was chilly and damp. Great masses of black clouds obscured the skies; the ground was soaked with the vast quantities of water that had fallen.

Charley was speaking to me, "Come, my boy, we are to march in a few moments. The surgeon says there is no room for you in the ambulance, but if William and I can get you down there, I will find you a place, or I will know the reason why."

Sick, weak, and half delirious, they bore me to where the ambulances were standing, near the regimental headquarters. They were all loaded, with one exception, and in this they quickly placed me with my blankets and baggage. Just at this moment a surgeon emerged from one of the tents, and approached the ambulances, and something like the following dialogue took place: Charley, with a military salute and much politeness, remarked:

"Surgeon, that sick man in Company H is unable to march; if we leave him on the ground he will die, and I have put him in that ambulance."

With a fearful oath the surgeon answered:

"Sergeant, that ambulance is reserved for the use of the officers if they should need it. So, pull your man out, and if he is too cowardly to march to the front, let him die like a d——d dog on the ground."

With a voice perfectly cool, and yet as keen as a scimitar, Charley replied:

"You are mistaken in the man, sir; he has always done his duty; he is now very sick; if he is taken from that ambulance, you will do it, and if it is done, I will report it to every officer in the regiment, and will publish the facts in every newspaper in the state of Maine."

I trembled as I thought what the results of the controversy might be to Charley. I knew him well; he had seen much of the world. As a sailor, he had frequently weathered Cape Horn, and four years of his life had been passed in a whaling voyage, amid the icebergs of the northern seas. He was a kind-hearted, Christian gentleman, yet as immovable as the hills of his native Vermont. The surgeon evidently saw that he had caught a Tartar, and with a volley of oaths turned on his heel and walked away. Another sick man was placed in the other compartment of the ambulance, and we moved forward.

I wish I could describe that journey. The day was cold and raw; the rain came pouring down at intervals; the roads were rough and muddy. Our ambulance formed a part of the long line of ambulances, baggage wagons and artillery filling the roads for many miles. At times we moved very slowly; perhaps for an hour we would not move at all; then the train in front would close up rapidly, and for a mile or more our horses would gallop over the rough road. The space that I occupied in the carriage was about two feet in width by six in length. Lying upon my back, with my head toward the horses, a thin, low partition separated me from my sick companion, whose groans of pain sounded hoarse and hollow. I was burning up with a fearful heat, and I was so *tired*. At times I would distinctly understand my situation, and could hear my driver as he talked to his horses, or sang songs; one of which was then very popular with the old soldiers who had fought on the peninsula. I remember the refrain, it ran something like this:—

McClellan leads the van,
McClellan leads the van;
We will show our deeds
Where'er he leads;
McClellan leads the van;

Then all would become blank; dark, weird forms would flit around me; I would see green hills, great forests, crystal streams of water, and familiar faces; then there would be rushing columns of soldiers, and scenes of carnage and death. Slowly the hours passed away; night came and went; another day and night slowly followed, and the third day had measured more than one-half its length before the ride was completed.

It was my first night in the ambulance. The train had been slowly toiling along in a narrow, muddy road that wound its tortuous way through a dense forest. It finally came to a dead halt. My driver, whom I had learned by his language to be a coarse, rough fellow, was growling because the train did not move on. An officer who had charge of the train, came riding back, and accosted the driver with, "Well Sam, unhook your horses, we are to stop here for the night."

"Stop here," answered the astonished Sam, "what shall we do with the sick fellers? I reckon they're pretty well gone for it, by the way they have groaned and raved all day."

"That is none of my business," gruffly replied the officer. "All I have to do is to haul them as long as they are alive; the more that die the fewer we shall have to haul," and with a coarse laugh he rode on.

I heard Sam mutter as he hitched his horses close by the side of the carriage:

Perhaps it don't matter, but I swear I do like to see men a little human like. I pity these poor cusses groaning and talking about home; rough fare is good enough for a fellow when he is tough and strong, but when he wilts he wants something tender like. The Lord only knows what is to become of us all, before we get out of this infernal scrape. A fellow can't look a foot ahead, and see how soon his own time will come.

I heard this much, and then his voice grew indistinct. I experienced dizzy sensations, and soon all was dark.

It must have been midnight. I thought I heard familiar voices. I could not be mistaken. The curtain at the rear of the ambulance was raised, and William's voice was heard saying, "Yes, here he is," and

Charley broke in with—"Say, old fellow, how are you? we have come back to find you, and for three blessed miles we have looked in every ambulance to see if you were there." Three miles they tramped, after a hard day's march, in search of me. But he continued, "We have brought your supper. We did not have much of a variety to select from, but I found a piece of soft bread at a sutler's today, and I have toasted that, and sprinkled sugar upon it, and have brought it to you, and now you must eat." The food was held to my lips. It was sour, dry, tough, and smoky, but had it been ever so tempting I could not have eaten it.

The noble, generous fellows! Their kindness caused a great lump to gather suddenly in my throat, and it was impossible for me to swallow. With kind words of encouragement, and promising to visit me again as soon as possible, they bade me goodbye, and were gone.

It was about the hour of noon, on the second day of my ambulance ride, when Sam thrust his head inside the carriage with—"Here is a biling spring; guess I will fill your canteen with water." A few moments after, the canteen was placed at my side, and the ambulance rolled swiftly on.

My lips and throat were parched with a burning heat. With weak and eager hands, I seized the canteen and pressed it to my lips. The water was so cool and delicious. Suddenly the carriage came in contact with some obstacle. There was a fearful jolt, and the canteen slipped from my nerveless grasp. The water went pouring down my neck. I had not strength to take the canteen up again, and I had the grim satisfaction of having three pints of icy water roll in tiny wavelets along my back for at least two hours. At that time, I had not very pronounced theological convictions or prejudices, but I did have a strong dislike to "pouring."

The second night came, and we halted again on the muddy road in the great dark forest. The regiment was now so far away that my comrades could not return. I knew that I was better; the fever had partially subsided, but I was so weak and faint! Slowly the hours passed away. My companion had ceased to groan, and I supposed he was sleeping. I knew that Sam was busily at work over a fire that he had built by the roadside. I could hear him mutter and talk as he stirred the fire or piled more fuel upon it. A savoury odour seemed to fill the air. He is preparing his supper, I thought, and then I fell asleep.

I was awakened. Someone was speaking to me. I listened. It was Sam's voice. "Say there, old feller, don't you want some supper?" and before I could reply, he rattled on, "I drew a Secesh chicken back along the road today, and have made some broth for you fellers, but I find that your companion has become uncommon quiet, so I will give it to you."

He rolled up the side curtains of the carriage. A great fire was burning close at its side, sending its light far out in the darkness, among the great pine trees, until each one looked wild and weird, like grim giants standing as sentinels in the gloom. My head was bolstered up, and the change of position afforded so much relief! The fire was warm and nice, and flooded the interior of the carriage with its cheerful light, and as tenderly as a woman the rough fellow, with a spoon, fed me the delicious broth. It was to me the "elixir of life." I know that it was very childish, but the tears ran thick and fast from my eyes, and fell upon the great, hard hand that was so kindly ministering to my wants. Sam pretended not to notice them, but in his comical way continued to talk.

> I understand there has been an uncommon demand for poultry in Virginny, the last few days. The chivilry have had lots of visitors whom they did not expect. A great many fellers from the Northern states have seemed determined to come down this way. They didn't even stop for an invite, and chickens are mighty hard to find; I hardly know when I can draw another. The old woman where I got this one, flourished her broomstick over my head, and threatened my life if I did not drop her chicken, and I have put all the broth and meat in this pail for you; it will last you a week.

I tried to thank him, but gratitude choked my utterance. My head was laid back upon its hard pillow. The fire continued to make the inside of the carriage comfortable and warm.

Sam sat down upon an old log, drank his coffee from a black tin cup, and ate his hard tack with a keen relish. I never knew his full name, or the state from which he enlisted, and if living I know nothing of what position he may fill in life, or how his fellow-men may regard him, but I do know that under his rough and coarse exterior he had a true, manly heart, and deserves a kingly crown.

"Cheer up," shouted Sam, on the afternoon of the third day, "you are almost home." He gave his whip a sharp crack; the weary horses went on at a sharp gallop, and the ambulance stopped at the street of Company H.

I was indeed at home. Kind comrades were there to welcome me,

William, Charley, and a dozen others to assist them. I was quickly taken from the ambulance and led to a tent. I glanced over my shoulder, and saw some men as they removed my companion from the carriage; his form seemed cold and rigid; he was dead. I then understood why he had ceased to groan, and the meaning of Sam's words when he said that he was "uncommon quiet." My tent-mates went to thank Sam for his kindness to me. The noble fellow brushed his rough hand across his eyes and drove rapidly away.

Our camping-ground was a small pine knoll at "Stoneman's Switch," near Falmouth, Virginia, and but a few miles from the city of Fredericksburgh, where the great battle was fought. Here our regiment passed its first winter in Virginia. The tents of our company were built on both sides of our company street. The walls were of logs, and some three feet in height, and the sharp roofs were covered with thick cotton cloth. They were each about eight feet square, and usually contained four men. In each tent was a small fireplace made of sods cut from the muddy soil, and in these little huts, through the cold, chilling storms of that long winter, our regiment found but poor protection. Wood was so scarce that it had to be carried a long distance, and then it was of the poorest quality.

At first the men could obtain sapling pine and white-wood trees by carrying them two miles, but this supply soon failed. When the trees were all gone, they were obliged to dig out the stumps and roots, and carry them that long distance for firewood. Our regiment suffered severely from exposure and sickness, and as I recall those long, dreary weeks, I can only wonder that the little graveyard on the hillside does not contain the ashes of a greater number of our men than it does. We buried some of the bravest of our men there,—noble fellows, who had hoped that if they were to die for the country they might have the privilege of dying on the field of battle, but that boon was denied them.

A few of us visited this old camp-ground after the close of the war, as we were marching from Richmond to Washington, in 1865. The tents were all destroyed, the streets were overgrown with weeds, the parade-ground was covered with grass—all was changed; the only places that remained in any degree in their natural condition were the little sacred mounds containing the remains of our comrades. Those hillsides of Virginia contain that which is far more precious to our nation than all the gold and silver of its mines—the priceless ashes of our noble dead.

It was a most fortunate thing for me when I arrived at the regiment, sick, to be surrounded by kind friends, each of whom helped me to get well. My tent-mates did all they could to make me comfortable, and to prepare food that would tempt my appetite. It is amusing to think of the ordinary and extraordinary dishes that were served upon our table, and the various forms in which hard tack made its appearance. I will enumerate a few of the forms that I remember:—first, in its natural condition, those dry, juiceless, flinty sheets or cakes that every soldier will so distinctly remember; second, broken in small pieces, soaked in cold water, fried in pork fat, served hot, known as "Burnside stew"; third, pounded fine, mixed in water, baked in thin cakes, called "Washington pies"; fourth, burned to a crisp, boiled in water, to be eaten with a spoon, and this was called "Potomac chowder."

Each day some of the boys in our company would go out on a foraging expedition, and if they found any delicacy, they would usually share it with me. "Orlando B——," our captain's cook, made me a daily visit, and generally left a small package, the contents of which would inform me what the officers "bill of fare" had been for that day. All this, with a naturally elastic constitution, soon put me upon my feet, and in a few weeks, I was as well as ever.

Of all the many frauds perpetrated upon the government during the war, one of the greatest was that of a certain class of men, who secured commissions as surgeons and assistant surgeons, men who knew but little of medical science, and evidently cared a great deal less than they knew.

When a regiment was in camp, there was usually, at nine o'clock in the morning, a bugle call, known as the "sick call," or as the boys used to render it, "come and get your quinine." Then the sick in each company, who were able, would march in charge of a sergeant to the surgeon's tent where they would be examined, excused from duty, and have their medical wants supplied. If they were not able to march to the surgeon's tent, they would remain in their own tents, and be visited by the surgeon or one of his assistants.

One of the latter class came under my own observation, and it was very amusing to follow him in his daily visitation of the sick. I do not think any person in his regiment ever had any possible conception as to how he came by his commission; but he had one and retained it until he was dismissed from the service.

Let us follow him in a series of his morning calls. He is a large, robust man, but he moves with that peculiar languor of one who has been tired from his birth. The boys have whispered around through the regiment that he is terribly afflicted with an insect known as "*pediadus (humanus) capitis,*" and that a lack of energy on his part has enabled them to firmly intrench themselves upon his person. He enters tent number one; we listen, and the following ensues.

The medical man gives his back a most vigorous scratch, and asks the patient, "What ails you?"

Patient answers, "A severe cold."

Surgeon, "Let me see your tongue."

This member is duly exhibited, the surgeon counts a small handful of pills from a tin box, hands them to the patient with the instructions, "Take one each two hours."

Patient number two is reached. Another scratch; "What ails you?"

"A severe attack of rheumatism, sir."

"Let me see your tongue." Another handful of pills; "One each two hours."

Patient number three is accosted with "What ails you, sir?" with a more vigorous scratch.

Patient replies, "I am just recovering from a severe attack of typhoid fever."

"Let me see your tongue; one of these pills each two hours."

And thus, the farce goes on, until he has visited half a hundred patients, made many ineffectual attempts to dislodge the tormentors from his back, prescribed for a score of diseases, decided each patient's condition by an examination of his tongue, and furnished remedies from the same box of pills. Fortunately for both the men and the government, the pills were never taken, and consequently many of the men recovered.

Drawing rations is one of the most interesting events in a soldier's life. Rations are usually drawn once in three days.

"Company H, fall in for rations," shouts a sergeant, standing at the head of the company street, and out from twenty tents tumble the men for rations. Haversacks, tin cups and cloth bags are carried to receive the treasure. Nine cakes of hard tack a day, twenty-seven cakes for three days' rations are counted out for each man. Three spoonfuls of sugar and coffee are dipped out to every man, for each day's rations, and a small piece of meat.

Wonderful rations, and most wonderful times we used to have in eating them. Many laughable incidents would occur. One man in our company was always eating hard tack; at all times and under all circumstances he was grinding the dry, hard cakes. He carried them in his pockets; and on drill, guard mountings, dress parade and review, crunch, crunch, would go those tireless jaws upon the flinty substance. The captain grew nervous, listening to the endless grinding of the bread, and at last became quite desperate; and one day when the grinding was unusually brisk, he called out savagely: "Keegan, why on earth are you always crunching hard bread?"

And Keegan with great innocence replied: "The juice, sir, I am very fond of the juice."

At another time an English recruit who was in our company found a few green apples very early in the season, and hastily stewed them for sauce. Just as the dish containing the sauce was removed from the fire, the order was given to fall in for inspection. In his haste he upset the dish of sauce upon his equipments and uniform. The regiment was quickly in line, the division inspector, accompanied by the colonel and staff officers, soon reached our company. Each man presented his rifle for inspection as they passed along the line. The officer took the rifle this man presented, but to his surprise and horror his gloves of immaculate whiteness were covered with a soft, sticky substance. He looked at them a moment in disgust, and then with an oath demanded of the man, "What is that?"

And the culprit with his peculiar drawling brogue made answer: "It is nothin' but green apple sass, sir."

For once military authority and decorum was powerless.

Receiving the mail was always a season of joy and disappointment. Each letter received was like a messenger from home, and was an additional cord binding our hearts to our loved ones. Perhaps, if on the march no mail had been received for weeks, we hear the brigade bugle, that old, familiar call, "*Dan, Dan, Butterfield, Butterfield.*" We listen in suspense. Clear and shrill comes the bugle notes upon the air—"Come and get your mail, come and get your mail." It soon arrives at the regimental headquarters, and is quickly distributed among the companies. The orderly sergeant stands in the street and cries out, "Fall in for your mail."

The men need no second invitation; eagerly they watch and listen; name after name is called, until every letter has been delivered, unless it is just after the battle, and as names are called, someone answers dead, dead. Some are joyous over the messages they have received, others are disappointed, but comfort themselves with the thought that the next mail will bring them the prize, while a few look on sadly and think there are no friends to send them tidings of sympathy and love.

In our company was a young man who occupied the position of a sergeant, a brave, quiet, gentle manly fellow. He had left a good situation, to fight for the old flag. He was always at his post, and took great pride in discharging every duty in a soldierly manner. He was one of the best soldiers in the regiment. While we were in camp at Stoneman's Switch, he was sick for a few days, and was excused by the surgeon from all duty. While he was in this condition, the regiment was from camp for several days, and none but the sick were left behind.

Our quartermaster was a large, rough, overbearing man, one who disgraced his uniform every day by his brutal treatment of the men; and to say that he was most cordially despised by every man in our company would be putting it in a very mild form.

While the regiment was from camp, the quarter master came to our company street, and seeing this sergeant standing at his tent door, ordered him to get an axe, and go up to the quartermaster's tent and cut him some wood. The sergeant informed him that he was sick, and not able to walk so far, but with bitter abuse he was ordered to obey. The sergeant replied that he was sick, and excused from all duty, and that he was also a non-commissioned officer, and not supposed to do such work when he was well. At this point the quartermaster knocked him down with brutal force, and kicked his prostrate form, and then returned to his tent.

A few days after this the regiment returned to camp. The quartermaster reported that the sergeant had refused to obey his orders, and the latter, without a hearing, was disgraced, and reduced to the ranks.

The weeks passed away. The young man felt his disgrace most keenly. His noble nature was stung to the quick by the great injustice that had been done him. He never murmured, but manfully performed the duties of a private soldier. He never spoke of the matter except when the boys gave him their sympathy for his encouragement; but everyone in the company knew the pent-up anguish of his heart.

Gettysburgh was reached. Little Round Top shook in the roar of conflict. Ever at the front, this man was among the first to fall. When the first lull in the battle came, his comrades stooped over him. The life-blood was gushing from a fatal wound. He was dying.

His thin, blue lips curled in scornful derision, and he muttered, "They reduced me to the ranks, but I will show them I am not afraid to die." Colonel Chamberlain was sent for. That gallant officer came and knelt by his side. "I was disgraced," hoarsely whispered the dying hero."

You are now exonerated, and promoted to a sergeancy," exclaimed the chivalrous officer. A sweet smile played upon the wan features; a look or satisfaction came to the hungry eyes, and he was dead. In the national cemetery at Gettysburgh is a little mound marked Sergeant George H. Buck, Co. H, 20th Maine Volunteers.

The quartermaster returned to Maine at the close of the war. A few years later, telegrams were flying over the state with the intelligence that there had been an attempted robbery of the Lime Rock Bank at Rockland, that the burglars had been arrested, and that among them was a prominent business man of that town. As the members of our old regiment read his name, they saw it was the ex-quartermaster of whom I have been writing. He was tried, found guilty, and sentenced to serve a term of years in the state prison. As I saw him in the labour gang at Thomaston, dressed in his convict's garb, I could not help thinking of the little affair at Stoneman's Switch, and of Sergeant Buck's honoured grave at Gettysburgh,

Chapter 4

Three Visits to Fredericksburgh

Fredericksburgh is an old city in the county of Spottsylvania, Virginia. It is situated on the southern bank of the Rappahannock river, and is about sixty miles from Richmond. At the breaking out of the rebellion it contained about four thousand inhabitants. The valley of the Rappahannock is so narrow at this place that it hardly permits the passage of the river, the southern bank of which rises in natural terraces many feet above the river's level. On the first of these terraces rests the city, and upon those in rear of and above was fought the great battle of Fredericksburgh. On the north side of the river the land rises so high that artillery planted upon its heights commands the city on the opposite side, and also affords a fine view of the heights above, where the army of General Lee was intrenched.

The North had become impatient at the long delays of General McClellan, and when General Burnside assumed command, public sentiment strongly demanded a forward movement. "*On to Richmond*" was the cry; and the brave General Burnside decided that the advance should be made by the way of Fredericksburgh. The army was reorganised, and divided into three grand divisions, commanded by Generals Hooker, Sumner, and Franklin. On the night of Wednesday, December 10th, 1862, the work of building pontoon bridges across the river began. On Thursday and Friday there was a great deal of fighting where the bridges were being built.

Our movements were tardy and slow, and this enabled the enemy to concentrate his forces, and fortify his position. The city was filled with sharpshooters, who poured a most deadly fire upon our men, who were engaged in the work of building the bridges; and as a last resort, our artillery planted upon the northern bank of the river shelled the town most vigorously and drove the rebels out. When

Friday night came, the divisions of Franklin and Sumner were nearly all across the river. The darkness was intense, but what a magnificent view met our eyes as we stood upon the Stafford hills on the north bank of the river.

Far above the city, on St. Mary's heights, in a crescent-like form, shone the campfires of General Lee. Thousands of General Sumner's men were encamped within the city, and their campfires, burning upon the streets and squares, shone up brightly and cheerfully in the darkness. Far down on our left, confronting the hosts of "Stonewall Jackson," Franklin's men were encamped, and their long line of flitting campfires showed us what an immense army there was prepared for battle on the morrow. Fifty thousand men, under the command of General Hooker, encamped on the northern bank of the river, were to cross tomorrow.

What thoughts filled our minds as we looked at the strange scene! Oh, that we could read the future, and be able to tell what a day would bring forth! What would be the result of tomorrow's battle? Why had the scores of rebel batteries on yonder heights remained so silent while our men were crossing? Had General Lee become frightened as he looked down from his lofty position, and saw the vast Union Army marshalling for the assault? and had he ordered a retreat to Richmond without a battle? or had our men been drawn into a fatal trap? Had Lee reserved his bolts of thunder, to hurl them upon our men in tomorrow's conflict?

A vague suspicion filled our minds as we looked; and as we thought of the fearful carnage, the very air seemed tremulous with ominous sounds.

There was but little sleep that night; the men sat around their campfires, and talked of the morrow. Patriotic songs were sung, and hearts beat high in anticipation of a glorious victory. Perhaps after all it is well for us that we are not able to discern the future. A knowledge of coming events might unman our hearts, and disqualify us to perform our duties.

Saturday morning dawned. Many of our men ate their last breakfast on that morning, little dreaming what awaited them on that fatal day. As I have already intimated, the rebel army was well posted and strongly intrenched. Their right was commanded by "Stonewall Jackson"; Longstreet commanded the centre, and General A. P. Hill their left.

The morning was quite warm, and a thick fog enfolded the contending hosts. Franklin's men, who had crossed the river on pontoons, three miles below the city, on the previous day, were early in motion, and the sounds of battle came rolling heavily up from our left, and the conflict soon opened in our front. The rebel artillery that crowned the heights and encircled the city poured a fearful storm upon our men who were within its streets, and our artillery thundered a terrible response. It was an artillery duel, in which it seemed that the gods were the combatants, and were hurling those iron globes with almighty power. It was soon apparent that our tremendous cannonade had made but little impression upon the rebel works, and that if they Were taken, it must be at the point of the bayonet.

But what a fearful undertaking! It is not necessary to search the pages of ancient history, or the military records of Europe, to find deeds of heroic valour, but only to look at the divisions of Howard and French as they form their lines to make that charge. Never did brave men undertake a more desperate enterprise. At a double-quick they rushed toward the rebel lines. The crescent-shaped hills above them were crowned with fire, as a score of rebel batteries opened upon them. Thick and fast came the plunging, bursting, shrieking messengers of death, but they heeded them not, and with wild cheers pressed onward.

They had almost reached the base of the ridge upon which the rebels were intrenched, when the long lines of rifle-pits behind the stone wall and far up the hillside, gleamed with fire, and twenty thousand rifles poured their deadly contents upon them. Their artillery was so posted that every gun could be turned upon any given point, and thus from the front and along either flank was poured the cruel iron storm. Men fell by hundreds, battalions melted away, the line was shattered, it staggered, then halted, and the next moment fell back repulsed, and sought shelter in a small ravine. They were reinforced by fresh troops, and charged repeatedly upon the heights, but only to be hurled back over those fatal slopes that were raked by the rebel guns.

The First Visit

It is late in the afternoon; Hooker's division is ordered to cross the river; it is a critical moment. On yonder field the battle is undecided; the river, city, and hillsides are throbbing in the fearful conflict; fifty thousand men are hastening to reinforce the shattered and bleeding columns that have been repulsed; banners wave, bands play, the soldiers cheer, and the rebels shell our advancing columns; but in the thrilling excitement of that hour the shells have lost their terror. We rushed across the pontoon bridges, and charged up through the city, until we reached its outskirts, where our brigade formed a line of battle about one-fourth of a mile from our most advanced position. For an hour we lay flat in the mud upon our faces, to escape the shells that were screaming and crashing over our heads.

A terrible struggle was raging around us. New lines were rapidly formed to take the place of those mown down by the fire of the enemy. Charge after charge was made upon the rebel lines by our troops with that same reckless valour they had exhibited in the earlier part of the day. Again, and again were the blue lines thrown back from those heights girded with death. The field was thickly covered with the fallen, many of whom were dead; others were wounded and unable to leave the field, mangled and bleeding, trodden under the feet of the charging columns as they advance and recede, having been victims by scores, of bursting shells and plunging shot.

In the midst of all this confusion our brigade bugle sounded the charge. In a moment's time our men were on their feet, charging at a double-quick through gardens, over wire fences and deep ditches. The air was filled with iron hail. It was the first baptism of fire that our regiment ever received, but with the inspiration derived from such a man as Colonel Ames, it was a very easy thing to face danger and death. The ground over which we charged was dotted with the forms, and stained with the blood, of our brave comrades who had charged over the same ground at an earlier hour. We pressed on until our most advanced line was passed, and then halted under the cover of a little elevation of ground.

Above us and almost within speaking distance was line after line of earthworks filled with rebels, while above them was the artillery vomiting fire and death incessantly. The utter impossibility of taking the rebel position was manifest to every man in the regiment, but we blazed away at the enemy, and they at us. The ground was covered with guns, blankets, knapsacks, haversacks and canteens, while the dead forms of our comrades were lying grim and ghastly around us. These placed in front of us afforded slight protection from the enemy's guns. Night came on with its friendly mantle of darkness, and through the long hours of that December night, we remained prostrated upon the wet, muddy ground. There could be no sleep; the groans of the wounded, and the scattered firing kept up between the contending lines, made a strange medley for those who listened. There was a singular conflict in our breasts. We were wishing the hours away, and yet dreaded to have the darkness disappear.

Sunday morning came; there was no aggressive movement made on either side. Our generals had evidently decided that it was impossible for us to carry the heights. Our army was at the mercy of General Lee, but evidently, he was not aware of our situation. Our troops were crowded back in the narrow streets of the city, and upon the bank of the river. Our only means of recrossing was upon pontoon bridges, and the enemy had artillery enough in position to blow every pontoon in our possession out of the river.

It was impossible for us to advance, and equally impossible for us to retreat, if the enemy was disposed to prevent it. Our position was much more desperate than that of General Lee after the Battle of Antietam. If General Lee had opened his guns upon our army, situated as it was on that Sabbath morning, its destruction or surrender would have been a foregone conclusion. Why Lee did not seize the opportunity, I do not know; but the fact that he did not, goes far to prove that he was not so skilful a commander as his admirers would have us believe.

Our brigade was in close quarters on that memorable Sabbath, and the Johnnies kept a strict watch over our movements. It used to be the old adage at Donneybrook Fair, "Wherever you see a head, hit it," and with our enemy it was, "Wherever you see a head, shoot it"; and as soon as we understood that they desired us to remain quiet, we were very willing to gratify them. There were only a very few exceptions to this rule. Here and there was a man who was so reckless that he would stand up and fire at the rebels, and thus bring upon us the fire of the entire line. One man in Company B took special delight in this. He was cautioned by his comrades, and ordered by his officers, to desist, but heeded them not. He saw a rebel far above him, on the hillside; rising to his feet, he took deliberate aim, and fired. A sharpshooter saw him; a bullet came singing through the air, and with a dull thud it struck in the man's brow, and he fell a corpse, a victim of his own rashness. Thus, through the entire day we lay, hungry, covered with mud, and benumbed with cold.

At about ten o'clock on Sunday evening, under cover of the darkness, we were relieved by another brigade, and fell back to the city. We spread our blankets upon the sidewalks, and endeavoured to get a little sleep. Notwithstanding the grave situation of the army, as a regiment we were much elated. We had fought our first battle, had made a most brilliant charge with unbroken ranks, where veteran regiments had faltered in fear. Colonel Ames passed among the men and complimented them for their gallant conduct; and we all appreciated such words of praise, coming from so brave and brilliant an officer. Sunday night passed, and Monday came and went, but no movements of importance were made on either side.

Burnside was preparing to re treat from his perilous position, and Lee was strengthening his lines in fear that another assault was to be made. Late on Monday night our brigade was pushed up close to the enemy's lines, and in the darkness the work of recrossing the river began. It was a most dangerous undertaking, and upon its success depended the salvation of the army if not of the government. The pontoons were covered with earth, that no noise should reach the enemy and inform him of the movement we were making. Swiftly, and in silence, the troops moved on. At two o'clock in the morning we were withdrawn, and marched back through the city, and to our surprise found that the army had nearly all recrossed the river. I think that our brigade was the last one to leave the enemy's front, and our regiment was the last of the brigade to recross the river.

The battle had been fought and lost. Ten thousand Union soldiers had been killed and wounded. Burnside had blundered in crossing the river, Lee had blundered in allowing him to recross. With sad hearts we marched away from the field of battle, and thus closed my first visit to Fredericksburgh.

My Second Visit

to Fredericksburgh was made in May, 1864. The flames of war had been sweeping for several days through the dense thickets of the wilderness. Grant had begun that desperate march from the "Rapidan to the James." A long line of ambulances and baggage wagons, heavily laden with wounded soldiers made its weary way from the battlefield to Fredericksburgh.

Saturday night, Sunday, and Sunday night, had passed away while we were making this brief journey. On Monday, at noon, we entered the city. The growling of a distant cannonade was heard far away at Spottsylvania. There were but few of the inhabitants that showed themselves outside of their homes, and those looked dark and threatening, with no sympathy for the boys who had gone down in defence of the stars and stripes.

The baggage wagon, drawn by six mules, in which twelve of us had been carried from the wilderness, halted by a little churchyard, where we were unloaded, and placed under the shade of some great trees. Slowly the wounded were taken from the carriages. By scores, hundreds and thousands they came. The church, the yard, every square, and many of the buildings, were filled with the suffering soldiers. Scores had died by the way, and hundreds of others died here. I was very hungry, but there was no food; my shattered leg had not been dressed since it was injured; it was inflamed, swollen, and painful, but I forgot it all as I watched the acute suffering of those around me—humanity shot and mangled in every conceivable form!

The surgeons worked with untiring zeal in attending to the most serious cases. There was a fearful lack of bandages, lint, and everything necessary to dress the wounds. Through Monday night and Tuesday, the air was filled with the groans of the suffering heroes. What a terrible thing is war, and what a fearful responsibility rests upon the instigators of that most unholy rebellion!

On Tuesday I was surprised to hear my name called, and to see approaching me an old schoolmate, known as Freddie Ward when we were boys together, and who was then a member of the 17th Regiment U. S. Infantry. He had been in search of food, and had obtained two cakes of hard bread, and a tin cup half filled with coffee. He needed no invitation to divide. We sat on the ground, and ate the priceless food; we forgot the war and all our surroundings; once more we were boys together in the good old state of Maine; and thus, we passed most delightful moments as we talked *of home*. He remained with me until evening, when our train was once more in motion. We climbed slowly and painfully into our wagon; the mules started off at a brisk pace. The great carriage lumbered and rattled down the principal street leading toward the Rappahannock River; and for the second time I bade goodbye to Fredericksburgh.

My Third Visit

was on a beautiful May evening in 1865. A long line of infantry marched along the northern bank of the Rappahannock river, and encamped just opposite the city of Fredericksburgh. Their uniforms were stained and ragged, and their flags were torn to shreds. They had evidently seen much service in the open field. It was the First division of the old Fifth Army corps, commanded by Major-General Chamberlain. They were fresh from the surrender of General Lee at Appomattox, and were marching from Richmond to Washington. The tents were quickly pitched, and the weary soldiers lay down to rest, but I had a strong desire to revisit the city. In the deep twilight I crossed the river, and passed up one of the principal streets. The indications of war only existed in the buildings, battered and riddled by shot and shells.

I reached the little churchyard. It was not filled with suffering humanity as it had been just one year before. A few worshipers had entered the sanctuary; a sweet song of prayer was rolling out so softly on the still, evening air; I listened, the words were so familiar:

Jesus, lover of my soul,
Let me to thy bosom fly,
When the nearer waters roll,
While the tempests still are high"

I passed on, as nearly as possible over the ground where our regiment made its charge, and then climbed to the heights from which we had been re pulsed. There were no indications left of the fearful struggle. The breastworks had been levelled; the green grass covered the graves of blue and gray alike, so that the one could not be told from the other. I sat for a few moments on a little knoll. How peaceful and quiet! The air was soft and balmy; the tinkle of a cowbell came faint and low from a distant field; a little group of children were playing and laughing merrily in a yard just below me; the songs of the worshipers were indistinctly heard in the distance. I thought of the war now ended, of the brave comrades we had left on so many bloody fields, of the sacred dust scattered so lavishly upon the slopes before me. I could stay no longer; the silence was oppressive; and with noise less steps I retraced my way down the hill, through the little city, across the river, to my regiment, rolled myself in a blanket, and tried to sleep.

CHAPTER 5

Hooker's Campaign—Chancellorsville

General Hooker superseded General Burnside in the command of the Army of the Potomac, on the 26th of January, 1863, and quickly the army responded to the genius of its new commander. At that time Hooker was the favourite with the army. There was something magnetic in the brilliant and reckless daring of the man, and he possessed the wonderful genius of imparting his own enthusiasm and daring to every man in his command. When it was known that he was to be our leader, a new inspiration seemed to be given unto us all. We had all admired General Burnside, and had thought that his failures were largely due to the fact that he did not have the hearty support of his corps commanders, that they had taken advantage of his noble, manly nature, to work his ruin.

We knew that Joe Hooker was not that kind of a fellow, that no corps commanders would trifle with him, that he would deliberately shoot any man who would dare to disobey him, whether he wore the coarse uniform of a private soldier, or the golden straps of a major-general. The whole army seemed to be invigorated with a new life. Excellent rations were issued to the men. There was drill and discipline, and the tall, erect figure of "Fighting Joe" became a familiar sight to the soldiers' eyes as he daily dashed here and there through the various corps of the army. Every man was hopeful, and we used to boast, around our campfires, that we would handle the "Johnnies" without gloves when the spring campaign opened.

The Army of the Potomac at that time must have numbered one hundred thousand men, and it is very doubtful if it was ever in better fighting trim than when it marched for Chancellorsville. A short time before the army marched, our regiment was vaccinated, and by some blunder of the medical director, the smallpox was introduced, and there were several cases of this dreaded disease in its most violent form. On this account, and to our great disgust, we were detached from the brigade, and encamped on what was known as Quarantine hill, and were not permitted to advance with the army; but as the battle opened, we were detailed to guard a telegraph line running from Falmouth to Hooker's headquarters—our regimental line extending, I think, from Falmouth, to where the line was carried across the river—and were situated in such a position that we could learn much of the situation, although the columns of troops were concealed from our view by the forest trees.

Hooker's advance was made in secrecy and with great rapidity, so that no one knew where the blow was to fall. For once the newspaper correspondents "were at sea," and consequently the papers in Washington and New York did not publish the coming campaign in advance, to the rebels, as had been their custom. Our army was separated from the rebels by only a narrow river, and the movement was made so quietly that they did not know we had broken camp. A portion of the army, under the command of General Sedgwick, moved down the river, below the city, where the troops of Franklin had crossed at the battle of Fredericksburgh, and there they successfully effected a crossing.

The rebels received the impression that the whole army was to cross below the city, and hurried reinforcements there, and so failed to guard the forts above; but the remainder of the army, numbering nearly eighty thousand men, were rapidly marching up the river, and crossed the several fords, the last corps having crossed before the rebels knew of our advance. At five o'clock on the morning of April 29th, a horseman dashed through the streets of Fredericksburgh, with the startling information that the Union Army had crossed the river above the city. The bells were tolled, and great alarm prevailed. General Hooker's headquarters were at Chancellorsville, ten miles from Fredericksburgh, and his line of battle was formed in a most advantageous position.

The whole army was elated with their remarkable success. The river had been crossed without opposition, they were intrenched on chosen ground, and General Lee must either fight them there, or retreat to Richmond without a struggle. General Hooker issued an address to his men, congratulating them on the successes they had so easily gained, and all were happy. But as these hours passed, General Lee was not inactive; he had been surprised and outgeneraled thus far, but heroically he worked to repair the disaster. He had some advantages yet. He was familiar with the country where the battle was to be fought; he could move his troops along these familiar roads, and conceal them in the forests, until he had massed them in one place, and then hurl them all upon the weakest place in our extended line; and this we shall soon see he turned to a good account.

Our extreme right was held by the Eleventh corps, composed of German troops, under the command of General Howard. For several hours it had been apparent at army headquarters, that the rebels were moving. All signs seemed to indicate that a large body of troops were moving through the dense forest, toward the right of the Union line.

Hooker dispatched couriers to Generals Slocum and Howard, on the right, to be prepared for an attack on the flank. General Sickles was ordered out with Birney's division, to make a reconnoissance in front, to ascertain the position and strength of the rebels. Through the dense wilderness Birney's men gallantly advanced, until they struck the rear of the rebel column that was massing upon our right. From prisoners captured, Sickles learned that Stonewall Jackson, with a force estimated at forty thousand men, was preparing to attack our right. The prospect was encouraging. Sickles sent the information he had obtained to General Hooker, and asked for another division of the Third corps to be sent to his support, and he would fall upon Jackson's rear, and thus have the rebel chieftain between two fires. Hundreds of prisoners had already been taken.

From our point of observation, we were dis cussing the probability of General Lee retreating to Richmond, when a sullen, booming sound comes from our extreme right. Every man springs to his feet. There can be no mistake. From far up in the front, where Howard holds the line, there comes a sound of awful import. More distinctly we hear it now. Cheers and yells of men mingle with the crash of musketry and the roar of artillery. In a moment we comprehend it all. General Lee has been massing his men, and now, like a thunder bolt, hurls them upon our lines. It is a fearful moment. The roar increases; the yelling of the charging columns is drowned in the awful roar of the guns, and to our dismay it comes nearer.

Our right flank is falling back. The news soon runs along our picket line—"Stonewall Jackson has charged upon Howard, and the Germans have broken, and run back to the river!"

Like all the movements of this famous leader, Jackson, the blow had fallen like a bolt from the skies. At five o'clock General Howard was sitting at the door of the house where he had established his headquarters, and had heard the opening of the battle. He rushed to the scene of conflict, but only to find his men falling back in wild disorder. It was a terrible moment. Our flank was turned and demoralised, and thirty thousand rebels, wild with the excitement of victory, were pouring in upon our flank and rear.

Unless that awful tide was checked, we had lost the battle, and an army with it. Instantly Hooker was in the saddle. With a soldierly instinct he comprehended the danger, and understood what was to be done. Jackson's advance must be checked. A kind providence favoured us at that moment. General Berry, of Rockland, Me., was near at hand, with a division of veteran troops. Hooker knew his man, and shouted, "Berry, sling your men into the breach; don't burn your powder, but take them up on the bayonet!"

At a double-quick, and with a line of glittering steel, they sprang before the gray hosts that outnumbered them five to one. The rebels halted; they had encountered a foe that they could not drive, but Jackson urged them on. Our artillery came to the rescue, and poured a deadly fire upon the rebels. Sickles, Pleasanton, and other officers, threw themselves heroically into the breach, with what men they could muster. Union bravery was too much for rebel strength, and as the sun went down our men held the position, and changed a rout to a victory.

It was an anxious night to us, as we thought of our comrades and of the terrible battle they were fighting.

How ardently we hoped that victory would be theirs on the morrow. It was eleven o'clock, a most beautiful evening, the sky was cloudless, and the moon shone down in its loveliness upon the hostile forces. There was an unbroken quiet all along the lines, but suddenly there was a fearful roar—we could hear the cheering of men, the rattle of musketry, and the fearful booming of artillery. "Jackson making another charge," we all cried, as we heard the fearful onset, and with compressed lips we waited for further developments. But the conflict seemed to be receding from us. It must have been our boys who made the charge. Yes, General Ward's brigade had been massed on our extreme right, and had made this midnight charge to regain the ground lost by Howard in the afternoon. The rebels were surprised and unable to resist the assault, and fell back. Our men rushed on, and regained the line of works from which the Eleventh corps had been driven.

Sunday morning came,—a most beautiful day, designed for the

worship of God, but destined to be a day of bloodshed and death. It had been a busy night with our boys. New lines of defence had been constructed, and the old ones made stronger. Reynolds was on our right, Slocum in the centre, and Sickles on the left. The battle was opened, about sunrise, by the rebels advancing from the place of concealment where they had massed their forces, upon the divisions of Sickles and of Berry. The lurid flames of war soon spread along the line for about a mile, and in a most reckless manner the flower of the Southern Infantry charged upon the Union position.

In close columns they plunged from the woods, upon the divisions of Berry, Birney, Williams and Whipple. No bloodier struggle ever raged on the American continent than where Sickles on that Sabbath morning stayed the tide of the rebel advance. His artillery hurled shells, shot, grape and canister through the solid columns of the enemy. Line after line went down, but only to be replaced by new lines ever appearing from the pine forest beyond. Slowly Sickles was pressed back, his lines were in good order, and every inch of the ground was disputed. They reached a stone wall, and here a desperate stand was made. General Berry was mortally wounded.

The situation rendered our men desperate, and the rebels were repulsed; but once more they charged, pulling their hats down low over their eyes, and with that well-known peculiar Southern yell they came. The ground is raked by our artillery, and is soon covered with their dead. For four hours the rebels breasted that iron storm, in their endeavour to push our men back to the river. At eleven o'clock we could tell by the firing that our men were slowly yielding ground. They had fallen back to Chancellorsville, and here the battle broke out afresh. The old brick house, which so many of the survivors will remember, was now filled with the wounded. Shells went tearing through the rooms, sending death and terror among the bleeding victims of war.

General Hooker, unmoved by danger and threatening disaster, had stood upon the veranda of this house, amid the missiles of death, and superintended the movements of his army. But unfortunately, in the early part of the day, he had been knocked senseless by a blow received from a falling column, that had been hurled from its position by a cannon shot. For hours the army was without an intelligent head. Sickles pressed and overpowered, was sending for reinforcements, but there was no one to order the movement of troops until General Couch assumed the command. A huge shell exploded in one of the rooms of the house, and a moment after, it was infolded in flames. The hour of noon was passed, and the rebels made another desperate endeavour to hurl our forces back into the river; but our men were so well posted, and our artillery was in such an excellent position, that they were pushed back in defeat.

While the battle had been raging at Chancellorsville, Sedgwick had charged and carried the heights at Fredericksburgh, but for some reason he did not press his attack upon Lee's rear, as Hooker had designed, and at a favourable moment Lee turned a large portion of his force upon Sedgwick, and hurled him back with great loss upon the river, which he gladly recrossed, and thus made his escape. Our hearts grew heavy and sad. Monday passed. There was heavy skirmishing but no general engagement. Tuesday, it was evident that our men were preparing to recross the river.

A cold rain storm came on, and through the darkness and storm, our brave men, discouraged, defeated and demoralised, came back across the river, and returned to their old camps. Never since the first Battle of Bull Run was the old Army of the Potomac demoralised as then. We had expected so much from the battle, and it had ended so ingloriously. We had one thing to encourage us:—Stonewall Jackson would never lead his men in another assault upon our lines. This brilliant and daring rebel chieftain was among the slain. In his death, we felt much as the French people did after their naval defeat at Trafalgar. They could build another fleet of vessels, but the English could not produce another Nelson. So, we could raise another army, but the Confederates could not have another Jackson.

The prime cause of our defeat at Chancellorsville has always remained a disputed point. But it is evident that many things combined to that result. The stampede of the Eleventh corps was most disastrous, as it forced Hooker to withdraw from his chosen line of battle, and also to change his line for the battle of the following day. The injury that Hooker received was also a very disastrous feature, as it deprived the army of its commanding general just at a time when an important disposition of the troops should have been made.

General Sedgwick's failure to obey orders, to press up from Fredericksburgh to Chancellorsville, was a grave mistake, as it enabled the enemy to throw his whole force upon a small portion of our army, and thus defeat them in detail. Our troops fought bravely, but in a disconnected mariner, while Lee, by rare generalship, massed his troops, and turned what threatened to be a defeat into a victory. The heavy rains, and the rough usage he had received, prevented General Lee from following up his advantage, which was a fortunate thing for us, as in our demoralised condition we could have made but a feeble resistance to his advance. We had received a fearful shock by this reverse, but the campaigns that followed proved that the germs of heroism still existed in the breasts of the old Army of the Potomac.

At the close of the Battle of Chancellorsville, public sentiment in the South strongly demanded that General Lee should no longer remain upon the defensive. They looked with hungry eyes upon the fertile fields of the prosperous North, and argued that by transferring the war to Northern soil they could feed their half-starved soldiers, that with Washington and Baltimore in the possession of the rebels, Europe would demand that the blockade of the Southern ports be raised, and that public sentiment in the North would demand a cessation of hostilities, and thus the whole situation would be changed. General Lee yielded to the pressure thus brought to bear upon him, and soon began the campaign that closed in his fatal defeat at Gettysburgh.

For a number of days, he succeeded in concealing his movements from General Hooker, but the latter was soon in hot pursuit of the rebels. Our own regiment for several days performed duty, guarding the fords of the Rappahannock River, above the city of Fredericksburgh, and then followed the army by the way of Morristown, Catlett's station, and Manasses junction, through Leesburg, and then crossed the Potomac River at Edwards Ferry. It was a most critical moment in the history of our country. General Lee, with a veteran army of one hundred thousand men, flushed with victory, was on Northern soil; behind him was a desperate South, determined to make his campaign successful.

Our foreign relations were in a very critical condition. England and France were both in active sympathy with the South, and were only awaiting a decisive rebel victory to acknowledge the Confederacy as a nation, and then raise the blockade. In the North public sentiment was much divided.

A portion of the people had been opposed to the war from the beginning, and our repeated defeats had strengthened their opposition. Another large portion was loyal to the government, but severely censured and criticised all the movements made to suppress the rebellion, and the little success gained by our troops in the field. Of the remainder, many were hopeful, but others were despondent, and feared that General Lee would be able to dictate his own terms to the defenders of the Union. When Lee crossed the Potomac, and his troops overran Maryland, threatening Washington and Baltimore, a torrent of abuse was poured upon the Army of the Potomac by its Northern critics.

Men gathered on the farms, in the stores, and on the street corners, and discussed the campaigns in Virginia. Each one knew just how it should be done, and thus, through those fearful months, a great many men helped crush the rebellion by criticising the army and evading the draft. In newspaper offices and halls of legislation enough military campaigns were planned by those who had never seen a battalion of troops, to have crushed all the rebellions the world ever saw, if one-half of them had been carried into effect. The Army of the Potomac was at first soundly berated for allowing Lee to enter Maryland, but as his forces advanced toward Pennsylvania, and the danger became more apparent, this tone of abuse was changed, and from ministerial studies and editorial sanctums, there came the most frantic appeals to the army.

These men felt that it was a gross violation of their rights as American citizens to have the rebels so near, and their peaceful minds disturbed by scenes of bloodshed and fears of personal danger, and they called upon the soldiers to avenge their sufferings with Spartan-like courage and sacrifice, exhorting them to shed their last drop of blood, if necessary, to hurl Lee's forces back across the Potomac. "Better try it on themselves, and see how they like it," muttered the boys in blue, as tired, footsore and hungry, they pressed on after the rebels.

"Confound those fellows," growled a sergeant one night, as he dropped a daily *Tribune* he had been reading, "I am tired and sick of them kid-gloved fellows telling us what to do, and eternally finding fault because we do not do more. I wish they had to try it themselves."

"Yes," chimed in another, "it is a mighty easy thing for them to tell us to shed the last drop of our blood in this glorious cause, but I notice the fellers who make that kind of talk never enlist."

"That's so, Bill," continued a third speaker, "and if they are drafted they either have a cramp in the stomach, or an old mother dependent upon them for her support. I wish they had to face the music."

"I move that we get up a regiment of Beechers and Greeleys," said another, "and arm them with sixteen shooters. Lord, wouldn't the Johnnies laugh to see them shoot?"

"That's good," cried a little ragged private, who was lying on his back, with his bare, blistered feet elevated over a knapsack, so that they would cool off in the evening air, "and give them nigger officers. They will probably shoot themselves, the niggers, or the rebels, and in either case it will be an almighty benefit to the government."

A loud laugh here ran around the circle of soldiers, and three lusty cheers were given for the "Beecher and Greeley Guards." But it was not all mirth and carelessness within the ranks, as the days passed by. If you could have seen these men as they toiled on in the intense heat, along those dusty roads, or sat with them around the campfires that flickered out through the darkness, you would have noticed that they were sober, candid, intelligent, thoughtful men, and while they indignantly rejected the class of criticism to which I have alluded, they had not forgotten the anxious friends at home, or their grave responsibility as defenders of the nation's life. Look for a moment at this little scene on a hillside in Maryland.

It has been a long, tedious day's march of thirty miles. The scanty supper of hard tack and coffee has been eaten. The thin blankets have been spread upon the hard ground for the soldiers' bed. They know that before sunrise tomorrow, the shrill blasts of the bugle will awaken the echoes upon the hillsides, calling them to "fall in" for another day's march, but they cannot retire yet; they are thinking of loved ones far away. Little packages are tenderly taken from the pocket over the heart, and carefully unrolled. Letters from home received weeks before are read again and again; the pictures of dear friends are eagerly scanned, until lines and features alike are blurred by the falling tears; and thus, around the campfires, amidst these sacred reminders, and beside the torn and faded battle flags, resolutions were formed that were to be felt upon the battlefield, resolutions that sealed the defeat of General Lee, before the thunders of Gettysburgh proclaimed it to the world.

We had expected to find the States of Maryland and Pennsylvania in arms to repel the invaders, but we were surprised at the in difference of the people. They gave us a warm welcome, but endeavoured to make money by selling us water, fruit, and provisions at most exorbitant prices. We usually purchased their entire stock; and as we had no money, told them to "charge it to Uncle Sam." They endeavoured to shame us by comparing our conduct to that of the rebels, but they soon learned that words had no effect upon hungry Yankees.

CHAPTER 6

Gettysburgh

On the 28th of June, General Hooker, at his own request, was relieved of his command, and it was given to General Meade. The latter had been in command of our corps. We knew him to be a brave and gallant officer, but feared a mistake had been made in changing commanders just as a battle was to be fought. Many rumours came back to us from the front, and from these we learned that Lee's troops numbered at least one hundred thousand, that he was concentrating his forces near Gettysburgh, and that a desperate battle would probably be fought near that place. We knew that the army of the Potomac did not number over eighty thousand men, that the authorities of the states of Pennsylvania and New York were moving so slowly in raising troops that but little aid would be received from them, and that unaided we must cope with our old foe.

On the first day of July we crossed the state line of Pennsylvania, and noted the event by loud cheering and much enthusiasm. And here, on the border of the state, we learned that our cavalry under General Buford, and our old First corps, under General Reynolds, had on that day encountered the rebels at Gettysburgh, and that on the morrow the great battle would be fought. Night came on, but we halted not. We knew that our comrades on the distant battlefield needed our aid, and we hastened on. It was a beautiful evening. The moon shone from a cloudless sky, and flooded our way with its glorious light.

The people rushed from their homes and stood by the roadside to welcome us, men, women, and children all gazing on the strange spectacle. Bands played, the soldiers and the people cheered, banners waved, and white handkerchiefs fluttered from doors and windows, as the blue, dusty column surged on. That moonlight march will always be remembered by its survivors. A staff officer sat on his horse by the roadside. In a low voice he spoke to our colonel as he passed.

"What did he say?" anxiously inquired the men.

"McClellan is to command us on the morrow."

McClellan, our first commander, who had been removed, criticised, and we thought he was forgotten; but our old love for him broke out afresh. He had never seemed one-half so dear to us before. Men waved their hats and cheered until they were hoarse and wild with excitement. It is strange what a hold little Mac had on the hearts of his soldiers. At midnight we halted, having marched more than thirty miles on that eventful day. The men threw themselves upon the ground to get a little rest and sleep. Sleep on, brave fellows, for the morrow's struggle will call for both strength and courage!

While they are sleeping, we will step across the country for a few miles and view Gettysburgh in the moonlight, that we may better understand the battle-ground of tomorrow. It has been a bloody day around this little country village. Early in the morning the cavalry under General Buford had met the enemy advancing in great force, and bravely contested the ground with him. General Reynolds, hearing the heavy firing, had pushed the First corps forward to Buford's support, and formed his line of battle upon an eminence west of Seminary Ridge. The conflict soon became general.

The gallant Reynolds was killed at the first volley, as he was riding to the front to ascertain the position of the enemy. General Doubleday assumed command of the corps. It was a fearful struggle. Hill's corps of the rebel army on the one side, and the First corps, much the inferior in numbers, upon the other.

General Howard arrives with the Eleventh corps. The rebels also receive reinforcements. Back and forth the contending lines press each other until late in the afternoon, when the Union troops are overpowered, and are hurled, bleeding and mangled, through the streets of Gettysburgh, and up the slopes of Cemetery Ridge. General Hancock arrives at this moment from the headquarters of General Meade, and assumes the command, and in concert with General Howard, selected the line of battle. The village is filled with the highly elated rebels, who loudly boast that they can easily whip the Yankees on the morrow.

Things look a little desperate on Cemetery Hill. Reynolds and thousands of his gallant men have fallen, but their courage saved the position for the Union Army, and on that hill our line of battle is being formed under the supervision of our brave generals,—Howard the one-armed hero, Hancock the brilliant leader, Dan Sickles the irresistible commander of the Third corps, and brave Slocum of the Twelfth. Sykes and Sedgwick with their respective corps will put in an appearance on the morrow. At midnight General Meade arrives and assumes command of the entire line. It is evident at a glance that the old army of the Potomac is "on deck," and that if General Lee expects to win Gettysburgh by fighting a few brigades of raw militia, he is very much mistaken. The ridge on which our line of battle is being formed somewhat resembles a horseshoe in shape. Cemetery Hill, facing the northwest, is the point nearest Gettysburgh and Lee's headquarters, and that point we will call the toe calk of the horseshoe.

To the left and rear is Round Top, which represents one heel calk, while Wolf's Hill to the right and rear represents the other. Howard, with the Eleventh corps, is stationed at Cemetery Hill. The First and Twelfth corps, under Generals Slocum and Wadsworth, formed our right, reaching from Howard to our extreme right at Wolf's Hill. At the left of Howard is Hancock and the Second corps, and at his left Sickles with the Third, in a somewhat advanced position, reaching unto our extreme left, near Little Round Top. It has been decided that General Sykes and Sedgwick shall be held in reserve to reinforce any part of our line upon which Lee may mass his troops. And thus, through the hours of that night our preparations for the battle were being made.

If General Lee had pushed on his forces, and followed up his advantage gained in the afternoon, he would have been master of the situation, but this delay was fatal to him. The Union line is formed, the artillery is in position. The rebels outnumber us both in men and guns, but we have the ridge, and are on the defensive. The tired men sink upon the ground to catch a few moments' sleep before the battle opens. All is still in Gettysburg!! save the groans of the wounded and dying. It is an anxious night throughout the great loyal North. Telegrams have been flashing all over the country, bearing the sad tidings of the death of Reynolds and the repulse of his troops.

Everyone knows that this battle is to decide, to a large extent, the fortunes of war. There is no sleep for the people. Strong men are pale with excitement and anxiety, as through the hours of night they talk of the coming conflict; Christians gather in their sanctuaries to pray that success may be ours on the morrow; mothers, wives and sisters, with pale, upturned faces, pray to God to protect their loved ones in the dangers of the battle. It is the most anxious night through which

America ever passed. God grant that we shall never pass through another like it!

At daylight, on the morning of July 2nd, we resumed our march, and in a few hours halted within supporting distance of the left flank of our army, about a mile to the right of Little Round Top. The long forenoon passed away, and to our surprise the enemy made no attack. This was very fortunate for our army, as it enabled our men to strengthen our lines of fortifications, and also to obtain a little rest, of which they were in great need. The rebels were also engaged in throwing up rude lines of defences, hurrying up reinforcements, and in discussing the line of action they should pursue, for, to use General Lee's own words in his report of the battle, they "unexpectedly found themselves confronted by the Federal Army."

The hour of noon passed, and the sun had measured nearly one-half the distance across the western sky, before the assault was made. Then, as suddenly as a bolt of fire flies from the storm-cloud, a hundred pieces of rebel artillery open upon our left flank, and under the thick canopy of screaming, hissing, bursting shells, Longstreet's corps was hurled upon the troops of General Sickles. Instantly our commanders discerned the intention of General Lee. It was to turn and crush our left flank, as he had crushed our right at Chancellorsville. It was a terrible onslaught.

The brave sons of the South never displayed more gallant courage than on that fatal after noon of July 2nd. But brave Dan Sickles and the old Third corps were equal to the emergency, and stood as immovable against the surging tides as blocks of granite. But a new and appalling danger suddenly threatened the Union Army. Little Round Top was the key to the entire position. Rebel batteries planted on that rocky bluff could shell any portion of our line at their pleasure. For some rea son Sickles had not placed any infantry upon this important position. A few batteries were scattered along its ragged side, but they had no infantry support.

Lee saw at a glance that Little Round Top was the prize for which the two armies were contending, and with skilful audacity he determined to wrest it from his opponent. While the terrible charge was being made upon the line of General Sickles, Longstreet threw out a whole division, by extending his line to his right, for the purpose of seizing the coveted prize. The danger was at once seen by our officers, and our brigade was ordered forward, to hold the hill against the assault of the enemy. In a moment all was excitement. Every soldier seemed to understand the situation, and to be inspired by its danger. "Fall in! Fall in! By the right flank! Double-quick! March!" and away we went, under the terrible artillery fire.

It was a moment of thrilling interest. Shells were exploding on every side. Sickles' corps was enveloped in sheets of flame, and looked like a vast windrow of fire. But so intense was the excitement that we hardly noticed these surroundings. Up the steep hillside we ran, and reached the crest. "On the right by file into line," was the command, and our regiment had assumed the position to which it had been assigned. We were on the left of our brigade, and consequently on the extreme left of all our line of battle. The ground sloped to our front and left, and was sparsely covered with a growth of oak trees, which were too small to afford us any protection.

Shells were crashing through the air above our heads, making so much noise that we could hardly hear the commands of our officers; the air was filled with fragments of exploding shells and splinters torn from mangled trees; but our men appeared to be as cool and deliberate in their movements as if they had been forming a line upon the parade ground in camp. "Our regiment mustered about three hundred and fifty men. Company B, from Piscataquis County, commanded by the gallant Captain Morrill, was ordered to deploy in our front as skirmishers. They boldly advanced down the slope and disappeared from our view. Ten minutes have passed since we formed the line; the skirmishers must have advanced some thirty or forty rods through the rocks and trees, but we have seen no indications of the enemy.

"But look!" "Look!" "Look!" exclaimed half a hundred men in our regiment at the same moment; and no wonder, for right in our front, between us and our skirmishers, whom they have probably captured, we see the lines of the enemy. They have paid no attention to the rest of the brigade stationed on our right, but they are rushing on, determined to turn and crush the left of our line. Colonel Chamberlain with rare sagacity understood the movement they were making, and bent back the left flank of our regiment until the line formed almost a right angle with the colours at the point, all these movements requiring a much less space of time than it requires for me to write of them.

How can I describe the scenes that followed? Imagine, if you can, nine small companies of infantry, numbering perhaps three hundred men, in the form of a right angle, on the extreme flank of an army of eighty thousand men, put there to hold the key of the entire position against a force at least ten times their number, and who are desperately determined to succeed in the mission upon which they came. Stand firm, ye boys from Maine, for not once in a century are men permitted to bear such responsibilities for freedom and justice, for God and humanity, as are now placed upon you.

The conflict opens. I know not who gave the first fire, or which line received the first lead. I only know that the carnage began. Our regiment was mantled in fire and smoke. I wish that I could picture with my pen the awful details of that hour,—how rapidly the cartridges were torn from the boxes and stuffed in the smoking muzzles of the guns; how the steel rammers clashed and clanged in the heated barrels; how the men's hands and faces grew grim and black with burning powder; how our little line, baptised with fire, reeled to and fro as it advanced or was pressed back; how our officers bravely encouraged the men to hold on and recklessly exposed themselves to the enemy's fire,—a terrible medley of cries, shouts, cheers, groans, prayers, curses, bursting shells, whizzing rifle bullets and clanging steel.

And if that was all, my heart would not be so sad and heavy as I write. But the enemy was pouring a terrible fire upon us, his superior forces giving him a great advantage. Ten to one are fearful odds where men are contending for so great a prize. The air seemed to be alive with lead. The lines at times were so near each other that the hostile gun barrels almost touched. As the contest continued, the rebels grew desperate that so insignificant a force should so long hold them in check. At one time there was a brief lull in the carnage, and our shattered line was closed up, but soon the contest raged again with renewed fierceness. The rebels had been reinforced, and were now determined to sweep our regiment from the crest of Little Round Top.

Many of our companies have suffered fearfully. Look at Company H for a moment. Charley, my old tent-mate, with a fatal wound in his breast, staggered up to brave Captain Land. "My God, Sergeant Steele!" ejaculated the agonised captain as he saw the fate of his beloved sergeant.

"I am going, Captain," cried the noble fellow, and fell dead, weltering in his blood.

Sergeant Lathrop, with his brave heart and gigantic frame, fell dying with a frightful wound. Sergeant Buck, reduced to the ranks at Stoneman's Switch, lay down to die, and was promoted as his life blood ebbed away. Adams, Ireland, and Lamson, all heroes, are lying dead at the feet of their comrades. Libby, French, Clifford, Hilt, Ham, Chesly, Morrison, West, and Walker are all severely wounded, and nearly all disabled. But there is no relief, and the carnage goes on. Our line is pressed back so far that our dead are within the lines of the enemy. The pressure made by the superior weight of the enemy's line is Severely felt. Our ammunition is nearly all gone, and we are using the cartridges from the boxes of our wounded comrades.

A critical moment has arrived, and we can remain as we are no longer; we must advance or retreat. It must not be the latter, but how can it be the former? Colonel Chamberlain understands how it can be done. The order is given "Fix bayonets!" and the steel shanks of the bayonets rattle upon the rifle barrels. "Charge bayonets, charge!" Every man understood in a moment that the movement was our only salvation, but there is a limit to human endurance, and I do not dishonour those brave men when I write that for a brief moment the order was not obeyed, and the little line seemed to quail under the fearful fire that was being poured upon it.

Oh, for some man reckless of life, and all else save his country's honour and safety, who would rush far out to the front, lead the way, and inspire the hearts of his exhausted comrades! In that moment of supreme need the want was supplied. Lieut. H. S. Melcher, an officer who had worked his way up from the ranks, and was then in command of Co. F, at that time the colour company, saw the situation, and did not hesitate, and for his gallant act deserves as much as any other man the honour of the victory on Round Top. With a cheer, and a flash of his sword, that sent an inspiration along the line, full ten paces to the front he sprang—ten paces—more than half the distance between the hostile lines.

"Come on! Come on! Come on, boys!" he shouts. The colour sergeant and the brave colour guard follow, and with one wild yell of anguish wrung from its tortured heart, the regiment charged.

The rebels were confounded at the movement. We struck them with a fearful shock. They recoil, stagger, break and run, and like avenging demons our men pursue. The rebels rush toward a stone wall, but, to our mutual surprise, two scores of rifle barrels gleam over the rocks, and a murderous volley was poured in upon them at close quarters. A band of men leap over the wall and capture at least a hundred prisoners. Piscataquis has been heard from, and as usual it was a good report. This unlooked-for reinforcement was Company B, whom we supposed were all captured.

Our colonel's commands were simply to hold the hill, and we did not follow the retreating rebels but a short distance. After dark an order came to advance and capture a hill in our front. Through the trees, among the rocks, up the steep hillside, we made our way, captured the position, and also a number of prisoners.

On the morning of July 3rd, we were relieved by the Pennsylvania reserves, and went back to the rear. Of our three hundred and fifty men, one hundred and thirty-five had been killed and wounded. We captured over three hundred prisoners, and a detachment sent out to bury the dead found fifty dead rebels upon the ground where we had fought. Our regiment had won imperishable honour, and our gallant colonel was to be known in history as the hero of "Little Round Top." We cared for our wounded as well as we could, although there was but little we could do for them.

Our dead were buried, and their graves were marked by the loving hands of their comrades. I suppose that their remains have since been removed to the National Cemetery at Gettysburgh, but somehow, I wish they had been left where they fell, on the rugged brow of Round Top, amid the battle-scarred rocks which they baptised with their blood as they died.

While the desperate encounter was taking place on Little Round Top, the fearful conflict continued to rage in front of Sickles' command, and when Longstreet's bleeding brigades fell back in defeat, it was not because they had not fought bravely, but because it was impossible to push back our line of battle. It was a fearful blow to the fortunes of the Confederacy when Longstreet was repulsed on that eventful afternoon. But important events were about to transpire on our right. General Ewell had been massing his troops through the afternoon, and swore with a fearful oath that he would take and hold the positions occupied by Howard and Slocum, or he would die in the attempt.

Just as the sun was sinking from view, the storm burst upon our lines. General Howard, with an empty sleeve pinned to his shoulder, stood calm and erect amid the bursting shells. That Christian gentleman, while scorning to exhibit the profane and reckless deportment of some of his brother officers, was nevertheless as heroic an officer as ever served in the Army of the Potomac. An eye witness on this occasion testifies that, while the shells were falling and bursting on every side of him, he stood leaning against a tombstone, surveying the movements of the enemy with his field-glass, and that his countenance was as unmoved as the marble upon which he leaned for support. His men (the Eleventh corps) remembered the surprise at

Chancellorsville, and were anxious to meet the enemy, to regain the prestige that they felt they had lost.

Under the terrible fire of artillery and musketry, the Southern infantry charged in a simultaneous attack upon the central position of Howard, and the long line of defences held by the soldiers of the First and Twelfth corps. Howard's artillery opened to receive them, and fired with such rapidity that the men were obliged to wait for the guns to cool. The infantry poured volley after volley upon the Southern columns; but in defiance of all this opposition the gallant Southerners swept across those fields covered with the dead, and like a ragged ocean wave broken and lashed by the fury of the gale, reached the breastworks of General Howard.

General Barlow's division, commanded by General Ames (formerly colonel of the Twentieth Maine Regiment), nobly breasted the avalanche that poured upon them, but they were pressed back, two batteries having been already captured by the rebels. But at this critical moment, the guns of Stevens' Fifth Maine Battery were brought to bear upon the assaulting column with double-shotted canister. Reinforcements arrive. General Ames rallies his shattered line, and gallantly leads them upon the foe. The Louisiana Tigers swarmed upon the muzzles of his guns. It was now a hand to hand conflict—clubbed rifles, bayonet thrusts, sabre strokes, stones, clubs, and whatever came to hand.

The struggle was brief, bloody and desperate. Many rebels were captured, and the remainder, but a feeble remnant of that gallant corps, went rushing wildly back over that field of carnage and defeat. A wild cheer went up from the victors. Chancellorsville has been redeemed, and the gallant German troops once more have a record of which they may well be proud.

The attack made upon the Twelfth corps had met with a slight success. Only one brigade had been left to guard a long line of rifle-pits, the remainder of the troops having been sent to reinforce the centre. The charging columns of Ewell swept over this feeble line, and as darkness came on, he held a portion of the Union rifle-pits, which perhaps would be the key to a rebel victory on the morrow.

That was a memorable night at Gettysburgh. Mingled sadness and joy filled the hearts of the Union soldiers,—sadness on account of the loss of so many of our noble comrades, joy that it had been a day of decided success to the Union Army. The people around Gettysburgh endeavoured in vain to learn from the Confederates what the result of the day's conflict had been, but, although the rebels were not disposed to talk, they could easily detect disappointment and defeat written upon their faces.

It was a gloomy night in the rebel camp. The Confederate leaders were now fully convinced that the old Army of the Potomac had overtaken them, and that their chances for success were nearly hopeless. In their council of war some even proposed that they should retreat that night. But there was too much at stake for that. A retreat from Gettysburgh would discourage the South, and destroy all hopes of intervention on the part of European nations. In fact, retreat would be almost as bad as death. And then Ewell, on the rebel left, had gained a slight advantage; and if he was heavily reinforced by a desperate advance in the early morning, they might regain all they had lost, and drive the Union Army from its position. Accordingly, General Rhodes' division was pushed up to reinforce Ewell, and other troops were concentrated near that point in the line to assist in the contemplated assault.

The rank and file of the rebel army were evidently discouraged and much demoralised, but their officers assured them of an easy victory on the morrow. They were told that the Union line was made up of raw brigades, which were already terrified by the slaughter, and that they could easily be crushed before the main portion of the Army of the Potomac could arrive.

Troops were also being moved within the lines of General Meade. The Twelfth corps was moved back to our right, and was also reinforced by two brigades from the Sixth. At daylight these troops advanced upon Ewell and Rhodes, to regain their lost rifle-pits. The conflict was sharp and bloody. The artillery crashed and roared. Inch by inch our men advanced and pressed the rebels back at the point of the bayonet, and before eleven o'clock the rebels were dislodged and driven back in defeat.

A cheer loud and joyous rolled along the Union line when it became apparent that the enemy had lost the only advantage gained in yesterday's battle. From eleven until half-past one all is quiet. Scarcely a shot is fired. Nothing is heard save the groans of the wounded and the low conversation of the men. We wondered at the meaning of that silence. Had Lee given up and was he to confess his defeat by a hasty flight? Or was it the momentary calm that usually precedes the bursting forth of the storm?

General Lee climbed to the cupola of the college building and there surveyed the field of death. He evidently became convinced that it would be useless for him to endeavour to gain any advantage on his left, where Ewell and Rhodes had just been thrown back with such fearful slaughter. He resolved to make one more desperate attempt to break the Union lines, and that the charge should be made upon Meade's left centre upon the troops of Hancock and Howard. It was a most desperate undertaking, and it speaks volumes for Southern chivalry and courage that they had officers and men to plan so brilliant a charge and to carry it into effect.

At half-past one o'clock one hundred and fifty pieces of rebel artillery opened on the Union lines. It was the most terrific cannonade that ever shook the continent. Bursting shells fell everywhere. They dropped down by scores around the little farmhouse where General Meade had his headquarters. Wounded men far in rear of the line of battle, lying weak and bleeding upon the ground, were torn in atoms by the bursting shells. It was a scene that cannot be pictured and will never be forgotten by those who saw it. One writer in speaking of it uses the following language:

> The air was alive with all mysterious sounds, and death in every one of them. There were muffled howls that seemed in rage because their missiles missed you, the angry buzz of the familiar minie, the spit of the common musket ball, hisses, and the great whirring rushes of shells. And then came others which made the air instinct with warning or quickened it with vivid alarm—long wails that fatefully bemoaned the death they wrought, fluttering screams that filled the whole space with their horror, and encompassed one about as a garment, cries that ran the diapason of terror and despair.

Our generals understood the importance of that terrible storm. Every cannon on Cemetery Ridge, from the centre to right and left, was pointed into the valley through which the charging columns must come. Not one of them replied to the rebel shots, but each one was crammed to the muzzle with fire and death. Woe to the brave men who provoke their fire! Yelling like incarnate demons the rebels charge—six gigantic brigades—the flower of the Confederacy—the old Imperial Guard of Lee's army. Their courage was worthy a nobler cause and deserved a better fate. They rushed down Seminary Ridge, and were coming across the plain that intervenes between the two ridges.

The rebel artillery—one hundred and fifty guns—were pouring their terrible fire above the charging columns, and pounding our line of battle with terrible vengeance, but not a Union gun replied. The enemy evidently concluded that our guns had been silenced by their terrific cannonade, and with renewed courage rushed on to dislodge the supposed Yankee militia from their rifle-pits. It was a grand spectacle, that long line of gray clad soldiers in a semi-circular form, charging under the crashing shells of their own comrades, upon a line of breastworks that appeared to be only tenanted by the dead. They are so near that you. can almost toss a biscuit within their lines.

The signal is given to fire. Instantly zigzag flames leap along our lines, and a horrible roar and frightful yells for a moment drown all other sounds. The rebels had advanced so near to our lines, and were coming with such force, that in many places they were not checked until they reached our breastworks, and when our infantry arose to receive them, they, to their surprise saw, instead of raw militia, bronzed faces and old familiar badges. "The army of the Potomac!" they exclaimed, as they went down in defeat and death. Such a conflict could not be prolonged. In a brief time, the rebels were defeated. It was not a retreat of six brigades rushing back to be reorganised. They had vanished—gone like leaves of autumn before the tempest.

A few officers went dashing wildly back on fleet horses, while here and there a broken and shattered battalion of brave soldiers returned to tell the awful story of death,—one colour sergeant manfully bearing his colours, the only flag that went back from that charging column to the rebel army Do you ask where these men have gone? If so, look at the four thousand prisoners within the Union lines, and the great windrows of dead piled upon the bloody plain.

The Battle of Gettysburgh has been fought and won for the Union cause. General Lee's army of one hundred thousand men with which he entered Pennsylvania, has been reduced by death, wounds, and prisoners to sixty thousand. Leaving his dead to be buried and many of his wounded to be cared for by his enemy, he gathers up his bleeding and defeated forces and retreats rapidly toward Virginia.

The Confederacy had received its death blow. New armies could be raised, munitions of war purchased, campaigns planned, and scores of bloody battles fought, but all this was to be but the heroism of despair. The prestige lost in the Pennsylvania campaign could not be regained. The fate of the Confederacy was but a question of time. The Union Army must have lost, in all, twenty-five thousand men. General

Meade was therefore at the head of an army of fifty thousand, who were footsore with long, weary marches, and completely exhausted with the hardships of the terrible campaign. Had General Lee been vigorously pursued, he could never have reached his native Virginia. Whether the army of General Meade was in a condition to make that pursuit or not is a disputed question, and one which perhaps a private has no right to discuss. Lee made good his escape, recrossed the Potomac, and intrenched himself in the wilderness along the Rappahannock River.

The North rejoiced over the defeat of the rebels, and resolved anew that the rebellion must be crushed and the country saved.

Thousands of loyal hands have assisted in the task of constructing the national monument and cemetery at Gettysburgh, and henceforth it is to be the Mecca of those who love to stand amid the ashes of the gallant dead, and draw inspiration from deeds of manly daring.

CHAPTER 7

From Gettysburgh to Rappahannock Station

On the fifth of July the Army of the Potomac turned from the battlefield of Gettysburgh, upon which they left sixteen thousand of their comrades killed and wounded, and began the pursuit of General Lee. The pursuit had been delayed too long, for it had given the rebel chieftain twenty-four hours' advantage. General Lee had left his dead unburied, and his wounded uncared for, and with his defeated army was making forced marches to endeavour to recross the Potomac River before our army could overtake him. On every hand there were indications of the defeat and demoralisation of his army. If ours had been a vigorous pursuit he would not have reached the Potomac, and the destiny of the rebellion would have been determined upon the plains of Maryland.

A freshet of unusual severity came on, the rain for days fell in torrents, the roads were almost impassable, and our advance was made very slowly. There was continual skirmishing with the enemy's rear, and occasionally indications of a battle. In one of these skirmishes, near Fair Play, Company E of our regiment lost eight men, two of whom were killed, and the remainder taken prisoners, not one of whom ever lived to rejoin their regiment. We found the enemy intrenched at Williamsport, Maryland, a beautiful village on the Potomac River. We had at last brought the enemy to a halt, and we were once more facing him. We were all anxious for a battle to be fought, for we knew that if Lee escaped across the river, it meant many long, weary marches and bloody battles for us.

A council of war was held, and it was found that many of the corps and division commanders were unwilling to make the attack.

The army had sustained a sad loss in the death of General Reynolds, and in the severe wounds received by Generals Hancock and Sickles. In all probability, if they had been in that council of war, the Army of the Potomac would have been hurled upon the position of Lee, and his retreat would have been impossible. When the advance was finally made, we found that the enemy was making a rapid retreat in the direction of the Shenandoah valley.

We crossed the Potomac at Berlin, and pushed on for several days down the Loudon valley, the Blue Ridge being between the two great armies. There was occasional skirmishing as they came in contact with each other through the gaps of the mountain chain. On the 23rd our division relieved the Third corps, in Manassas gap. The scenery was bold and grand. The ragged, perpendicular hill, overhanging crags, huge boulders, thick growth of stunted forest trees, and dense under brush, all combined to make up a picture, which for rugged beauty is seldom excelled. We supposed the enemy to be intrenched in force in our immediate vicinity, and expected an attack every moment.

Our rations were exhausted, and we were almost in a state of starvation, but fortunately for us we found blackberries of the most luscious quality, and in great quantities, the bushes being literally covered with them, so that the men easily secured enough to satisfy the demands of hunger. When we reached the lofty crest, we found that the enemy had retreated, but from this point we obtained a magnificent view of the beautiful Shenandoah valley, and as we looked over on its fertile fields, smiling so sweetly in the sunshine, we were reminded of Moses, when, from the heights of Pisgah, he surveyed the promised land, but like him, were not permitted to go over and enjoy it. The beautiful scenery repaid us for the toilsome ascent. When the bugle sounded the recall, we descended, carrying with us very pleasant memories of the scenery in Manassas gap.

We continued our march until the Rappahannock River was reached, where we halted, and for a month guarded Beverly Ford. While here Colonel Chamberlain, who had commanded our regiment since the promotion of General Ames, the previous winter, assumed command of the brigade. In those eventful months, Colonel Chamberlain had, by his uniform kindness and courtesy, his skill and brilliant courage, endeared himself to all his men, and had done much to give his regiment that enviable reputation it has since enjoyed. Our regiment was especially favoured in its two first commanders, and those who came in the line of succession were well worthy to follow such illustrious predecessors.

Lieutenant-Colonel Gilmore here took command of the regiment. Then back and forth across the country we marched and countermarched. When we advanced, the enemy retreated, then both would halt; when he advanced, we kindly retreated. Neither commander evidently dared to become aggressive, and bring on a general engagement. There was much heavy skirmishing, an occasional battle, and if either side gained any advantage there was no disposition shown to follow it up and gain important results.

The men became sour, weary and discouraged; there seemed to be no established plan of action; we would go into camp, and have orders to arrange and police our company streets and parade ground, as we would probably remain for weeks. We would all forget our weariness, and work with a will, and then when everything was in "apple-pie" order, it would be "strike tents," and then march half-a-dozen miles, and go through the same experience again. Thus, days and weeks passed away. The monotony of this life was occasionally broken by some events of considerable importance.

In the month of August, 1863, while our regiment was encamped near Beverly Ford, on the Rappahannock River, a report was circulated through our corps that five deserters had been arrested, were being tried by a court-martial, and would probably be found guilty and be executed. This caused quite a ripple of excitement in camp. Years before we had read of deserters being shot, and our boyish hearts had been thrilled with the vivid descriptions given; but we had never witnessed such a spectacle. We had seen death in almost every form, but this was something new.

One of the most solemn events that occurs in army life is the execution of soldiers. There are several offenses in the army punishable by death. There are times when the offenders are deserving of much sympathy, but military laws must be enforced with an iron rigor, or there would be no safety for the army at all. We may have much sympathy for the weary soldier, who, in the darkness of the night, falls asleep upon his picket post, and death for such an offense may appear to be a severe penalty, but when we remember that his hours of sleep may have allowed death to visit his comrades, and defeat to overtake an entire army, we understand why such severe penalties are inflicted.

But when the crime is desertion, there can be but little sympathy for the offender, especially if he has enlisted for the bounty received, with the intention of deserting at the first opportunity. Where the case has been aggravated by several enlistments, bounties, and desertions, the offender justly forfeits all claims upon human sympathy; and yet, after all, under the most aggravating circumstances, it is a very solemn thing to see human beings led forth to be shot like dogs, and those who witness such scenes receive an impression that can never be shaken off.

The court-martial found the deserters guilty, and sentenced them all to be shot. The 29th of August was the day when the sentence of death was to be carried into execution, and the whole Fifth corps was to witness the spectacle. The regiments were massed in columns by divisions around a hollow square. The lines were so formed that nearly every man in the corps could obtain a view of the whole situation. The lines were all formed, and for some moments we waited for the arrival of the solemn procession. It soon made its appearance, and while the description of it may not impress my readers with much force, I can assure them that it made a deep and lasting impression upon the minds of those who witnessed it. Every detail had evidently been arranged for the special object of making a solemn impression upon the interested spectators.

Let us for a moment imagine the scene. On a broad level field, the old Fifth corps with its bronzed veterans and tattered flags, closed in solid columns around the open square. The impressive silence was not broken by a single sound. Each line of soldiers looked more like the section of a vast machine than a line composed of living men. The silence was suddenly and sadly broken by the sounds of approaching music,—not the quick, inspiring strains with which we were so familiar, but a measured, slow, and solemn dirge, whose weird, sorrowful notes were poured forth like the meanings of lost spirits. Not a soldier spoke, but every eye was turned in the direction from which came the sad and mournful cadences, and then we saw the procession.

First came the band of music, of which I have spoken. Each musician seemed to comprehend the solemnity of the occasion, and this knowledge inspired them with ability to discharge the responsibility. Slow and measured was their step; sad and painful was their music; solemn as eternity was the impression that swept over us. Next came a detachment of the provost guard, numbering sixty men. The provost guard consisted of men who were detailed from the several regiments, and in their selection special regard was made to the soldierly qualities of the individuals.

This detachment, as well as the one of the same size making up the rear of the procession, was composed of the finest looking men that could be selected from the entire provost guard. Each one was tall and erect in form; all were well drilled and neatly clad; with the precision of drilled veterans they kept step to the slow and solemn music. This is the firing party. Next followed a black coffin carried by four men, and close after that came one of the condemned men, then another coffin, and following that the second criminal; and thus, in regular order they came, the rear of the procession being made up of the second detachment of the provost guard, of which I have already spoken.

This detachment, like number one, was composed of sixty men. The prisoners were all clad alike, in blue pants and white shirts, each man's hands were manacled behind him, and a guard was on either side. The five prisoners were marched to the centre of the square where the graves had already been prepared. Each prisoner was also accompanied by a priest or chaplain. It was reported at the time that there were two Protestant chaplains, two Catholic, and one Jewish priest, each prisoner, I suppose, being allowed to select one of his own religious belief. The coffins were placed near the open graves that were to receive them.

Of what could those men have been thinking as they marched to the gateway of eternity? I can imagine how men may face death under almost any circumstances, but to be thus marched to the place of execution, between the massed columns of their own comrades, and keep step to the music of death, must have awakened emotions in their breasts, that can only be rivalled by the stern events of the judgment day.

Four of the condemned men walked steadily, and to all outward appearances, with perfect unconcern, to the place of death. One was weak and tottering, and was evidently leaning heavily for support upon his attendants. When the coffins were properly arranged at the graves, each prisoner sat down upon the foot of his coffin, in such a manner that he would directly face the detachments of the provost guard. Then followed a long, low conversation between the condemned men and their spiritual advisers. It was a most affecting scene. Five men! beings of deathless destiny! men for whom the Redeemer died! about to be hurled through the iron gateways of death for crimes committed against their bleeding country.

Faithfully and well did the men of God perform their duties toward those who were about to die, and eternity, I suppose, will record the results. The last exhortation was given, the last word spoken, and the clergymen withdrew from the presence of the condemned. Each of the doomed men was then blindfolded with a thick and heavy bandage. The officers in charge then stepped back upon a line with the soldiers who were to fire. The sixty men were ready to perform their sad duty. One rifle in each twelve was loaded with a blank cartridge, so that not one of the firing party should know that he had taken the life of a fellow being. The second detachment was placed in such a position that they could complete the work if any of the condemned should survive after the first fire.

After the bandages were placed upon the eyes of the men, there was a moment of awful suspense. To the anxious spectators it seemed to be an age. Then clear and sharp the voice of the commanding officer rang out "Ready!" and instantly each of the sixty guns obeyed the command. Once more the officer's voice was heard, "Aim!" and sixty rifles were brought into position, twelve being aimed at the breast of each victim. Intently we watched and listened. At last we heard the fatal word, "Fire!" There was a gleaming flash, a line of curling smoke, a sharp crash like the report of a single rifle.

We looked again. The provost guard was standing at "Shoulder arms." Five bleeding forms were lying limp and lifeless upon the ground where they had fallen; the deserters had met their doom. Law had been enforced; the penalty inflicted; the outraged government avenged. The lines were quickly in motion, and the regiments marched to their respective camps, each soldier feeling more keenly than ever before the solemn responsibilities of his position.

The only advantage gained by the enemy in all these marches and counter-marches was the destruction of the railroads and bridges to such an extent that it employed our army nearly all the fall and winter to reconstruct them. On the 17th of November our regiment under the command of Major Ellis Spear was in camp at "Three Mile Station." The enemy held the railroad, a few miles distant, at a point known as Rappahannock station, on the north ern bank of the Rappahannock River. The position was naturally a very strong one, as it was a high eminence commanding the country for miles around.

Upon these heights they had constructed strong works, and these were garrisoned by the rebel brigades of Hoke and Hayes. It was determined to carry this fort by assault. Eighty men were detailed from our regiment, and were placed under the command of Captain W. G. Morrill, to act as skirmishers. Gallantly this line advanced under a fearful fire, until they reached the railroad embankment, which afforded them an excellent shelter. Then a portion of the Sixth corps came in upon their right to storm the fort. But these brave men were determined not to be outdone, and dashed forward with the Sixth Maine regiment, and entered the fort simultaneously with them. Many prisoners and a number of guns were taken. This was one of the most brilliant events of the campaign.

As is usually the case, many deeds of valour were performed by both officers and men, that have never found their way into print. Seth McGuire, a private of the Twentieth Maine, was well in advance of the assaulting column, and was determined to be the first man to mount the rebel breastworks; but before he reached the coveted position, a minie-ball shattered his leg. The wound unfitted him for service, and thus the regiment lost one of its bravest members.

The gigantic form of Morrison, one of the Aroostook boys, was rushing to the front, when a twelve-pound shell tore his knapsack from his shoulders and hurled him with great force across a pile of rocks. Springing to his feet he dashed on, and was the first man to enter the works at the point where he reached them. Seeing at a glance that he was alone, he sprang over the works, and fell in the trench as if he was dead, and remained under the rebels' feet, until the Union line of battle reached the works, when he arose and joined in the capture of the fort.

Another man belonging to our regiment was missing from the detachment, when it returned to the regiment. Darkness came on, and he did not return. The wounded had been borne from the field, but he was not among them. We knew that he could not have been taken as a prisoner. He also had a brother in the same company. As the long hours of the night slowly passed, all decided that he must have been killed in the desperate charge. He had been seen in the front, nearly up to the fort, and there they had lost all trace of him. His brother passed a sleepless night, for he supposed that he was cold and lifeless on the battlefield. The next forenoon a squad of men was sent from the regiment to search for his body and bury it when found. The bereaved brother sadly accompanied them. But they searched in vain; he was not to be found upon the battlefield. The graves of those who had been buried, were all marked, and his name was not among them.

It was nearly noon, and the squad was returning to the regiment; they saw a thin, blue smoke curling from a little fire in a clump of small trees; they approached it, and to their joyful surprise discovered the object of their search. He had fought through the battle, and pursued the rebels as far as any of our men were allowed to go; and then being tired had lain down in the bushes to take a nap. Had slept all night, and nearly all the forenoon, and when discovered was coolly engaged in making coffee, regardless of the anxiety in his regiment and the squad searching for his remains that they might have a soldier's burial. The survivors were all loud in their praises of the gallant manner in which Captain Morrill led them into the battle, and the heroic bravery he there displayed.

On the following day our regiment crossed the river at Kelley's Ford, marched a few miles from the river, encamped, and on the next day recrossed the river at the same ford, and passed a cold, uncomfortable and sleepless night near the river. And thus, for two weeks we were moving from point to point. The weather was cold and stormy, the roads were almost impassable, and the men suffered much from cold and exposure. On the 26th, we "struck tents" at four o'clock in the morning, and marched in the direction of the enemy. We crossed the Rapidan River at Gold Mine Ford late in the afternoon and continued our march until eight o'clock in the evening. It was Thanksgiving Day in Maine. We thought of the pleasant gatherings and well-loaded tables at home, and turned from these pleasant pictures of peace and plenty to the soldiers' fare, heavy marching, hard-tack, salt pork and coffee. I do not wonder that our hearts for a few hours were a little homesick at the contrast.

On the 29th we came up to the enemy at Mine Run. We found him strongly intrenched upon a ridge of land from which he could not be dislodged without a great sacrifice of life. Our commanders halted, for some cause not known to us. That halt was fatal. The rebels improved it by adding to the strength of their position, which was soon made almost impregnable. Our brigade occupied the picket line close up to the enemy's works, and between us was the deep stream of water known as Mine Run. For a day or two there was an incessant firing along the picket line, but both sides soon grew weary of this, and all was quiet. The weather was intensely cold, the long nights were frosty, and the soldiers, being thinly clad, suffered intensely.

On the 30th the battle was to begin at eight o'clock in the morning, and at that hour our artillery opened upon the enemy, and theirs quickly made reply. In our advanced position the shells of the combatants passed over us. If I could reproduce the sounds that filled the air—the screaming, hissing, hooting shells—as they passed over our picket line! but that is impossible. There was also picket firing and skirmishing all along the line, but no general engagement, took place. The artillery fire gradually grew less, and the rumour reached us that the army was to fall back. General Meade did not think it wisdom to attack the enemy in their intrenched position, and had consequently ordered a retreat.

On the night of December 1st, the army began its retreat. Our picket line was withdrawn at four o'clock on the morning of the second. We recrossed the Rapidan at Germania Ford, and retreated as rapidly as possible. The old soldiers will not forget that retreat, the cold night, the rough, frozen roads, how we, sleepy, hungry, and nearly worn out, dashed along the roads and through the woods to escape before the enemy could capture us. As a regiment we point to the retreat from Mine Run as the fastest record of speed we made in our three years' service. One fellow in our regiment always declared that he was so sleepy that he could not possibly keep his eyes open, and that with head fallen back upon his knapsack, he had actually marched five miles through the woods, sound asleep; but I do not vouch for that fellow's veracity.

On December 3rd we reached the Rappahannock River, and on the day following went into winter quarters at Rappahannock station, where the battle had been fought on the 7th of the previous month.

And thus the campaign of 1863 closed. To us it had been an eventful one. For seven months we had been actively engaged, and had marched many a weary mile. There had been numberless skirmishes with the enemy, in which our men had honoured the State whose seal they carried upon their banner. At Round Top we had crossed bayonets with the sons of the South, and had given them an exhibition of Northern courage at which they had so often sneered. Our officers had patiently borne with us the fatigues of that campaign, and had bravely led us in those scenes of danger and death. Our colours were torn and riddled by the enemy's bullets, and our brave comrades had been killed and disabled by scores.

No pen can describe, no brain can estimate, the amount of suffering through which we had passed. But we were there, the broken and scarred remains of the old Twentieth Maine, there in winter quarters to reorganise and prepare for the coming campaign, one that was destined to eclipse all others in the battles fought, the bravery displayed, the sacrifices made, and the results gathered

CHAPTER 8

Rappahannock Station

The campaign of 1863 had closed, and once more the old Army of the Potomac went into winter quarters. On the 4th of December our regiment encamped at Rappahannock station, for the purpose of guarding the railroad bridge at that place. Our camp was on the crest of a hill upon the north bank of the river. The hill overlooked for a long distance the blue river that rolled swiftly at its base, the rail road bridge, a vast expanse of country, and the fortifications upon the opposite side. We were upon historic ground. The rebels had strongly fortified this position, and it had been garrisoned by the brigades of Generals Hoke and Hayes.

A detachment of eighty men from our regiment, under the command of Captain W. G. Morrill, had co-operated with a portion of the Sixth corps in its capture, on the 7th of the previous November. The assault was one of the most brilliant and successful of the war. Maine was well represented by several regiments, and in the little cemetery on the hillside we built a wooden monument and dedicated it to the memory of the brave soldiers of our State who fell in the gallant charge. In the trenches and among the rocks we buried the rebel dead, who fell in their brave defence of the position.

When we returned and encamped, the breastworks were torn down, and upon the rocky surface of this elevation we levelled our parade ground, made our streets and built our tents. It was a beautiful place for an encampment, healthy from its elevated position, and picturesque in every sense of the word. Our tents, built of logs and covered with tent cloth, were large and quite comfortable. Good water was plenty, wood was easily obtained, the men were healthy, and this winter's experience was the most pleasant that we enjoyed while in the army. There was but little fatigue duty, and only a small section of picket line to sustain, and a large portion of our time was devoted to such amusements as we could devise in camp. The principal feature in these were the practical, good-natured jokes we used to practice upon each other. In our company there were about thirty men, nearly all of whom were less than thirty years of age.

As I recall the names of those brave fellows, and think of the amusements of that winter, I am almost tempted to assert that it was the happiest period of my life. Many recruits came to us during that time, and of course they were proper subjects for practical jokes. One fellow from the backwoods of Maine reached the regiment late in the afternoon. He soon revealed to a number of the boys that his only fear in becoming a soldier was that he would not be able to stand on "a picket post." He felt that it would require a great deal of practice to do this in a skilful manner, and since he had decided to enlist, he had not had a moment's time to practice it.

Of course, the boys had a great deal of sympathy for him, and kindly promised to assist him, for which he was very thankful. They informed him how difficult a thing it was for them when they first began. They accompanied him to the lower end of the street, where a post some four feet in height and six inches in diameter was set upright in the ground, the upper end being sharpened nearly to a point. With a little assistance the recruit succeeded in reaching its sharpened top, and in the evening twilight, for nearly two long hours he managed to maintain his position, and received the compliments of his comrades. He then went to his tent, proud of the fact that he had mastered so difficult a problem in so brief a time.

Another recruit, fresh from the schools and refined society, but who had never seen much of the world, came to our company. The boys saw at a glance that he was a glorious subject for a practical joke, and anxiously waited for an opportunity. It soon came. The young man was very confidential, and before he had been with us a whole day revealed all his plans. He had enlisted, knowing that his education and polished manners would give him rapid promotion. Of course, he would be a private but a few weeks, so he had brought an officer's uniform with him, and had the whole suit packed in his knapsack.

 Seeing that we were deeply interested in his plans, he asked if we could advise him in any way that would assist in his promotion; he would do anything to gain success in that line. Various things were spoken of by his advisers, which, if done, might aid him in his commendable ambition. One remarked that extravagance in the use of government stores was the great evil of the army, and when the officers noticed that a man was prudent, and looked out for the interests of the government, he was always rapidly promoted. We all took the hint. Only the day before this conversation, fresh ammunition had been issued to our regiment, and that which we had carried so long having become worthless by exposure to air and moisture, was thrown away. The cartridges were scattered along the street and through our tents.

"Yes, that is so," continued another, "now, there are those cartridges; it is too bad to have them wasted, and I have no doubt the colonel would promote any man who would gather them up and carry them to his tent, but I won't do it."

"Neither will I," said speaker number three, "I enlisted to shoot rebels; I am perfectly willing to wade in blood, but I won't do such work as that if I am never promoted."

After this patriotic declaration he yawned, and turned over in his berth as if he would sleep; but the bait had been swallowed. The recruit glided from the little group of soldiers, went to the cook house, borrowed two large camp kettles, and then through the tents and streets he went, until the kettles were nearly filled with cartridges, and he had all the load he could possibly carry. Then staggering along with a kettle in each hand, he walked to the colonel's tent. He passed the guard who was on duty there, and did not halt until he had reached the doorway. He then gave a smart knock, with the assurance of one who is confident of receiving a warm welcome.

One of the field officers answered the summons. The expectant recruit made known his business. The officer glanced down the street and saw the laughing soldiers. He took in the whole situation at a glance. There was a scowl, an oath, a vanishing officer, a door closing with a fearful slam, and Company H yelled and howled with delight. The sounds of merriment must have grated harshly upon the ears of the poor fellow who had been the victim. This episode crushed his expectations, and we never heard him utter the word promotion again.

These jokes were not confined to each other, but the men in the ranks took great delight in practicing them upon the officers whom they did not like, when it could be done innocently. At one time a regiment in camp was living upon very poor rations. The bread was mouldy, hard, and unfit to eat. There were no rations of meat, and as for the coffee and sugar, the grip of the quartermaster could be detected in every spoonful. There was a chaplain in the regiment who was supposed to look after the interests of the men, especially if they were sick, but the boys thought that this one paid too much attention to the officers and too little to them, as he never came to their tents or spoke with them when he met them. He was a remarkably sleek and well fed looking individual.

One day he, together with some officers from another regiment, passed through a company street just as the men were eating dinner. The chaplain had his hands behind him, and wore a self-satisfied look. A wag by the name of Dick sat on the ground by his tent door, trying to eat the musty hard-tack. Assuming almost an idiotic look as the chaplain approached, he inquired very innocently, "Chaplain, will you be kind enough to tell me what the two capital letters, B.C., stand for, when they are printed together upon anything?"

"Oh, yes," blandly answered the chaplain, raising his voice so loud that it would attract the attention of all the men in the street, "it means before the birth of our Saviour, previous to the beginning of the Christian era." He proceeded to give quite a profound theological exposition of the matter, and then inquired, "But, my man, why did you ask so unusual a question?"

"Oh, nothin'," answered the innocent Dick, "only we have seen it stamped on these sheets of hard-tack, and were curious to know why it was there."

At this point the listeners all exploded with laughter, while the chaplain saw that he was sold, and walked rapidly away. But of all the "shining lights," or men possessing remarkable qualities, in Company H, it is safe to say that our company cook ranked all others. He is living now, (1882), and if he reads these lines, I know he will forgive the description I give of him, and also thank me for revelations here made that he never knew before. He was a short, thin, frail man, with one leg shorter than the other, and the longer one much more crooked than its mate. Of course, he could not march in the ranks, and I think he never carried a rifle. But no man in the Army of the Potomac could rival him in the art and science of cookery.

Among mess pans, camp kettles, and dish cloths, Daniel shone peerless and alone. He was a generous, kind hearted man, and for the boys who went out with him when the regiment was mustered, he had a profound respect, and could never do too much for them. But like all old veterans, he had a great contempt for recruits, which he was always anxious to display. As I think of his kindness to me I almost feel condemned for the many jokes the other fellows played upon him.

Like many other men in positions of trust, Daniel learned some crooked ways. He learned by observation that the longer he boiled the rations of fat pork, the more lard would rise to the surface of the water when it was cooled. He quickly took advantage of this discovery, and, by purchasing flour at the sutler's, soon built up quite a business in frying doughnuts and selling them to us at the rate of about ten cents apiece. We used to complain to him that the doughnut business sadly interfered with our rations of meat, but he always gave us to understand that he knew his own business. There were but few of us who had any money to buy with, but we were all exceedingly fond of doughnuts, and many were the schemes we devised to come into possession of the coveted stores.

One fellow would invite Daniel to his tent, to ask his advice upon some very important matter, and he was never known to refuse a request of this nature. While he was thus occupied, some graceless scamps would enter the cook-house, break open the well-known box under the table, and bear away half a peck of the stolen luxuries. Soon after, we would see him coming from his tent, wrath pictured on every feature, and vengeance ringing in every step, to make known to us his loss. How deeply we would sympathize with him! Someone would chance to remember that he saw a recruit coming from the direction of the cook-house a short time before. A hint was enough, and upon their luckless heads he would pour the vials of his wrath. Then in the kindness of his heart he would bring forth the remainder of the doughnuts and divide them among his sympathizers as a reward for their honesty.

The last joke we played, however, was rather overdone, and completely destroyed this branch of the cook's business. It was pay day, the soldiers had lots of money, and the cook had planned for a rich harvest. The rations of pork had been so large that he did not think it wise to issue them all to the men. Round after round of pork had been laid carefully away. Of course the boys understood all about it. This day had been a busy one for Daniel, and as a result of his economy and industry he was in possession of two large camp kettles filled with liquid lard. He had placed them under the table to cool, while two kettles of similar size filled with water were sitting upon the floor of his cook-house. This building was covered with cotton cloth; its walls were made of pine logs, pitchy and dry; the chimney was made of barrels, which were, of course, as dry as tinder.

Morrison, Daniel's most trusted friend, called at the cook-house, and informed Daniel that the sutler wished to see him a moment. The summons was quickly obeyed. When his form vanished through the tents, the barrels were set on fire and the kettles of lard exchanged positions with the with the kettles of water. Soon spiral tongues of flame are seen encircling the sooty barrels. Someone cries fire! The cry is caught up, and *fire! fire! FIRE!* resounds along the line. "Company H's cook house is on fire!" yell a hundred men.

At that moment we see Daniel advancing on the double-quick; never before had those illy mated legs done such uniform service. Breathless and with flushed face he crossed the door-sill of that establishment where he alone was king. Seizing what he supposed was a kettle of water, he hurled it upon the greedy flames, and without waiting to notice the result, the contents of kettle number two followed those of number one. A black flame of fire sprang fifty feet into the air, and in a moment the whole cook-house was a mass of fire.

It was with much difficulty that we prevented the flames from spreading through the whole encampment. Poor Daniel was completely demoralised. He sat down by the smoking ruins of his home and wept. A few of us gathered around him and sympathized with him over the fatal mistake he made in putting away the water instead of the lard. To our surprise he shook his head as if he did not believe our theory of the disaster. Lieut. Bickford, commanding the company, came down to where we were talking, and with a frown on his face and a smile of mirth twinkling in his eyes, asked us the cause of the fire. Morrison and others gave various theories in relation to it.

But unfortunately for us, the lieutenant was an old soldier, and had known us for some time. As he turned away he remarked, "Morrison, you and Gerrish and Tarbell and Gilmore must rebuild that cook-house immediately." There was no appeal from this decision, and for two long days we toiled in the work of rebuilding. Daniel did not exult over us in our misfortune; but there was a look of satisfaction upon his face as he took charge of the building squad, to which position he had been assigned by the lieutenant commanding.

Out on the picket line

As already stated, during the winter we were encamped at Rappahannock station, our picket duty was light. And as there was evidently no enemy in our immediate front, this duty was far more pleasant than that which usually falls to the soldier's lot. The usual rigor and discipline was much relaxed. A corporal and three men would be placed upon each post, and around a good fire of oak logs the hours passed pleasantly away. The practical jokes and fun were not confined to the camp, but were often indulged in on the picket line. As we look back to those months we smile as we remember how often we were made the victims of our comrades' wit.

No opportunity for fun was ever allowed to pass unimproved, no matter whether the victim was an officer or a private. There was an officer in our brigade who was distinguished throughout the command as an ardent admirer of "red tape," or, to use the phrase coined by the boys for the occasion: "He was always on his military." When this officer was in command of the picket line there was no comfort or rest for himself or any other person. At such times he evidently comprehended the vast responsibilities that rested upon him, and acted accordingly. He would be up at all hours of the night, prowling along the picket line, evidently hoping to find some luckless fellow asleep.

If a sentinel failed to challenge him, as laid down in the "tactics," woe be unto him. He would not allow four of us to remain upon a single post and relieve each other, as the other officers did. The regulation plan of the reliefs tramping the length of the line to relieve the men each two hours must be carried out. No sentry was allowed to have a fire on his post, and the reserve picket forces must sleep on their arms, to be ready at a moment's warning in case the enemy should advance. Thus, for three days and nights he would strut and parade along the picket line, and each man would sputter, growl and swear at such a display. Each one felt inspired to vex and aggravate him as much as possible, without committing any act for which he could be punished.

One night, in the month of March, 1864, I was on picket, and this officer was in charge of the line. He had established his headquarters, with the reserve, in a piece of oak woods about one-third of a mile in rear of the picket line. For two days he had been in charge, making it just as uncomfortable as he could for the men. The rain had been falling in torrents, but the storm had now cleared away. The stars shone down through the mists, and their feeble light partially dispelled the darkness and gloom.

The air was damp and chilly, and a thick fog enveloped us like a mantle. The ground was soft and muddy. This officer had passed along the line after dark, and given orders for every man to be on the watch, to exercise a double caution, for he had no doubt but that Moseby's guerrillas would attack our line before morning. The reserve were ordered to "fall in," and were then commanded to sleep on their arms and be ready to repel the enemy.

Every soldier knew that, in all probability, there was not a rebel within ten miles, and that this was only an exhibition of "red tape." My relief went on at eleven o'clock, to remain two hours. I had been standing in the darkness about an hour when a soldier on the adjoining post spoke my name in a low voice. I went to where he was standing and found that he was a recruit who had recently joined our regiment, and that this was his first service on picket. He told me that he had been standing there for three hours. The relief must have passed him in the darkness, and he was nearly frozen. He was very angry, and denounced the corporal for thus passing him, saying it was simply an old soldier's trick played upon him because he was a recruit; but he wanted them to all understand that, although he had just enlisted, he was not a simpleton.

When he had finished his tirade, he asked me what would be the most effectual method of arousing the corporal and also of informing the commanding officer of the situation. He was evidently determined to have the corporal court-martialled, and thus teach the old soldiers a lesson. I, of course, gave him the information he needed, and informed him that if he should fire his gun he would probably arouse the corporal, and also have a chance to state the facts to the officer in charge. I then hastened back to my post. A moment after, a flash of fire glared through the gloom, there was the sharp crack of a rifle, and a minie-ball went whistling forth in the darkness.

For a moment all was still, and then there was an excitement. Clear and shrill I heard the officer's voice ring out through the forest, "Fall in!" "Fall in!" There was a rattle of bayonets as the guns were hastily taken from the stacks, and then "Forward!" "Double-quick!" "March!" and one hundred men under the command of this irrepressible officer came dashing out toward the picket line. The officer was on horseback, and his steed sank deep in the mud at every plunge. In this ludicrous condition they bore down upon the picket post where I was standing.

There was no time to lose. Twisting the laugh from my features, I prepared for the desperate work of halting the charging column, and with all my power yelled, "Halt! Who comes there?" The officer informed me of his rank, but of course I must receive the countersign over the point of the bayonet, at such a perilous time, before I could believe him, and to do this he must dismount in the mud. He gave the magic word, and then inquired about the firing. I told him it was down on our left, and that evidently our man had fired at some object, or else some person had fired at him. In a moment he was mounted and leading on his command. Again, he was challenged, this time by the offender himself.

"Who fired that gun?" roared the officer.

"I did," answered the enraged soldier.

"At what did you fire?"

"Nothin', sir," was the reply, "only I have stood here three hours and want to be relieved." The men chuckled aloud with laughter. The officer was speechless with rage, and demanded, "How long have you been in the service?"

"Four days," responded the veteran.

There was no remedy. The man was a recruit and knew no better. The officer summoned the corporal and ordered him to instruct the man how he could be relieved from his duty without firing his rifle. He then rode slowly back to his tent, and we all fancied that from that hour he was more of a man than he had ever been before.

The following month, four of us were stationed for three days at a point on the picket line where a physician resided, and we took possession of his stable, spread our blankets upon the straw, and thus had very comfortable quarters. We were instructed to protect the property from any raid our soldiers might make upon it. The physician was a man some sixty years old, and one of the "chivalry" in every sense of the word. He was proud, pompous, and a genuine "Secesh." Once in a while he would come out to the stable and chat with us. He did not attempt to conceal his sympathy with the South, and would talk about the superiority of the Southern troops, and of the certain success of the Confederacy.

We replied very respectfully to his insults, but decided that, if it was possible, we would play some joke upon him before we were relieved, that would give him reason to remember us.

In calling upon his patients in his professional work, he drove a spirited horse harnessed to an old-fashioned gig. This gig was a clumsy affair, with two huge wheels and a seat long enough to hold three persons. One night about twelve o'clock, I was awakened by Dick, who slept by my side, punching his fist into my ribs and saying, "We have got him; let's get up and harness the old doctor's horse into the gig and ride into camp." By this time all were awake, "Lord, won't the old fellow storm when he finds it out?" chuckled Mac, and we began to make arrangements for the ride. Three of us would go, and the fourth would remain on guard. We must leave before daylight, or the old man would be awake.

The old carriage was taken from the stable, and the wheels with noiseless revolutions rolled through the door-yard. The horse was led around by a back passage so that his steps upon the yard would not awaken his owner. The old harness, patched and tied together in many places, was taken from the peg where it was hanging, an old whip that had probably cracked and snapped around the ears and heels of the slave in the "good old days," was taken from a beam where we had observed it the day previous, and we began to prepare for the forward movement. It had been so long a time since we had harnessed a horse, that our movements were slow and awkward; but after a time, our perseverance was rewarded. The horse was harnessed and all was ready.

Three of us mounted to the seat, the reins were pulled taut, the whip cracked along the side of the nag, and away we went. There was something in the situation that imparted an inspiration of joyous excitement. The horse was a rapid roadster, the roads were quite smooth, and we made remarkable time. We decided that it would be best for us to reach the regiment about the time of morning roll-call, as we would make quite a display riding into camp before the whole regiment. So, we rode up and down the roads, talking and laughing, while our horse was making his best time, until we heard the regimental bugle blow for roll-call.

Just as they were breaking ranks, they were surprised by seeing us drive down across the parade ground at a three minute gait, behind a smoking steed. In a moment they took in the whole situation, and with wild cheers three hundred men made a rush for us. "It was now a race for life." The old horse displayed speed that we never dreamed he possessed. Back and forth between the charging lines we dashed; the huge wheels seemed to smoke as we rushed to and fro over the parade ground. We turned square corners, made angles and described circles. The whip cracked and cut across the shoulders of the assailants when they were within reach. We cheered; the carriage creaked and groaned, while the horse dashed madly on.

Our line of communications was cut; we were flanked, surrounded, over powered, but would not yield. We were turning a square corner to escape the enemy, when a score of them caught the wheel of our carriage, and in a moment after we were sprawling upon the ground, and the horse dashing down at a break-neck rate over the rocky hillside toward home, while the air was filled with pieces of the carriage and harness. The boys gathered us up, and voted on the spot that it was one of the most remarkable defences ever made in the history of the war. But how to meet the doctor was the question that confronted us; not that we feared the wrath that he would pour upon us, but he perhaps would report the matter at headquarters, and the officers might misunderstand the nature of the harmless amusement in which we had participated, and punish the innocent offenders.

Fortune favoured us. In our company was a sergeant, whose name was Joe, brave, witty, generous, and always ready for any emergency. We reported the situation to him, and informed him of the disloyal sentiments of the doctor. He studied a moment and then exclaimed, "By Jove, I can fix him!" His arrangements were rapidly made; wearing his sergeant's chevrons and side arms, and having tucked a revolver in his belt, and a huge package of papers in his breast pocket, and having secured the services of three of the boys, who were to accompany him with their rifles, we all glided quietly from camp without attracting attention. We three who had ridden in with the doctor's team went in advance along the road that led to his residence, Joe and his command proceeding some forty rods in our rear. We had passed over two-thirds of the distance to the doctor's house, when we saw him coming with long rapid strides.

He recognised us, and of course began to give vent to his rage. "You unprincipled Yankee scoundrels, horse thieves, if I live to get to your headquarters, if I don't punish you for this outrage! I, an honoured citizen of the State of Virginia, to be thus robbed and outraged by you Northern vandals!"

In vain we endeavoured to reason with him, and offered to pay him for all the damage done. This only added fuel to the flames of his wrath. At this moment, a sergeant and a file of soldiers with fixed bayonets arrived upon the scene. The physician, noticing that he was an officer of some grade, poured forth his tale of indignation to him. When he stopped for want of breath to proceed further, Joe, with a gravity that could not be surpassed, asked, "Is this Dr. ——?"

"Yes sir, that is my name," replied the other.

"Then sir," said the sergeant, placing his hand upon the physician's shoulder, "you are my prisoner."

"For what?" demanded the astonished Virginian.

Joe, with the importance of a commanding general, made answer:—

First: for treasonable utterances made against the United States Government.

Second: for riding several times to the enemy's lines, and giving them important information in regard to the Union Army.

Third: entertaining rebel officers or spies at your house, and secreting them from the Union soldiers.

For a moment the old fellow was dumbfounded. Joe, with solemn gravity, had rattled off charge after charge in such a manner that it sounded almost like a death warrant. The doctor then protested his innocence. Joe touched the bundle of papers in his pocket, and informed him that he had all the proof he needed. The doctor then admitted that he had often spoken in favour of secession, that once, and but a few weeks before, he had ridden nearly to the rebel camp, to visit a patient, but claimed that no rebel officers had been at his house since our army had advanced the previous November. The tables were turned, and he began to beg. He would do anything in the world if the officer would only let the matter drop.

For a long time, Joe was immovable. "An unconditional surrender" was his only terms. But at last a compromise was effected. The doctor was to return home, he was never to come inside the Union lines again while we were encamped there, and if any officers went to his house or came in contact with him, he was never to mention the matter of the horse. With many words of counsel as to his future conduct, Joe ordered him to be released, and he hastened to his home. We followed him, while Joe and his guard returned to camp.

The doctor never mentioned his harness and carriage that had been destroyed. The horse was uninjured, and from that time the professional visits were made on horseback. We were relieved on the following day, and returned to camp, and I can assure my readers that the tents of Company H rang with shouts of laughter as we made known the adventure of Sergeant Joe.

Milk, of course, was a luxury in the army, and many were the expeditions made from the picket line at Rappahannock station to secure the coveted article. Having learned one day from a contraband that came within our lines that there was a plantation about three miles out, where several cows were kept, two of us arranged to go out and secure some milk. The only possible danger was that we might fall in with some of the rebel cavalry, who were occasionally scouting in that vicinity; but we decided, if we went out before daylight, that even this danger would be removed, and so, the next morning, about four o'clock, two of us sallied forth. I was armed with a camp kettle that would contain twenty quarts. My companion carried his rifle.

The distance was greater than we anticipated, and when we reached the plantation, day was dawning. We soon ascertained that the cows were in a yard near the house. The programme was for me to enter the yard and milk the cows, while Sam was to stand guard, and give the alarm in case of danger. The cows were wild, and some little time was consumed in skirmishing around the yard before I could begin to milk. My position was such that my back was toward the house, and very near the fence that enclosed the yard. I was meeting with great success, and several quarts of the precious fluid already repaid me for my industry. I was thinking of the rebel cavalry, when, in the dim, gray light of morning, a huge form towered upon the fence above me, and sprang with terrific force to my side, and at the same moment a loud, unearthly yell saluted my ears.

I thought Moseby, and his whole gang of cut-throats were upon us. I sprang to my feet, upset the pail, rushed through the herd of astonished cattle, climbed the fence, and dashed toward the picket line. After I had run an eighth of a mile, I thought of Sam. I looked around, expecting to see a squad of the enemy following me, but to my surprise saw Sam coming, roaring with laughter, and motioning for me to return. I returned, and demanded the cause of my alarm. Poor Sam could only roll on the ground and ejaculate between his bursts of laughter, "It is so good, so good." (*The Gray Raiders* published in 3 volumes, each containing 2 *Accounts of Mosby & His Raiders During the American Civil War* is also pulished by Leonaur.)

After a time, I learned that while I was milking, a coloured lady of gigantic proportions had come out of the house with a milk-pail, and proceeded to the yard. Sam, from his outlook, saw her, but she did not know of our presence. Sam saw that she intended to climb the fence near where I was milking, and decided that it would be a grand chance to settle some old scores with me, and so, when she descended from her elevated position, he had given me the benefit of the yell. It had operated in a double capacity, for the negress had rushed to the house in a fright while I was running away. We returned to the yard, and secured some milk. Sam promised me most solemnly that the boys in camp should never hear of it, but before the close of that day it was known to every man in the regiment.

Chapter 9

The Wilderness Campaign Opened

The spring of 1864 was a memorable period in the history of the Army of the Potomac. It had been thoroughly reorganised and consolidated, and was greatly inspired by the intelligence that Lieutenant-General Grant was to make his headquarters with the Army of the Potomac in the coming campaign. We had never seen this general, whose wonderful campaign in the southwest had given him a world-wide reputation, but we had great faith in his ability, and rejoiced to know that he was to lead us to battle. The army was in good condition, healthy, well fed, and full of enthusiasm.

It was an inspiring scene at Rappahannock station on the first day of May, when we broke camp and marched forth to enter upon the spring campaign. Several regiments had been added to our brigade, which was commanded by General Bartlett. Our division was under the command of General Griffin, while General Warren commanded the corps. It was a beautiful morning; summer was blushing in its new born beauty; the sun shone warm and bright from the soft blue sky, the air was warm and balmy; the birds were singing their sweetest songs; and all nature smiled in peace and loveliness.

Man, who prides himself as being the noblest work of the Creator, was the only being that seemed to be out of harmony, for, in the midst of all that was peaceful and joyous, he was preparing for strife and sorrow. On every hand were indications of the bloody struggle about to open; bands were playing warlike music; the shrill, keen notes of the bugles were ringing out over the hillsides and down through the meadows; long lines of soldiers were forming the ranks of war; banners were waving; and soldiers cheering as the general officers rode along the lines.

Our brigade crossed the river on pontoon bridges at Rappahannock station, and marched to a camping ground east of Brandy station, where the Fifth corps, now composed of thirty thousand men, was being concentrated. The army was all being rapidly marshalled, and we knew that a most desperate battle was soon to be fought. Our men were anxious for the campaign to open, hoping it would be the last one of the war. General Grant's presence gave the men such an inspiration that their enthusiasm was almost irresistible.

On the fourth of May, upon pontoon bridges, we crossed the Rapidan River, a dark, swift-rolling stream of water, and entered a huge, dense forest of pine trees. It was a proud and yet a solemn spectacle to see that great army of one hundred and fifty thousand men entering that dense forest to encounter a desperate enemy, they knew not where. We passed the old battlefield of Chancellorsville, and were pain fully reminded of the great struggle that raged there one short year before. We crossed a section of the line of battle held by the rebels at that time.

As we passed by where a rebel battery had been stationed, we saw small piles of railroad iron cut into pieces some twelve inches in length, which they frequently fired from their cannon when their stock of shells became exhausted. They were grim reminders of the welcome we should probably receive in a few hours from the hands of the Southern soldiers. That night we encamped on the Orange and Fredericksburgh turn pike, near the old Wilderness tavern. We under stood that we must be near the rebel army, but not an enemy had been seen, and not a gun had been fired. The picket lines were established. The sun sank from view, and the weary soldiers lay down upon the ground to rest. The tall dark pines bowed and waved their heavy plumes in the evening breeze, and all was quiet. In nature we observe that a peaceful calm often precedes the most fearful storm, and thus it was with the elements of strife in the wilderness.

On the fifth of May we were awake at an early hour. It was a beautiful morning. The rising sun sent its rays of light down like golden needles through the tops of the pine trees. Little fires were kindled, our coffee was quickly boiled, and we sat down to our rude breakfasts with appetites such as are unknown in lives of luxury and ease. The men were all in excellent spirits, but it was an easy task to distinguish a contrast in their dispositions. Some were laughing and cracking their jokes about hunting for the Johnnies through the forest, of the grand times we should have marching down to Richmond and entering the rebel capital, how when the war was over, "we would hang Jeff Davis to the sour apple tree," and then go marching home.

Another class more thoughtful and equally brave were lying upon the ground silent, alone, thoughtful, with compressed lips, seeming not to notice what was transpiring around them. They were thinking of wives and little ones far away, and wondering if they would ever see them again. Others were leaning against the trees, writing letters to their loved ones at home. It was well that they did this, for before the sun went down that day, some of them were cold in the embrace of death. Cavalrymen soon came back with the thrilling intelligence that General Lee's army in great force was rapidly advancing. There was no time to lose. The field of battle which our commanding generals selected, stretched its length for six miles through that great forest.

The trees were all cut down for a distance of some ten rods in front of the line, and their trunks trimmed of all their branches, and piled up for breastworks, from behind which we would give the enemy a warm reception. Building the breastworks required but a few hours' work, and before twelve o'clock they were completed. General Warren rode along our lines, and was received with the most enthusiastic cheering. At noon we again boiled our coffee and ate our hard-tack. The Sixth corps, under the command of General Sedgwick, joined us on our right, while our left was to connect with the Second corps, commanded by General Hancock.

At one o'clock in the afternoon our division was ordered to advance, and attract the attention of the enemy, while the left of our line of battle was fortifying its position. Our third brigade occupied the centre of the division. This brigade was formed in two lines of battle, our regiment being in the second. When the order was given to advance, the three brigades forming the division went forward on the double-quick, cheering as they charged. We soon encountered the enemy, and pressed his advanced lines back upon his reserve. The ground was covered with a second growth of pine trees, stunted and covered with limbs, many of which, dry and dead, came nearly to the ground. Seldom, if ever, was a battle fought under such circumstances.

The rebels evidently knew but little of our force, position and intention, and it is safe to say we knew less of theirs; and thus, the two great masses of men were hurled against each other. The rebels fought like demons, and under cover of the dense underbrush poured deadly volleys upon us. The air was filled with lead. Minie bullets went snapping and tearing through the pine limbs; splinters flew in every direction; trees were completely riddled with bullets in a moment's time;

blood ran in torrents; death lost its terror; and men for a time seemed transformed to beings that had no fear. Major Spear, aided by the field and line officers, gallantly led the regiment on. Our lines were broken. It was a disorganised battle; every man fought for himself and by himself, but all faced the enemy with heroic daring, and were determined that the tide of victory should set on the Union side.

With remorseless determination the rebels poured their deadly fire upon our men, and they, with irresistible power, pressed back the foe. The rebels retreated across a small field that had been cleared in the heart of the great forest, and reforming their lines in the edge of the woods prepared to receive us. By this time our regiment had worked its way well up to the front line. General Bartlett, in person, led our brigade in its charge across the field. As we stood for a moment and looked upon that field, and saw where the bullets were falling into the dried soil, and the little clouds of dust arising so thickly, we were re minded of heavy drops of rain falling just before the shower comes in its full force.

The order was given to charge. The right of our regiment now rested upon the turnpike; and across the field we dashed. *Zip, zip, zip,* came the bullets on every side. The field was nearly crossed. We dashed up a little swell of land on its farthest side and were under the shadow of the trees. A red volcano yawned before us and vomited forth fire, and lead, and death. Our lines staggered for a moment, but with desperate resolution our men threw themselves upon the enemy's guns. It was not child's play, but more like a conflict of giants. North and South arrayed against each other, man against man. The sons of the Pine Tree State crossed bayonets with those who were reared under the orange groves of the far South.

The rifle barrels touched, as from their muzzles they poured death into each others faces; the ground shook with the roar of musketry; the forest trees were flaming with, fire, and the air was loaded with death. Foot after foot the rebels retreated, their gray forms mantled with fire as they went. Slowly and steadily we advanced, giving blows with a mailed hand as we pursued the foe. What a medley of sounds,—the incessant roar of the rifle; the screaming bullets; the forest on fire; men cheering, groaning, yelling, swearing, and praying! All this created an experience in the minds of the survivors that we can never forget.

The right of our regiment reached a small field, while our left was buried in the forest beyond. Major Spear ordered our colours to advance into the open field, and the regiment to form upon them; but just as this movement was being executed, we received a sharp and fatal volley from our right and rear. We at first supposed the brigade upon our right had mistaken us for the enemy, and had fired through mistake; but Major Spear was informed at that moment that the Sixth corps had failed to connect with our division, and consequently the brigade upon our right had fallen back, and the enemy was in our rear. Our only way of escape was by the left flank, while each man worked his way back to the breastworks. It was a very narrow escape for us, and it was only by a quick, daring dash that we escaped from the snare in which we found ourselves. The regiment regained the line of breastworks, losing heavily in killed and wounded, but capturing many prisoners. Company H entered the battle with thirty men, and came out with eighteen.

Many deeds of daring were done that day by members of our regiment, which, if all recorded, would fill a large volume. I will only mention a few that have come to my knowledge. Captain Walter G. Morrill, of Company B, discovering that the enemy was coming down upon our right flank, marshalled a fragment of his own company, and a few men from other commands, formed a little line of battle along the turnpike, and for some minutes held a large force of the rebels in check. It is doubtful if the brave captain would have retreated at all, if a minie-ball had not gone crashing through his face, and hurled him to the ground. Regaining his feet, he bound a handkerchief around his face, and continued to fight until he was blinded and choked with blood, when his brave men assisted him to the rear. Three of our men in a clump of bushes, saw a dozen rebels close upon them. They called upon them to surrender, and the "Johnnies," not mistrusting for a moment how small the Yankee force was, threw down their guns, and were brought within our lines.

Lieutenant Melcher, whose company was the left of our regiment, did not learn that we were flanked, and with a small squad of men continued to advance until he discovered that the firing was all in his rear. Then he went out on the turnpike and looked in the direction of the breastworks, and saw a line of rebel infantry stretched across the road behind him. He went back to his men, told them of the situation, and mustered his force. He found that he had fifteen men, among whom were Sergeants Smith, of Company F, and Rogers, of Company H.

A council of war was held. They must decide to do one of three things: continue to advance and capture Richmond; remain where they were and be taken prisoners; or cut their way through the rebel line of battle and rejoin their regiment at the breastworks. Not a single man would listen to the thought of surrender. Some, I think, would have dared to make the advance upon Richmond. It was finally decided to cut their way through the enemy's line, and escape. It was a dangerous undertaking, but they were men who dared to face danger and death. With loaded rifles and fixed bayonets, they moved with noiseless tread toward the rebel line.

They were guided by the firing, which, however, had much abated, and soon through the pine trees they caught a glimpse of the rebels. With a yell the little band charged upon a force that could have brought a regiment to contend with each man in that little squad. There was a flash and a roar. Melcher's voice was heard calling upon them to surrender. The rebels, of course, were surprised, and their line was broken and divided. The squad of fifteen lost two or three men in the shock, but swept on to our line of battle, bearing with them thirty prisoners, which they had torn from the rebel line in their mad charge.

Sitting in Alderman Melcher's pleasant parlour, in Portland, a short time since, talking over that eventful day, I was shown, among other relics of the war, a receipt dated May 5th, 1864, given by the provost marshal of our division to Lieutenant Melcher for the thirty rebel prisoners he turned over to our provost guard on that day.

Before daylight, on the morning of May 6th, our line again advanced upon the rebels. Our regiment was at this time at the left of the turnpike, with our left flank resting upon it. We quickly learned that the enemy was prepared to receive us. Minie-balls came singing spitefully from the thickets in our front; their batteries also opened upon us, and shells went crashing and tearing through the trees. We were at close quarters with the rebels, and they had an excellent range of our position. We were ordered to halt, and lay under their fire all day. Late in the afternoon a fearful battle was raging upon our right; the enemy had massed his forces upon the Sixth corps, and was evidently determined to drive it back from its position. Suddenly there was a wild, fearful yell, a terrific crash, and the tide of battle rolled backward.

A portion of the Sixth corps had given way, and the enemy followed up the advantage thus gained, until they had completely turned our flank, and the firing was almost in our rear. Some of the regiments in our brigade showed signs of alarm at this situation, but the sons of Maine were determined to hold their position, even if they were surrounded and destroyed in so doing. The enemy's advance on our right was finally checked, and our line was re-established. At dark we were relieved and went back to our breastworks to remain for the night. The next morning, we again advanced. Our regiment, with the One Hundred and Eighteenth, was ordered to charge in upon the enemy.

We drove their skirmish line rapidly back, and soon came to the line of battle, which was strongly fortified and supported by artillery. We were not strong enough to carry them by assault, but under the murderous fire they were pouring upon us, we deployed a skirmish line, reformed a line of battle, and returned their fire as well as we could. On this day we lost a number of our brave men. Lieutenant Lane was wounded in the head by a piece of shell, fell into the hands of the enemy, and died a few days afterward. Lieutenant Sherwood was wounded and died before the next morning.

That night the army moved in the direction of Spottsylvania, our regiment and the One Hundred and Eighteenth remaining until midnight, when we rapidly followed them. In these three days' battles our regiment had lost about one hundred and twenty-five men in killed and wounded. One of the latter thus describes the situation in the Wilderness, as it came under his own observation:—

> At the critical moment of the first day's battle in the Wilderness, when brave Sergeant Crocker had gallantly carried our colours out into the open field, just as Major Spear received the order to retreat, I was wounded, a minie-ball passing through my left ankle. It is impossible to describe the sensations experienced by a person when wounded for the first time. The first intimation I had that I was wounded was my falling upon the ground. My leg was numb to my body, and for a moment I fancied that my foot had been carried away; but I soon learned the true condition of my situation. Our regiment was rapidly retreating, and the rebels as rapidly advancing. The forest trees around me were on fire, and the bullets were falling thick and fast.
>
> If I remained where I was, the most favourable result that I could hope for was captivity, which, in reality, would be worse than death by the bullet on the field. I stood up, and, to my joy, found that my leg was not entirely useless. I could step with it, and so long as it remained straight I could bear my weight upon it, but when bent at the knee it refused to bear me up, and I would fall to the ground. Under existing circumstances, I determined to retreat. I threw off all my baggage and

equipments, and turned my face toward the line of breastworks, which we had that morning built. Fear lent wings to my flight, and away I dashed. Frequently my wounded leg would refuse to do good service, and as a result I would tumble headlong upon the ground, then rising, I would rush on again, and I doubt if there has been a champion on the sawdust track in Maine for the last five years who has made such a record of speed as I made on that retreat through the Wilderness.

In my haste I did not keep so far to my right as I should have done, and consequently was obliged to cross the lower end of the field over which we had made our charge. It was a sad spectacle, that lonely field in the forest. Here and there a wounded man was limping painfully to the rear; dead men, and others wounded too severely to move, were scattered thickly upon the ground.

As I was crossing the lower corner of the field, to my surprise and horror the rebel line of battle came out on its upper edge, some quarter of a mile from where I was running. Almost at the same moment the rebels appeared in the field. A Union officer, whom I have always supposed to be General Bartlett, our brigade commander, also came out into the field, not twenty rods from the rebel line. He was on horseback; not a staff officer was with him; his uniform was torn and bloody; blood was trickling from several wounds in his face and head; he had evidently been up to discover why our line of battle had not connected with the Sixth corps. The rebels saw him, the moment he emerged from the forest, and called upon him to surrender, while a wild yell rang along their line as they saw their fancied prize. But they did not know the man with whom they had to deal.

Shaking his fist at them in defiance, he put spurs to his horse and dashed away. He was a target for every rifle in the rebel line. Five hundred guns were pointed at him, and five hundred bullets whistled around him, the enemy pursuing as they fired. It was a brilliant ride for life, with all the odds against the daring rider. Bravely he rode in the midst of that storm, as if death had no terror for him. His steed was a noble animal, and at a three-minute gait bore his master from his pursuers. Each seemed to bear a charmed life. Over one-half the distance across that field had been passed, and yet the rider sat erect upon the steed that was bearing him onward with such tremendous speed.

A deep ditch must be crossed before they could gain the cover of the forest. A ditch dug many years before, five or six feet deep, and ten or twelve in width. The rebels knew the ditch was there, and sent up a wild yell of delight, as they fancied the officer would be delayed in crossing, and so fall into their hands. The horse and rider evidently saw the obstacle at the same moment and prepared to meet it. Firmly the rider sat in his saddle, and gathered the reins of his horse with a firm hand. I never beheld a nobler spectacle than that presented by the gallant steed his nostrils dilated, his ears pointed forward, his eyes seeming to flash with the fire of conscious strength as he made the fearful leap.

For a moment I thought they were safe, but rebel bullets pierced the horse, and turning a complete somersault he fell stone dead, burying his rider beneath him as he fell. Again, the rebels cheered and rushed on, but to my surprise, the officer, with the assistance of a few wounded soldiers, extricated himself from his dead horse, ran across the edge of the field, and made his escape. I also entered the woods and continued to run at the top of my speed until I reached the breastworks, where I found our line of battle. I passed beyond these and went back a mile or more to our division hospital in the rear.

Many wounded men had already arrived. The surgeons were busily at work. Rough tables had been erected under the trees around the house where the hospital had been established. Wounds were dressed and limbs amputated with a fearful rapidity. Only the most serious cases were attended to. Groans and shrieks filled the air as the fearful work went on. Those were terrible hours. How plainly they are pictured upon my mind! Of course, my wound would receive no attention where there were so many others of a dangerous character.

Under a tree, without a blanket, I lay and listened. The line of battle was now well formed, and the conflict was raging in all its horror. How can I describe it? For a few moments, perhaps, all would be quiet; then upon the right, where the Sixth corps was in line, there would be a yell, followed by a terrific musketry fire lasting for ten minutes, while all along the remainder of the line there would be silence; then suddenly a volley on the left; then all along the entire line, until it seemed as if the

Wilderness itself throbbed under the terrible concussions. Thus, the battle raged that afternoon and night, the day and night that followed them, and the succeeding day. At times the firing would seem to be falling back, the volleys appearing nearer and nearer; then the tides would change and roll back in the other direction. All the time wounded men were streaming back from the line of battle, and such rumours as were in circulation in regard to the situation of the army.

One wounded man would say: "Just as I was wounded there came a report that Lee had seized the fords in our rear, and there is no way to escape;" another would come back with the story that the rebel army had flanked our line of battle, and was in our rear,—scores of reports, all different, and yet all agreeing that our army was outgeneraled, and that we were defeated. We thought of our comrades who had perished by hundreds, of the Northern homes to be made sorrowful when the intelligence reached them of their death and of our defeat. We had expected so much from General Grant, and now he was to be defeated as other generals before him had been. We forgot our wounds, in the midst of these sorrowful thoughts, and many of those brave men wept like schoolboys over the grave situation.

The third night came, and instinctively we all knew that some great movement was being made. The night was very dark and gloomy. Orders came for the wounded to be placed on board the ambulances and baggage wagons, as the army was to move. The few ambulances were properly reserved for the use of those who were the most seriously wounded. Thirteen of us were placed in a baggage wagon drawn by six mules. We were informed that our destination was Fredericksburgh, and that no cavalry could be spared from the army to guard us from attacks by the rebel guerrillas. Consequently, rifles were placed in the wagons, and every man who had two sound hands was expected to use a rifle in case an attack should be made.

The work of loading the wounded was a long and tedious one. Many of them, who would doubtless have recovered if they could have remained quiet, and been cared for, were placed in the ambulances, and in riding over the rough road the arteries of their amputated limbs, hastily and imperfectly secured, would break forth again, and the precious life would soon ebb out through the crimson tides.

Slowly the long train of wagons, laden with its suffering freight of wounded humanity, took up its line of march. The road was rough and uneven; the pine trees stood thickly by the way on either side, and clasping hands above, formed a dark green canopy over us. As we jolted wearily on, the old Army of the Potomac was moving in the opposite direction, guided by a master's hand. It has obtained a grip upon the throat of the Confederacy, a grip that will not be relaxed until treason gasps and dies.

CHAPTER 10

The Battle of Spottsylvania

General Warren's corps was to lead in the advance from the battlefield of the Wilderness to Spottsylvania Court House, and at nine o'clock in the evening of May 7th, his columns were in motion.

Our regiment was for a brief time detached from the brigade, and remained upon the picket line after our division had moved from its old position to take up its line of march to Spottsylvania, which was about thirteen miles southeast of the battle-ground in the Wilderness. At one o'clock in the morning of May 8th, we were withdrawn from the picket line, and proceeded to follow them. It was with sad hearts that we turned from the field, where for three days had rolled the tides of war. Eighteen thousand of our brave men had fallen. A large portion of these had been sent to the rear, wounded, and the remainder were resting in soldiers' graves, beneath the tangled thickets of the pine forest where they had fallen.

It was sad to think of the brave fellows who had crossed the Rapidan and entered the Wilderness but a few days before, so full of life and activity, now cold and lifeless—mustered out forever. But such is war, and we distinctly under stood that we were marching to other fields of strife, where the atmosphere would be impregnated with a thousand clangers, where we would meet death in its most bloody form. The morning was dark, the road was rough, and our advance was necessarily slow. The men moved on in silence, but few words were spoken, each seemed busied with his own thoughts. The steel shanks of the bayonets rattled against the canteens, and occasionally a horse's iron-shod hoof would clang against a rock; aside from this, nothing was heard but the irregular and ceaseless tramp of the men, as the weary column pressed on.

Daylight dawned, and as the sun arose we were reminded of the fact that this was the Christian Sabbath, a day made memorable and sacred by the resurrection of the Prince of Peace, and that those whom he died to save were here engaged in deadly war. At the hour when the sacred stillness of that beautiful Sabbath was being broken by the clanging peals of the church bells in our Northern communities, the stillness of that morning at Spottsylvania was broken by the thunders of the artillery of General Longstreet's corps, as they opened a deadly fire upon the advanced brigades of General Warren, as they emerged from the forest in battle line at Alsop's farm, upon the high, open plain, two miles from Spottsylvania Court House.

General Lee had anticipated that some movement was about to be made by General Grant, and had thrown Longstreet's corps, now commanded by General Anderson, out to Spottsylvania, to check the advance of the Army of the Potomac, should it be made in that direction; and this was the force with which General Warren had come in contact. General Robinson, commanding our advance, promptly returned the enemy's fire, but he was soon severely wounded, and his men were pressed back. General Warren soon arrived, and with great gallantry rallied his men, reformed their line, and checked the enemy's advance. The Army of the Potomac, and the country at large, are under great obligations to General Warren, who, by personal daring, prevented what, for a time, seemed to be a fatal disaster to the Union cause.

The Fifth corps was soon in position, and held the enemy in check until the Sixth corps, under Sedgwick, came up. Our regiment arrived at the scene of conflict at ten o'clock in the morning. We had heard for hours the roar of battle, and knew that our comrades had encountered the enemy. We learned upon our arrival that our own brigade had been desperately engaged, and had suffered a severe loss. We changed our position several times on that day. At different periods we formed to charge, and would then be withdrawn. At six o'clock in the evening we were again pushed up to the front, where our lines were being formed, to assault the enemy's position near Laurel hill. The troops were in three lines, our regiment being in the third.

It was the design of our commander to make the assault under the cover of darkness, but unknown to us, the rebels were also preparing to make an assault, and just at dark, when forms could be but indistinctly discerned at a short distance, there was a heavy crash of musketry, and a wild, savage yell, as they rushed upon our first line of battle, which soon gave way and fell back upon the second. The confusion was indescribable; it was only with the greatest difficulty that we could tell friend from foe. As we rushed up to reinforce our comrades, the glare of the guns revealed to us the desperate character of the conflict.

Just as we reached the battle, our men gave way and fell back, leaving us in the breach thus made. The rebels came on with terrible energy, to follow up the advantage they had thus gained. Their advance was almost irresistible, and our regiment was borne back for a short distance by the force of the enemy's advance. We were alone; the other regiments had all fallen back; our men were in just the right mood to fight,—weary, hungry, discouraged, mad. In such a condition it is as easy to die as to run, and so they decided to hold their position until ordered to leave it. We were outnumbered, flanked, almost surrounded; there were rebels in front of us, on both flanks, and to the rear of us; it was an easy task to find a rebel anywhere. The situation was as desperate as any we occupied during the war, but officers and men alike were determined to fight, to sell their lives as dearly as possible, a willing sacrifice upon the altar of the country they loved.

It was a struggle at close quarters, a hand-to-hand conflict, resembling a mob in its character. The contestants for a time seemed to forget all the noble and refined elements of manhood, and for that hour on Laurel hill they were brutes, made wild with passion and blood, engaged in a conflict as deadly and fierce as ever raged upon the continent. Men were transformed to giants, the air was filled with a medley of sounds, shouts, cheers, commands, oaths, the sharp reports of rifles, the hissing shot, dull, heavy thuds of clubbed muskets, the swish of swords and sabres, groans and prayers, all combining to send a thrill of excitement and inspiration to every heart. Many of our men could not afford the time necessary to load their guns, the situation being too desperate for that, but they clubbed their muskets and fought.

Occasionally, when too sorely pressed, they would drop their guns, and clinch the enemy in single combat, until Federal and Confederate would roll upon the ground in the death struggle. Our officers all fought like demons. The revolvers and swords, which up to that hour had never seen actual service, here received their baptism of blood. Every man in that little band was a hero of whom his native state may well be proud. The enemy evidently did not comprehend how weak we were, for if they had, with their vastly superior force, it would have been an easy matter to have captured us all.

As the moments passed the valour of the men increased; many of those who were wounded refused to go to the rear, but with the blood pouring from their wounds continued to fight. And thus, blue and gray fought for victory. Upon the one side was the hot, brilliant, fiery blood of the South fighting for slavery and the Confederacy; upon the other was the naturally cool and sluggish blood of the distant North, now in flamed to a boiling heat as it fought for liberty and the union of states. The lumberman of the North crossed bayonets with the Southern planter, and both lay down to die together.

At last, to our great joy and surprise, the enemy fell back, leaving us victors upon the field, and also leaving a large number of prisoners in our hands. When our wounded went back to the rear, after the conflict ended, they found a picket line, and line of battle formed in our rear, but their officers would hardly believe that our regiment was out in their front. We established a picket line of our own, while our noble fellows lay down to sleep upon the ground where they had so bravely fought. Silent and motionless lay the dead and the living through the remaining hours of the night.

At daylight we were relieved, and ordered to the rear. Bearing our dead comrades with us to a place where we could give them a soldier's burial, we marched to the position assigned us, having won much honour and praise from our commanding generals for the gallant conduct we had displayed. Our loss had been heavy. Brave Captain Morrell had fallen dead in the thickest of the fight, Lieutenants Melcher and Prince had been wounded, and many others had been killed and wounded in our battle on Laurel hill, but this bloody strife was only the beginning of that which was to soon follow—only the battle in embryo.

The two great armies of Grant and Lee were once more facing each other. The North and South had each placed their greatest army under the command of their greatest leader, and were watching the result with breathless anxiety. Like gladiators, these two leaders were watching each other, to seize, if possible, some advantage. Lee, keen, quick, skilful, perfectly familiar with every hill, valley and road in the country where he was fighting, with the advantage of being on the defensive, holding his forces well in hand, was at the head of an army which, for the sacrifices they made, and the bravery displayed, has not been excelled in the present century.

Grant, cool, silent, persistent, with that stubborn, bulldog tenacity that has so distinguished him, had the serious disadvantages of being in a country comparatively unknown to him, and obliged to carry on an offensive campaign. He was equal to the emergency, and with an ability that astonished the world, he marshalled those great army corps, and successfully carried them through that unparalleled campaign.

As our line of battle was formed, on the ninth of May, General Hancock with the Second corps was on our right, Warren with the Fifth corps was in the centre, Sedgwick, in command of the Sixth, held the left, and General Burnside, with the Ninth, was at the left of Sedgwick. This day was spent in in trenching our position. There was a little skirmishing and some firing by the sharpshooters. It was a sad day, however, for the Union Army, for on this day we lost one of our ablest corps commanders. General Sedgwick was at the front as usual, superintending the erection of his fortifications, when he was shot dead by a rebel sharpshooter. He was beloved by all the army, and his death cast a deep gloom upon all.

The command of his corps then devolved upon General Wright. The tenth was an eventful day. Early in the morning the gallant Hancock had captured a portion of the Confederate wagon train, had gained an advanced position in the enemy's front, and was about to press his advance still further, but General Meade had determined to storm the enemy's position on Laurel hill, and the assaulting column was to be composed of the Fifth and Sixth corps. An attack was made upon this position of the enemy, at eleven o'clock, by the brigades of Webb and Carroll, and again, at three in the afternoon, by the divisions of Crawford and Cutler. These were but the preliminary struggles, and in both our men were repulsed.

At five o'clock the greater attempt to carry the strong position of the enemy was made. The Fifth and Sixth corps fought together; they struggled manfully up the side of the steep, rough hill, whose crest was crowned with the rebel forces; they penetrated the enemy's breast works in one or two places, but were finally over powered and hurled down the hillside in defeat. Again, they charged, and were again repulsed with fearful loss. Down on our left, at a later hour, two brigades of the Sixth corps charged the enemy's position in their front, captured a line of breastworks, nearly one thousand prisoners, and several pieces of artillery.

Darkness came on, and the battle ceased to rage. It had been a bloody day; our losses had been fearful, and we had gained no decided advantage over the enemy. Under such circumstances, many other leaders would have thought of retreating from a campaign where in six days' time he had lost nearly thirty thousand men; but in that gloomy situation General Grant never for a moment faltered or despaired of ultimate victory, and that evening he wrote that memorable dispatch to the Secretary of War, closing with that historic sentence that so thrilled the heart of the anxious country:

I PROPOSE TO FIGHT IT OUT ON THIS LINE IF IT TAKES, ALL SUMMER.

The eleventh was a day of heavy skirmishing; a sharp, irregular fire ran along the lines. It was evident to all that preparations were being made by our commanders to assault some position in the enemy's line. In the afternoon it began to rain in torrents, and the night that followed was dark and drear. It was whispered along the line, that evening, that General Hancock was to lead an assaulting column upon the enemy's position. We all knew that, if the report was true, there would be warm work, for of all the gallant generals in the Army of the Potomac, there was not one more brilliant and brave than General W. S. Hancock, and, if such an assault was to be made, he was the man to undertake it. Grant decided that this blow should fall upon Lee's right centre, which he considered to be the most vulnerable point in his whole line.

At midnight General Hancock with his gallant corps left his position on our right, and moved through the darkness, guided by the compass, and took a position between the Sixth and Ninth corps, and there waited until the hour should arrive when the blow should be given. His corps was formed in two lines of battle; the first was composed of the divisions of Barlow and Birney, the second, of Gibbon and Mott. At the appointed hour, through a dense fog, moving swiftly and with noise less tread over a rough ground covered with a thick wood, he made the movement. He struck the rebel line at a salient point of an earthwork, where Johnson's division of Swell's corps was intrenched.

With wild cheers the commands of Barlow and Birney threw themselves upon the rebel line. The enemy was completely surprised, and the battle was of short duration. Generals Johnson and Stewart, with the entire division of over three thousand men, were made prisoners, also thirty pieces of artillery and many colours, were captured.

The historian records a singular incident that occurred on that memorable morning. General Stewart, at the outbreak of the rebellion, belonged in Baltimore, and was an old army friend of General Hancock. When the former was captured, Hancock cordially offered his hand to the prisoner, and exclaimed, "How are you, Stewart?"

The haughty rebel, in a most absurd manner, refused to accept his hand, and replied, "I am General Stewart of the Confederate Army, and under the circumstances I decline to take your hand."

The gallant Hancock instantly rejoined, "Under any other circumstances, General, I should not have offered it."

We afterward learned that, in that charge, we had nearly captured General Lee and severed his army in twain. Hancock's men pursued the flying rebels for a mile in the direction of Spottsylvania Court House, until they were checked by the fugitives who had rallied behind an unfinished line of breastworks. Rebel reinforcements quickly arrived from the corps of Longstreet and Hill, and Hancock's men were pushed back to the line of works they had captured.

Lee instantly resolved to retake the position he had lost, and Grant was determined to hold the advantage he had gained. Our troops opened fire all along the line, to prevent the enemy from concentrating his forces to crush Hancock. Charge after charge was made by the troops of Burnside and Warren, but the enemy's position was so strong that it could not be carried. In the meantime, the storm of war was raging desperately around Hancock, and Griffin's division of Warren's corps was sent to his relief.

Five times in rapid succession did General Lee hurl his massed forces upon Hancock, to retake the breastworks that Johnson and Stewart had lost. The combatants fought desperately, hand to hand, and at times the flags of both North and South were planted upon the breastworks simultaneously, and within a short distance of each other. The carnage on both sides was most fearful, but the rebels were each time repulsed. Although the rain poured down in torrents, General Lee would not give up the idea of recapturing the line he had lost.

The afternoon passed, and midnight came before the shattered lines of the enemy were withdrawn at the close of a combat that had raged for twenty hours. Lee was defeated and Hancock was left in possession of the field and artillery that he had so gloriously won. Thus, ended the Battle of Spottsylvania, which was one of the most desperate and bloody of the war. It had been fought principally by the infantry, and at such short range that the carnage had been fearful. Probably there was no battle of the war where the conflict was for so long a time carried on at close quarters as at Spottsylvania.

Could those old forest trees, seared and scarred by the missiles and flames of war, speak and tell this generation of the scenes they witnessed in those eventful days, relate the deeds of valour, the reckless courage, the terrible sacrifice of life, tell how men suffered and died to preserve the constitution, it would kindle such a flame of intense loyalty in the hearts of the American people that the old flag would be secure from the attacks of all enemies for generations to come.

Our regiment moved to the left, at ten o'clock in the evening of the 13th. We marched all night in the mud and rain, and were pushed close up to the enemy's front, near the Court House, where we re mained until the 20th. What bitter days those were! I need not remind my old comrades of them, for their events are burned in upon our life's experience, and can never be forgotten. Constant skirmishing was raging all along our line; we were ever on the alert to repulse any attack the rebels might make; there was no rest; minie-balls were ever singing through the air; a steady stream of men, wounded and dead, were borne to the rear. Officers can tell you truthfully, and in eloquent terms, of the movements of our army through that memorable battle, and the days that followed; they can tell you of the bravery of our soldiers and of the glorious victories they won.

But if you desire to listen to the true suffering, sacrifices and hardships of that fearful battle, talk not with them alone, but rather sit down with him who carried the rifle and endured the brunt of battle, with the soldier who slept in the mud behind the breastworks, with his equipments buckled around him and his hand upon his trusty rifle, or with him who stood out on the skirmish line, wearied, hungry, wet, cold, and almost ready to drop to the ground from fatigue, and yet who through those long hours maintained his lonely vigils and watched the stealthy foe. Those men had an experience in the sufferings and sacrifices of war of which men in official positions know comparatively nothing. Grand men! I never meet them now but that I feel like raising my hat and greeting them with veneration and respect.

On the nineteenth, General Grant, being convinced that Lee's positions could only be carried with a terrible loss of life, determined to make another flank movement to the left, and thus oblige the rebel commander to evacuate his elaborate line of defences. General Lee, mistrusting that such a movement would be made, determined to prevent it, if possible, and for this purpose he suddenly threw General Swell's corps upon the right of our army, which had been much weakened by the withdrawal of troops. This position was held by General Tyler's division of heavy artillery, who were guarding our line of communications from Spottsylvania to Fredericksburgh.

Ewell swept down upon this road in great force, and attempted to capture our wagon train, but Tyler's men made a most desperate defence. These men had just been taken from the forces around Washington, and had never been under fire before, but they fought like veterans, although they did not use the caution that men do who have often been under fire, and so lost heavily. They repulsed Ewell, and captured several hundreds of prisoners, before the detachments of the Fifth and Sixth, sent to their relief, could reach them. This was the last fighting that took place around Spottsylvania. The wounded were sent back to Fredericksburgh, and the dead were buried as well as we could possibly bury them.

Another flanking movement was begun. Hancock's corps and General Torbett's cavalry moved in the advance, early in the morning of the twenty-first, and soon the whole army was marching in the direction of the North Anna River. Over thirty thousand of our men were sent to the rear, and left upon the battlefield where we had fought since the campaign opened, but the tireless brain of Secretary Stanton had organised twice that number of recruits in the various Northern States, and his strong arm, made almost superhuman by the responsibility of his position, was pushing these men rapidly to the front, to replete the shattered ranks.

The eyes, not merely of all the American people, but of the civilized world, were now turned upon the two great leaders, Grant and Lee, as with their huge armies they contended for their respective governments. But the suffering was not all confined to the army and the soldiers, but pervaded the whole land north and south;—so many homes being shadowed by mourning, so many hearts being filled with woe for the slain who had fallen upon those ensanguined fields! May God save the nation from another experience like that!

Chapter 11

North Anna to the James

This was to us a memorable march—one that is very difficult for me to describe. It is not so much my desire to give the movements of the several army corps, through those eventful days, as to give some of the experiences of a private soldier who toiled on in the ranks.

For nearly three weeks we had been under an unceasing fire. The days had been long and tedious, and the nights had been passed in marching, fighting, and sleepless activity. Of course, our ranks had been most sadly thinned by the ravages of the campaign, the regiment itself being now reduced in size to the appearance of a company, while the brigade was but a skeleton of its former strength. The men in the ranks did not look as they did when they entered the Wilderness; their uniforms were now torn, ragged, and stained with mud; the men had grown thin and haggard; the experience of those twenty days seemed to have added twenty years to their age.

I wish that I could truthfully picture the scene as we are closing the march on one of those sultry days. We have marched full thirty miles; the day has been one of those so heated that the atmosphere seemed close and stifling like that of an oven; the sun has disappeared, and the stars are beginning to twinkle down through the gathering gloom. With slow and irregular steps our men are moving wearily on, seemingly unconscious of everything around them.

Colonel Spear gives the command, "By the right of companies, to the rear into column." The regiment in obedience to the command, breaks into companies. Then the word, "Halt," "Halt," "Halt," sounds through the regiment, as the various company commanders give their respective orders. Then the orders, "Front face," "Order arms," "Fix bayonets," "Stack arms," "Break ranks," follow each other in rapid succession. Our equipments are hung upon the stacks of rifles, our haversacks and blankets are thrown upon the ground, and we are to rest for the night.

If the company musters fifteen men at the roll-call when we halt, it is above an average number, for many of the men have fallen out, unable to keep in the ranks. Just at this moment an order comes to the orderly-sergeant to make a detail of five men for picket, who are to report to the adjutant's tent in ten minutes, and one-third of our weary men are thus detailed to go out on the picket line for the night, where they can expect to obtain neither rest nor sleep. Of the ten who remain in the company, five at least are so footsore and weary that they are entirely unable to do anything in making preparations for their evening meal, but fall upon the hard ground to rest, as gladly as the weary child sinks into its mother's arms. The remainder go in search of wood and water; they soon return with a few fence rails and well-filled canteens, and then the cooking operations begin.

There was nothing very elaborate in our cooking apparatus. A black tin cup or pail sufficed for the coffee-pot, and were held patiently over the fire until their contents reached a boiling point. If we were fortunate enough to have rations of meat, they were easily disposed of. Salt pork was eaten raw, with a keen relish; fresh beef was broiled on the coals, and was considered as one of the luxuries. An hour was usually consumed around the little campfires, at the close of a day's march, in preparing and eating our suppers. Those who were too weary to assist in obtaining the wood and water are cordially invited to make free use of them, and if they are unable to do that, their comrades boil their coffee for them, and assist them all in their power.

We always used to draw an inspiration from the cup of hot coffee, and after supper there would be joking, talking, and laughter, reminding us of the old days at Rappahannock station. Our beds were not "downy beds of ease," to say the least; and I shall always believe that the soil of Virginia is at least several degrees harder than that of any other State in the Union. We always found, when we camped for the night, that the ground would not adapt itself to our wants; there was always a hummock where we wanted a hollow, and a hollow where it was desirable to have a hummock, and no matter how frequently we changed positions, the result was always the same.

I never knew whether this strange phenomenon was due to the geological formation of the country, or to the fact that the sacred soil itself was so hostile to the Yankees who were desecrating it, that it was determined to add to our misery. I only know that we twisted and turned ourselves in all sorts of shapes, as we vainly endeavoured to put ourselves in harmony with those hollows and hummocks.

We were usually awakened a great many times through the night. Frequently a roar of conflict from the skirmish line would be borne back to us, and we would be called to arms for the purpose of repelling the enemy if he should advance; then the firing would die away, and we would just get asleep, when we would be awakened by someone giving us a vigorous kick. This would come in so peremptory a manner, that we, in our half-awakened condition, would suppose that it must be given by some person having unusual authority, then we would rub our eyes and ask, "What is wanted?" and some lazy old straggler, who was looking for his regiment, would ask, "Is this the One Hundred and Seventy-fifth New York?"

Under such circumstances it would be a fortunate thing for the old bummer that we could not reach our rifle. One night, after a most outrageous day's march, we were endeavouring to obtain a little sleep, when a Constant stream of stragglers was passing through our company, disturbing us and asking for regiments and brigades of which we had never heard before. About midnight, with many others, there came a lieutenant in a *Zouave* uniform; he was evidently very proud of his rank, red cap, and the gilt lace upon his dress. He halted in our company, stirred up Dick Quinlan from a sound sleep, and asked, "What regiment is this?"

Dick rubbed his eyes a moment, and answered in a stentorian voice:

"The Ninth Ireland, sir," while the officer, who was undoubtedly grateful for the information thus received, went on his way rejoicing. Long before sun rise in the morning, the reveille would awaken us, and it would not seem as if we had been asleep at all, so rapidly had the brief night passed away; and then with aching heads, hungry stomachs, and weary limbs, we would begin another day's work, not knowing what hardships and dangers it contained. I wonder how men endured so much. Some are surprised that so many of our men died from exposure and disease; but as I recall those weary days, I only wonder that so many men survived them at all.

On the twenty-third of May, our regiment reached the North Anna River. Our brigade was ordered to cross the river at Jericho ford. The current was very swift, and the water nearly up to our armpits, which made the crossing a very difficult task to perform, but it was soon accomplished, and we then formed a line of battle to guard the men who were employed in building a pontoon bridge across the river. The bridge was soon completed, and then our whole corps crossed, and formed a line of battle, nearly all of which was in the woods. Our division, commanded by General Griffin, was in the centre, Crawford's was on our left, and our Second division was on the right.

At five o'clock a sharp attack was made upon our division by the rebel divisions of Heth and Wilcox, which we quickly repulsed, but three brigades, commanded by the rebel General Brown, were suddenly hurled with such force upon our second division that it was thrown back in disorder, to the exposure of the right flank of our division to the enemy's fire. For a moment it seemed as if this was a most serious disaster. The rebels rushed on, following up the advantage they had thus gained, while our brigade was ordered in at a "double-quick" to check them. It was a critical moment.

As we reached the spot, and were wheeling into position, the gallant Eighty-Third Pennsylvania regiment of our brigade, commanded by Lieutenant-Colonel McCoy, came around upon the flank and rear of the rebel line, and at a most fortunate moment poured in a deadly fire at close quarters upon the foe. So fearful was its effect that the rebel line reeled and staggered beneath its withering power, and the next moment broke, and ran from the field, leaving their commander, and nearly one thousand prisoners, in our hands. In this battle Colonel Spear and several of our men were wounded. After the enemy retreated, we built a strong line of breastworks, which were not completed until nearly morning. On the night of the twenty-sixth, we secretly recrossed the North Anna, and began another flank movement to the left. It was simply a renewal of the old experience, to fight all day, and march all night.

On the twenty-seventh, we passed the late residence of the rebel, John B. Floyd. It was a large plantation, with a magnificent dwelling, and numerous out buildings. The weather was very warm, and ripe strawberries peeped out and blushed at us from the thick grass that covered the land of the traitor. The twenty-eighth, we crossed the Pamunky River, at Hanover Ferry, sixteen miles from the city of Richmond. Our line of battle was formed some two miles from the river, and there we rapidly threw up another line of breastworks.

Heavy skirmishing was heard in our front and on either flank; occasionally a great shell would come tearing through the air above our heads, as if to remind us that our rebel friends had not forgotten us. We began to derive one satisfaction from the situation, and that was from the fact that we were now so near to Richmond that the sounds would be borne from the battlefield to that city, and each booming cannon would be a solemn reminder to the people of the rebel capital that justice was thundering at its gates, and demanding its dues. Upon the thirtieth our line was advanced several times, and we threw up two lines of breastworks. There was very heavy skirmishing, and scores of shells passed over us, but no one in our regiment was injured.

The day following, we were relieved by a portion of the Ninth corps, and moved to the left, and built another line of breast works. June 1st, we moved still further to the left, and built more breastworks. Late in the afternoon the rebels charged upon us in great force, but were soon repulsed. We found that it was much more to our advantage to have them charge upon our lines than it was for us to charge upon theirs. In the afternoon of the second we were ordered to some other point upon the left, and as we were advancing we came in contact with the enemy, who nearly surrounded us, so that it was only by cutting our way through their lines that we escaped being captured. We lost from the corps some five hundred men, nearly all of whom were taken prisoners.

On the third was fought the bloody Battle of Cold Harbor, which was one of the most desperate of the whole campaign. Early in that morning our whole army was in line of battle, prepared to assault the enemy's works at the appointed hour. Hancock was upon our extreme left, then came Wright, then the command of General Smith; upon the right of Smith was Warren's corps, while General Burnside held the extreme right of our position. The orders had been given to make the assault at four o'clock in the morning. The signal was given, and along the line our men rushed upon the rebel works. What a reception they met! Every thicket gleamed with the glare of rebel guns; every hill and ridge was crowned with rebel cannon.

Never before in that campaign had our men received such a baptism of death. The air was filled with the shrieking missiles of war, and every breeze was freighted with death. Our men came in contact with thickets so tangled with vines and thorns that to pass through them was an impossibility; there were bogs and marshes where no human being could walk, such was the mass of watery mire; and thus, our lines were broken and our commands were disconnected, and all the time there was poured from the rebel lines, which we could not see, those volleys of hurtling death.

General Barlow, of Hancock's corps, succeeded in reaching the rebel line, captured a strong position with several hundred prisoners, three guns and a battle flag, but the rebels soon overpowered him, and pressed him back. General Gibbon, of the same corps, also penetrated the thickets and reached the rebel breastworks. Colonel McKeen heroically planted the stars and stripes upon these, but in a moment after he fell mortally wounded, and our men were hurled back. These were the only troops, which charged in front, that succeeded in reaching the enemy's breastworks. General Burnside, on our right, struck the left flank of the rebel army, and inflicted a serious loss upon it, but our men being repulsed in front, he was also obliged to fall back.

The conflict was short, sharp, and bloody; we were repulsed at every point with great loss; in less than an hour's time we lost ten thousand men. Our regiment fought near Bethesda church, and lost quite heavily. The loss to the army, throughout the day, must have been nearly fifteen thousand men. Our men were now fully convinced that to carry the rebel position was an impossibility; and I do not believe that if the order to do so had been given, that a single man would have made the attempt. The situation was now a gloomy one; our losses through the campaign had been fearful; the army of General Lee was still between us and Richmond.

We now found ourselves, at a sickly season of the year, in the deadly swamps of the Chickahominy, where to remain with an army for any length of time, was an impossibility. The sun glared down upon us like a globe of fire, as he rolled through the brazen skies. The air was filled with malaria and death. The water was very poor and unhealthy. Sickness, as well as battle, was doing fearful work in our ranks. We were now in the position from which General McClellan had been driven two years before. It was a fortunate thing for the destiny of this nation, in this dreary period, that we had at the head of our army a man who knew nothing of the word defeat,—one who was equal to the emergency.

Undoubtedly General Grant was disappointed that the fruits of the campaign had not been more decisive, but he well understood that General Lee had lost heavily in the campaign, and that it would be a difficult task for him to replenish his decimated ranks, and so he conceived the idea of throwing his army across the James River, if possible, capture Petersburgh, cut the lines of railway connecting Richmond with the South, and thus compel the surrender of the rebel capital. It was a great undertaking to thus change a base of supplies by crossing a river in the face of an enemy, without having the army cut in two by an attack from his powerful adversary,—a task that required a great intellect, a strong arm, and a Spartan's courage.

Our leader possessed all these, and the movement was undertaken. To deceive the enemy, our line of breastworks was strengthened as if we were to remain in them. The rebels made repeated attacks upon us, but were always repulsed. Grant was rapidly maturing his plans to cross the James river. The various corps were to move in different directions, so that Lee would not understand where the blow was to fall.

Sheridan with his gallant cavalry was raiding upon the enemy's country, and cutting Lee's communications in every direction. Our corps, preceded by the cavalry of General Wilson, forced a passage across the Chickahominy at Long Bridge, and marched in the direction of Richmond. This was to conceal from General Lee the movements of the remainder of the army. The rebel commander, supposing that the attack was to be made upon that city, hastily retreated within its fortifications, and stood in its defence; while, in the meantime, the army of the Potomac was marching rapidly in the direction of the James River.

On the night of June 14th, a pontoon bridge, more than two thousand feet in length, was thrown across the river. Hancock's corps had already crossed on the ferry at Harrisons Landing, and a large portion of the army immediately followed upon the pontoon bridge. On the fifteenth, our corps reached the James, and began to cross over. At nine o'clock in the morning of the sixteenth our regiment was carried over on a small steam transport, named "General Hooker." The place of our crossing was at Powhatan Point.

And thus, closed the wonderful campaign from the Rapidan to the James. At its close, as we stood upon the opposite side of the James River and recalled it all, it seemed more like a fearful nightmare to us than a reality. We remembered the long days of weariness and pain, the many miles we had marched when we were so tired and hungry, the battles and skirmishes through which we had passed, and above all else we thought of our brave comrades so many of whom had gone down in blood and death. If there is a section of territory in all this Union that must forever remain sacred, it is that section of Virginia reaching from the Shenandoah valley to the James River, upon which was fought so many of the great battles of the war, and in whose bosom repose the ashes of so many thousand heroes.

That country must have changed much, my comrades, since we were there. Those rifle-pits we digged are now filled with earth; the breastworks are levelled down; the forts all dismantled. I presume we should hardly remember now at what points in the line our regiments fought, or where we buried our comrades. Those shallow graves are all over grown with weeds and bushes; but notwithstanding all this, I wish we could go down there again, and follow the indistinct trail of our army from the Wilderness to the James River. What points of interest we could visit!

I would like, some beautiful morning, just as the sun should be flooding the gateways of the coming day with his fleecy tides of golden light, to climb with a company of my old comrades the heights that encircle Fredericksburgh; or cross the plains around the ruins of the old Chancellorsville house; then enter the Wilderness, and lounge, through the sultry hours of noon, under the pine trees where we once fought the rebels, and plunged into the depths of death; and in the solitude of the evening climb around the heights of Spottsylvania, and recall the incidents that transpired in those distant days, when the tides of war surged over their rocky breasts; and thus continue our way to North Anna, Cold Harbor and the James.

I think that in some places we could easily locate the graves of our comrades. Eighteen years have passed since we buried them there, and I suppose that in all time no loyal man has visited them. No one who had any sympathy for the cause in which they died, has ever dropped a tear or a flower upon the little mounds that contain their ashes. The wild animals have passed over them; the friend of the "lost cause" has passed that way; but no Union soldier, no one who wept and prayed for them in their sacrifices and their death. I wish we could go down there, visit those graves, and scatter a comrade's tears and flowers upon the ashes of our brave comrades. I believe that we would derive an inspiration from the visit, that would prompt us to forget all political prejudices and parties, and to work, talk, vote, live, and die, if it was necessary, to perpetuate the principles for which they fought.

CHAPTER 12

In Front of Petersburgh

Those words sound very natural; we used to write them very often. How many letters, written to friends at home in the summer of 1864, began Camp of the ——, in front of Petersburgh. But many long years have passed since we wrote them last. In front of Petersburgh! yes, we were there, and we can never forget that fact; it was the first summer that we passed so near the beautiful capital of the Southern Confederacy—the Southerners gave us a *warm* reception—but we did not particularly enjoy the summer. There were very many inconveniences, which, to say the least, sadly interfered with our enjoyment, and had not circumstances beyond our control prevented it, I think we should have gone home some little time before the season closed.

I remember quite distinctly some of the inconveniences that we encountered. The weather was too hot, the dews at night were heavy, and gave us the chills, the water was poor, the bill of fare did not give entire satisfaction, the rooms we occupied were small, and poorly lighted, ventilated and furnished, the air at times was almost filled with dark-coloured insects of various and often of enormous sizes, whose sting or bite was deadly, causing, in that season, deaths in almost numberless cases, and last of all, there was so much noise and excitement that frequently there were whole nights in which we hardly closed our eyes in sleep, so that as a pleasure resort, "In front of Petersburgh" was a miserable failure, and I would advise all nervous people, at least, to avoid visiting the place, unless the regulations have been changed since we were there.

As I have stated in the previous chapter, we went there in June, 1864, and remained until the month of March, 1865, so that we know whereof we affirm. But in this chapter, I want to give some reminiscences of those months,—an account of some of the events that transpired and of some of the battles in which our regiment fought.

We crossed the James River June 16th, and, two days later, moved to the front, where we were received with a heavy fire. Our brigade was in the centre of the division, as we thus advanced, and was well concealed by the woods through which we marched, and consequently suffered but little loss. We reached the edge of an open field, where we halted, and threw up a line of breastworks. The second brigade had also made a gallant charge, and gained a position close up to the enemy's line. The first brigade, commanded by our own gallant Chamberlain, had made a desperate charge across an open field. Their brave leader led the van until he received a terrible wound, and was hurled from his horse. For this gallant conduct he was promoted to a brigadier-general on the field, by General Grant,—the only instance of the kind that occurred during the war.

This battle was followed by several days of marching and skirmishing, and then we took our position in the line that was investing Petersburgh. This was the first regular siege in which we ever participated. The city was very strongly fortified; its lines of defence were many miles in length, beginning on the bank of the Appomattox River, extending around the western side of Petersburgh, until they reached and crossed the James River, to the north-eastern side of the city of Richmond. These defences were elaborate, and consisted of redans, re doubts, and infantry parapets, with the outer line of defences, abatis, stakes and *chevaux-de-frise*, constructed by the most skilful engineers in the Confederate service; and behind these was the veteran army of General Lee. To hold that army in check we must have defences equally as elaborate, and quickly the work of construction began. We were so near the rebel lines that our work had to be done at night, under cover of the darkness. The weather was very hot, and we suffered much from sickness.

A battle would be raging at some point along our extensive line, nearly every day; and for six weeks, as we were in those works in front of Petersburgh, we lost men in our regiment nearly every day. The moods of the two armies seemed to vary like those of spoiled children. One day all would be pleasant and peaceable for a portion of the time, at least; the rebels would come outside their works, and we would clamber out over our breastworks, straighten up, get a good look at the situation, and not a shot would be fired from either line; in two hours from that time, perhaps, the great shells would be flying from either side, and if a man put his head above the breastworks, it was certain death.

The government exerted itself to supply us with good rations of food, and the sanitary commission, like an angel of mercy, sent its stores of vegetables and other luxuries to us frequently, and thus rendered us great service. It is impossible for me, in my limited space, to describe the fortifications we built, and the bomb-proofs in which we were often obliged to sleep. We shall never forget the latter—those little dens covered with logs and earth,—how often they saved our lives, and how frequently we fled to them in moments of danger.

The campaign became quite scientific, so that after the first few weeks, we learned to tell by the sound the nature of every missile that passed over us, and knew just which ones to dodge. Of course, the mortar shells had the most terror for us. The ordinary field-pieces or siege-guns, that threw shells directly through the air, did not disturb us much, as we lay behind our breastworks, but those confounded mortars, throwing those enormous shells up in almost a perpendicular direction, with such a peculiar aim that, when they reached a certain degree of altitude, they would descend plump within our lines, tearing up the earth in a most frightful manner, and filling the air with death-dealing missiles by their terrible explosions, so that our only safety was in the bomb-proofs. We always told short stories when we heard them coming.

As we became accustomed to the new situation in which we found ourselves, we learned to take all the advantages of it we possibly could. The bomb-proofs of course were damp and unhealthy, so we had our tents out in the open air, and fled to the bomb-proofs when danger threatened us. We also built dining pavilions, in which we used to eat. These were not very elaborate edifices, but answered their purpose; a few pieces of shelter tent were spread upon short posts, to protect us from the hot rays of the sun, the sides were left open to allow a circulation of air, a rough table and benches were constructed, and under those shelters we would dine in what, to us at least, was a metropolitan style.

But how often would those meals be interrupted in the most abrupt and amusing manner! We will relate one instance. It is one o'clock in the afternoon of a hot, sweltering day; the enemy has been shelling us in a most vigorous manner all the forenoon; an agent of the sanitary commission has made us a visit, leaving us potatoes, onions, soft bread, pickles, and a few other luxuries, and the event must be commemorated by a good square dinner. In the inspiration of the preparation we forgot Lee's army, the dreaded mortar shells and all else, and our feast is soon spread upon the table in our dining pavilion, while six rough, unshaved, sunburned fellows place their legs beneath the table, and prepare to devour the rations that have been dealt out to their mess.

They are a happy squad; they talk and laugh in high glee. The preliminaries on those occasions were very brief, and the food is quickly deposited within the plates of the hungry fellows, but just at that moment a noise that is utterly indescribable fills the air; it is a medley of shuddering, shrieking, agonising groans, as if the air was alive with demons, uttering their most demoniac yells with an infinite power—an incarnate hell that is descending upon us with lightning speed. The boys understand what it is; rules of etiquette are forgotten, and each voice utters those dreaded words,—a shell, a shell, and six men charge for the bomb-proof. In their hasty departure Horton came in contact with one of the four posts that supported the roof of the pavilion, and down came the structure.

Unfortunately for Wyman, the table was between him and the bombproof, and as he sprang over the former to reach the latter, his foot caught in the table somewhere, and as a result of the accident he entered the bomb-proof upon his head and shoulders, leaving the path along which he came strewn with potatoes, onions, and other articles in the culinary department. The dinner was almost a failure, and what rendered the circumstance more aggravating to the parties so directly interested, was the fact that the shell did not strike within several rods of them, and would not have done them any harm if they had remained at their table.

The boys learned to pass away the tedious hours, when there was nothing to do, by playing cards, and many of them became very skilful in their use; but, as is usually the case, the friendly games soon gave way to those where stakes were deposited, and so intense, though friendly, feelings were engendered. Four of the boys are thus occupied; the game of "bluff" has reached an exciting point; the little group around the table beneath the cotton canopy has become the centre of attraction for the whole company; the sum of money upon the board is rapidly increasing as each one in turn bets upon the value of the cards he holds; it is Wyman's turn; he glances at his hand and remarks, "I will raise it five," and a five dollar greenback drops from his hand upon the pile of stakes.

His next neighbour is Horton, who replies, "I will cover your five and go—"

The sentence was never completed. One of Lee's shells came plunging down through the air at that moment, and the game ended. I never knew what Horton was about to say after his word "go"; I only know that he did go—for the bomb-proof. And thus, the days passed, and notwithstanding all the dangers and fatigue, there were many elements of enjoyment in the summer's campaign in front of Petersburgh, and had it not been for the fact that so many of our men were being shot by the enemy's sharpshooters, the situation would have been quite endurable. Occasionally a shell would explode within our lines, and do considerable damage, so that our ranks were daily losing our best men, whose places were filled with recruits sent down to us from the North. On the 22nd of June, Captain Samuel T. Keene, one of our most gallant officers, was shot and instantly killed by a sharpshooter.

One of the most exciting events that occurred during the summer was the "explosion of the mine," on July 30th. For several days previous to that date we were aware that something of the kind was about to take place. The rebel fort under which the mine was being placed was to our right, and in full view; it was a very strong, six-gun fort, projecting out beyond the average line of the enemy's front. About four hundred yards behind it was Cemetery Hill crowned with a heavy battery which commanded Petersburgh itself. If we could seize that point and hold it, the capture of Petersburgh would be the result.

The plans of General Grant were all made, and if they had been carried out by the officers upon whom devolved their execution, there is no doubt but what they would have been successful. The explosion was to be made at an early hour in the morning; when it occurred, it was to be a signal for our artillery to open all along the lines, and at the same moment a division of Burnside's corps (in whose front was the doomed fort), was to rush over the ruins of the demolished fortress, and in the panic, seize Cemetery Hill; to General Ledlie's division was assigned the task of making the assault. This division was composed of two brigades, one of Massachusetts troops commanded by General J. J. Bartlett, and the other of troops from New York, Pennsylvania and Maryland, commanded by Colonel Marshall.

There was an accidental delay in exploding the mine, and it was nearly five o'clock in the morning before it took place. The fort was garrisoned by three hundred men. We afterward learned that the enemy had received an intimation of what was being done, but had no knowledge of the location or extent of the mine or the time when the explosion was to take place. The first intimation we had that the time had arrived was a dull, heavy roar, and the jarring of the ground upon which we stood. It seemed like the shock of a powerful earthquake; we looked, and saw that the air above where the fort had been was filled with smoke, dirt, men, guns, and pieces of fortifications, all falling in one mass of terrible confusion.

Then the crash of battle roared all along our lines, and the rebels for a moment seemed to be stricken with terror, not knowing of course but what other explosions were to follow. General Ledlie's column charged up into the ruined fort, and for several minutes there was no opposition; if they had only pressed on, Petersburgh would have been our prize, but they halted for a short time in the ruins of the fort. This inexcusable delay was fatal. In a short time, the rebels regained their senses; they saw that they must regain the position they had lost, and with a tremendous energy they charged upon Ledlie's men, who fought well to hold the crater, while other troops were hurled in to reinforce them, but the golden hour of our opportunity had been wasted, and the lives of thousands of our brave men were needlessly thrown away. Someone had blundered; it will be the task of the impartial historian to name that one.

Through all these disappointments and dangers, the men never swerved in their loyalty to the flag, their love for President Lincoln, or their faith in General Grant. To the North that summer was one of grave doubts and fears as to the results of that campaign, but, in the trenches, and behind the breast works, doubts did not exist—our soldiers expected to conquer the rebels; they had no other design. Their vote thrown at the Presidential election that November, is one of the most beautiful evidences of their loyalty and unwavering love for the government, even under the most discouraging circumstances. McClellan was our first commander, and, as such, he was almost worshiped by his soldiers.

The political friends of General McClellan well understood that fact, and it was a very *crafty* thing for them to nominate him as their candidate for the Presidency, but it was a very *cruel* thing for our old commander to accept such a nomination upon a platform declaring the war to suppress treason a failure. Yes, it was cruel in General McClellan to ask us to vote that our campaigns had all been failures, and that our comrades had all died in vain. And yet there were those who supposed that our love for him would cause us to do it. I can easily imagine that President Lincoln, in the midst of all his anxieties and burdens, had some anxiety upon this point. He loved the army with all the power of his great manly heart, and wondered if the boys understood how much sympathy he had for them, or whether they would rebuke him by voting for his opponent their old favourite general.

That grand old army performed many heroic acts through those years; they wrote their loyalty to country with the points of their bayonets in letters of blood all over those Southern fields, but never in its history did it do a more devoted service, than when those men, in the midst of dangers and death, laid down their rifles for a moment to exercise the rights of American citizens, when they sacrificed their love for the old leader who had abandoned them, and, almost to a man, cast their votes for Abraham Lincoln, and to prolong the war until the Confederacy should be crushed. The nation rejoiced at this exhibition of their loyalty, and Lincoln's heart was strangely cheered and melted to unusual tenderness by this spectacle of devotion. I hope the American people may follow the example thus set for them, and ever cherish and defend the principles which were so dear to those men.

After the explosion of the mine in front of Petersburgh, and the unsuccessful attempts to carry the enemy's position in the vicinity of James River, it became evident that the only way in which we could hope to drive the rebels from their positions, was to extend our lines to the left, and get possession of the great lines of railway along which the rebel army received its supplies from the South. With them once in our possession, Petersburgh and Richmond must be evacuated; but it was a most difficult task to perform.

Our army of course was much larger than that of General Lee, but he had the inside of the circle, and consequently his lines were much more contracted than ours. He was also acting upon the defensive, and in such a position that he could see any movement that was being made by our troops. The difficulty was this, if Grant moved any portion of his army to the extreme left, he would weaken some other point in the line by so doing. Lee knowing this, would either hurl his troops upon this weakened point, or upon the force moving to the left; and a success to him in either case would be very disastrous to us.

Arrangements were being silently made to make the movement, notwithstanding the dangers which attended it. On the fifteenth of August we were relieved by the Ninth corps, and marched back some distance to the rear, and encamped in a piece of woods. The change was a relief to us. At that time, we knew nothing of our destination, but we had been cooped up so long in the fortifications that any movement would have been hailed with delight. On that day letters came from home, and we lay down upon the ground, in the midst of vines and flowers, under the shade of the pine trees, and read the messages from our loved ones who were so anxious for our safety. At night we received marching orders. We were to move early in the morning, and so we consumed the remaining hours of that day and evening in writing letters home, explaining to them the situation, telling them we were to march in the morning we knew not where, and promising to write them when our destination was reached,—a promise which some of those brave fellows were unable to fulfil.

Chapter 13

The Weldon Railroad

On Thursday morning, August 18th, at six o'clock, we took up our line of march toward the left of the Union line. We knew that we were upon some expedition of importance, and that there would probably be heavy fighting. Our whole corps was moving, and we enjoyed the change from life behind the breastworks to the march, and with cheerful hearts we pressed on. We were moving in the direction of the Weldon railroad, which was one of the most important lines of communication that General Lee had with the South, and was consequently of great value' to him.

At twelve o'clock, the head of General Warren's corps struck this railroad, about six miles from the city of Petersburgh, and thus, without any opposition, we had grasped the coveted prize. Our division, commanded by General Griffin, remained to guard the point where we had seized the road, while the divisions of Ayers and Crawford pushed on toward Petersburgh. They had not proceeded far in that direction before they encountered a heavy force of the rebels. A severe struggle ensued, but Warren held his ground, with the loss of one thousand men, and from that moment the Weldon railroad was lost to General Lee; but the latter was determined not to give it up without another severe struggle to regain the possession of it, and he prepared to make another assault.

In the meantime, we were building breastworks. The trees in front of our line were cut down, and the logs were piled up in lines of fortifications, for we expected the rebels to make another attack at any moment. The weather was very rainy, and our situation was a very unpleasant one, but the men were much elated over the success of our expedition. On the day following the events just narrated, the rebels, through a plunging rain storm, made a savage attack upon the right of our corps, and pressed it back; in a moment all was excitement, and our brigade was ordered to double-quick to their relief. We all understood how vital it was for us to check their advance and hold our position upon the railroad, but before we reached the scene of conflict, our men had rallied and driven them back, and we returned to our own position in the line of defence. All that night, the next day and night following, we lay upon our arms, expecting each moment that the enemy would appear.

On Sunday morning, August 31st, we had orders to march, and began to pack our blankets, when the rebels suddenly advanced, and by so doing enabled our regiment to obtain the only bloodless victory we gained during our term of service. Our skirmishers were driven rapidly in, and brought the intelligence that the rebels were advancing in two lines of battle. One line evidently was to attack us in front, the other to turn our flank. Their artillery, numbering some thirty guns, also opened a brisk fire upon us, and for a time it looked as if we had bloody work before us, but each man was determined to hold his post, and never relinquish the position we had gained.

As the rebel line advanced, our regiment occupied a splendid position, where it was protected from the fire of the rebel line in our front, but where it could pour its volleys upon the line that was endeavouring to turn our flank. This enfilading fire from our regiment was very fatal to the rebels and our men enjoyed it very much, for they remembered how often we had been obliged to charge upon their lines, and be shot down by thousands, while they were screened from our fire, and we now rejoiced that for once the tables were turned, and that to our advantage. We loaded and fired with great rapidity, and our rude line of breastworks was wreathed in flame and smoke.

The rebels advanced manfully, determined to carry our position; but soon the gray line wavered, then halted, and a moment after fell back in defeat, being obliged to retreat under the same deadly fire through which they had advanced. They left all their dead and wounded upon the field, their entire loss being nearly two thousand men. Our division captured three hundred prisoners, thirty-eight officers, and four battle flags. After the repulse of the rebels, our breastworks were made so strong that General Lee did not make another attempt to recapture the Weldon railroad. From this time until September 30th, we had but little fighting to do, and our life was made up of the same old routine of duties with which we had become so familiar. Our picket duty was very heavy; then there was drill, dress parade, inspections, and fatigue, which served to keep us all at work a large portion of the time. Nearly every day we could hear the roar of battle at some point in the Union lines, where Grant, with steady and persistent energy was engaged in his mission of pounding the Confederacy to death. Occasionally we heard cheering intelligence from the army of Sherman, in the southwest, and of Sheridan, in the valley. Our line was very near the rebels, and there was frequently heavy skirmishing between the picket lines.

On the thirtieth of September our division advanced to Peeble's farm, which was about three miles from our line of breastworks. Our brigade was in front when we came up to the rebel position. They had a strong line of earthworks, well manned with infantry, and a four-gun fort commanding the road and field where we must advance. Their position was a very formidable one. Our line was formed for a charge, our regiment being upon the left of the brigade. As we advanced on the double-quick, their infantry opened a fearful fire upon us, and their artillery poured in grape and canister at a close range. Many of our men fell and our flag was riddled with bullets, but with wild cheers our men rushed on.

The rebel infantry remained behind their works until they fired their last volley in our faces, and then turned to run. The artillery men, seeing that they could not check our advance, endeavoured to save their guns by flight. The horses were attached to the guns, and three of them were carried from the fort before we could reach its interior, and the remaining one would have escaped in the same manner, had it not been for the gallant conduct of Lieut. A. E. Fernald of our regiment. This brave officer was in the advance of his command, and, seeing the situation, dashed through an opening in the wall of the fort, and called upon the men who were running off the gun, to halt.

The drivers hesitated for a moment, but a revolver pointed at the head of one of them had a very persuasive influence, and they halted the horses. The retreating rebels saw this movement, and the bullets flew thickly around the brave officer, but he persisted in holding the prize. One or two of the horses were killed by the bullets, so that it was impossible for them to remove the gun. Our men soon reached the spot, and the gun was in our possession. An officer of a Massachusetts regiment, who was the second man to reach the spot, with much anger claimed the honour of its capture for his regiment, but our plucky lieutenant would not yield the point, and retained the honour he had so heroically won.

We remained within the line of captured works, while the Ninth corps followed on after the retreating enemy. They had not advanced far before the rebels turned upon them with such vigour that our line was rolled back in confusion, and our division was ordered to advance on the double-quick, and check the rebels' advance. General Griffin entered into the spirit of the occasion, and soon formed us into line on a low crest of land covered with a scattering growth of wood. The enemy must advance in our front, and climb up the ascent, down which we could send our messengers of death to meet them.

Griffin saw that he was to contend with a force that was vastly his superior in point of numbers, and ordered his artillery to advance and take a position in his line of battle. A captain, commanding one of the batteries, pointed to our line of battle, which was but little more than a strong skirmish line, and, in much surprise, remarked, "My God, General, do you mean for me to put my guns out on that skirmish line?"

General Griffin, with much vehemence rejoined, "Yes, rush them in there; artillery is no better than infantry, put them in the line, and let them fight together," and the guns were placed in the line of battle, loaded to their muzzles with grape and canister. The rebels were not aware of the reception they were to receive, and just at dark came charging across the field in our front. Our infantry opened upon them furiously; nothing was heard but the clanging of the steel rammers and the sharp crack of the rifles. The enemy soon came within range of the artillery, and then those guns joined in the awful music.

It was enough to make us shudder, as we saw the fearful execution that our guns made on the advancing lines, but with a desperate determination they kept on, and soon they reached our line. Then it was a sharp, bloody strife; clubbed rifles were freely used; bayonets gleamed with blood; and then the brave line of rebels were rolled back in defeat, leaving their dead and wounded in our possession. It was one of the fiercest fights of the campaign.

Our brigade was that day commanded by Major Spear of the Twentieth Maine, and that regiment was under the command of Captain A. W. Clark. Both regiment and brigade won much honour. In our regiment we lost six men, and fifty were wounded, some of our bravest men being among them. Captain Weston H. Keene was killed, Captain Sidelinger and Lieutenant Alden Miller were wounded. Connected with Captain Keene's death there was a very singular incident. On the morning of the battle, Captain Keene remarked to a brother officer, that when entering a battle, it had always been his custom to send his money back to the rear by some non-combatant, for safe keeping, but that on this occasion he would not do that, and if he was killed the money would pay the expense of embalming his body, and sending it to his friends in Maine. That night, when the rebels were making their charge, at the most terrific moment of the battle, the gallant captain was killed, and his money was actually expended for the purpose named.

In Company H, among the wounded, was Sergeant James A. Horton, one of the bravest men in the regiment; he had never been off duty a single day for the two years; kind, generous and brave, he was beloved by all. When we stormed the fort, a huge canister-shot shattered his thigh; he was carried back to the hospital, where he soon died; his loving comrades had his remains embalmed, and forwarded them to his parents in Massachusetts.

We threw up a strong line of breastworks near the battlefield, and remained there until the first of December. There was nothing remarkable in our experience through those weeks. The day after the battle, Generals Grant and Meade rode along our line, and were loudly cheered by the men. General Meade suggested to General Griffin that it would be well for him to intrench his position, but Griffin, whose blood was boiling over the inspiration of the battle just fought, replied, "I don't need any breastworks; I can whip the whole rebel army with my little division," but the intrenchments were made, notwithstanding this remarkable fact. Our armies, under Generals Sherman and Sheridan, were gaining glorious victories at this time, and we rejoiced over their successes, and were all hopeful as to the result of the campaign.

On Tuesday, November 8th, our regiment voted for the candidates for the Presidency; Abraham Lincoln received one hundred and thirty-seven votes, George B. McClellan, thirteen. When the news of the re-election of President Lincoln by such an overwhelming majority reached the Army of the Potomac, the men were wild with excitement. From the Weldon railroad, along our entire line, past Petersburgh, across the James River, in the intrenchments away round to Richmond, our men cheered until they were hoarse.

The rebels heard the cheering, and supposing that we had learned of some greater victory to our arms, were anxious to know the news. At a point where the lines came within a few rods of each other, our men heard a voice from behind the rebel breastworks, "Say, Yank."

"Hilloa, Johnny."

"Don't fire, Yank."

"All right, Johnny."

"What are you'uns all cheering for?"

"Big victory on our side."

"What is it, Yank?" came the eager response.

"Old Abe has cleaned all your fellers out up North."

"You don't say so, Yank?"

"Fact; gobbled the whole concern, there is not peace men enough left in the whole North to make a corporal's guard."

Then there was an anxious conversation among the rebels, and the voice of the spokesman was again heard. "Well, Yank, we cheered when we heard that your little Mac was nominated, but we don't feel much like cheering now."

The rebels could scarcely believe that Lincoln was actually elected by such a majority. That fact cast a deep gloom over them, and was one of the most important Union victories of the war.

On December 6th, we were relieved by troops of the Second corps, and moved out in the direction of the Jerusalem Plank road, where we encamped for the night. Early the next morning we were marching down the Plank road; we marched all day, and learned that we were to make a raid upon the Weldon railroad, which the rebels continued to use, up as far as "Stony Creek station," from which place they transported their supplies by wagon around to Petersburgh. That night we encamped on the bank of the Ottawa River.

At two o'clock the next morning we were on our way, crossed the river, and marched past "Sussex Court House." It was a very hard day's march, and just at night we struck the railroad about two miles above "Jarrett's station." We immediately seized and tore up the railroad track for nearly twenty miles, and destroyed enormous quantities of rebel supplies. We encamped for the night, and our men went out to forage upon the country; it was a memorable night in the history of our regiment; we found it a good country for foraging; pigs, hens, cattle, and food of all kinds were found in considerable quantities; our men also found a large amount of the liquor known as "apple jack," and under its influence forgot all their hardships and passed a merry night.

They were inspired to act in various ways; one little fellow in our company entered the stately mansion of a venerable Virginian who had held high positions in the political circles of that state, and in defiance of the old gentleman's indignant threats, began to search the premises. The only things he found that were of interest or value to him was a drawer filled with the old gentleman's linen, and a box containing his stove-pipe hat. These he quickly confiscated, and soon after made his debut in the company, wearing a white linen shirt ten sizes too large for him, with a collar reaching far above his ears, its corners being at least several inches in advance of his chin, while on his head was a hat so venerable in its appearance that one would suppose it dated back to the days of the revolution.

Great fires were built of the railroad ties, and the rails were laid across them so that they would bend and twist in every conceivable form. Lines of men were formed, sham-battles were fought, and the night was one of wild hilarity and mirth. Many weeks had passed since our boys were on a time, and they seemed determined to make the most of it.

The day following, we moved down the railroad some six miles, and encamped, the men still foraging and destroying everything that could possibly aid the rebellion. We remained there for the night. The railroad had now been destroyed for a long distance, and much damage done to its rolling stock and warehouses. A cold storm of sleet and rain began to fall, so that in the morning we were covered with ice and frost. The enemy now made his appearance, and drove in our picket line, and we received orders to fall back.

The roads were very muddy—made almost impassable by the storm—but we marched twenty miles very rapidly, until we reached Sussex Court House, where we camped for the night. The following day we continued our journey until we regained our old position on the Jerusalem Plank road, and here our regiment built winter quarters. The men toiled hard and built the most comfortable and elaborate quarters we had ever enjoyed.

The terrible campaign of 1864 had closed. For desperate fighting and enormous losses of life, its parallel had never been known in our history. Including the losses in the army of the James, there is no doubt that, from the time when General Grant crossed the Rapidan and entered the Wilderness, to the closing of the active campaign the following winter, his losses in killed, wounded and prisoners, must have reached the enormous number of one hundred thousand men. It has been estimated that of these, thirty thousand returned to their regiments, leaving an actual loss of seventy thousand men. We had captured over fifteen thousand prisoners, sixty-seven battle-flags, and thirty-two pieces of artillery.

As we sat in our tents, that winter, and looked back over it all, it seemed like a terrible dream; but as we thought of the many brave men now gone, who were with us at Rappahannock station, the previous winter, we comprehended its stern reality. We were confident that we had gained great advantages over the rebels, and thought we could see the end drawing near. Our weeks in camp passed pleasantly away; our rations were good, and the men were healthy; there was much picket duty to do, and frequent skirmishes occurred along the line. Major Spear and several others went to Maine to obtain recruits for the regiment. The railroad was extended from City Point up to our encampment, so that we received our mail each day, and all were happy.

On the fifth of February, much to our disgust, we broke camp and marched in the direction of Hatcher's Run. The movement was made, to extend our left flank and to get nearer the Southside railroad, which was the last line of communication that General Lee had from Petersburgh to the South. I think that I will not attempt to describe that affair; the boys will all remember it, and there are some facts connected with that battle which we would not want everyone to know. We all remember the thick pine bushes, the tangled brush, the running vines, the thorn bushes, the streams of water, the deep holes filled with mud and mire, how the rebels fired on us, and how we fired in return, and how we got frightened, and "skedaddled" back through the woods like a flock of sheep. We recollect it all, but for the reputation of the regiment we will not speak minutely of those things here. There is an old adage, that:

He who wisely runs away,
Lives to fight another day,

—and we were all alive when the spring campaign opened the following month.

We did not return to our old quarters on the Plank road, but encamped near Hatcher's Run, so that we could hold the position we had wrested from the rebels at that point. We built rude, rough huts, and remained in them, waiting for the orders to come that would send us forth upon another campaign.

Chapter 14

Five Forks

The bloody campaign of 1864 had closed. The Army of the Potomac was encircling the rebel capital like a girdle of death. It stretched in its power from the James River, upon its right, to Hatcher's Run upon the left. It was evident to all that the time for the last great struggle was rapidly approaching. Grant, the great Commander-in-Chief of the Union Armies, was holding the throat of the Confederacy in a giant's grasp. Sherman, the invincible leader of the southwest, was sundering the Confederacy in twain, as he marched to the sea. Sheridan, the most brilliant leader on the continent, had destroyed the great army of General Early, in the Shenandoah valley. The Army of the Potomac was in winter quarters, but there was constant skirmishing between the hostile armies. Our brigade was encamped upon the left of the Union line, at Hatcher's Run, near the late battlefield of that name.

Our regiment was now quite large, as we had received many recruits from Maine, and since many of our old fellows who had been wounded in the Wilderness campaign, began to return. It is impossible for me to describe how warmly these men were welcomed to the regiment, and how glad they were to see their old comrades again. Many of them had been in the hospital at Augusta, and now, on their return to the regiment, brought us messages from home. One of these boys describes his return to the regiment, and the reception he received from his comrades, in the following words:

I had been away from the regiment since receiving my wound in the Wilderness, on the fifth of the previous May. In December, at Augusta, Maine, I had volunteered to return to my regiment, although my wound was yet unhealed. I had been detained a few weeks at Gallop's Island, in Boston harbour, and with hundreds of others had shivered and grumbled in the cold, miserable barracks that crowned that bleak island. I had been storm-tossed for a week or more, and nearly wrecked on the overcrowded Government transport, *De Molay*, and was then landed at City Point, in Virginia, where for a few days I was permitted to enjoy the very pleasant associations of the Distribution camp at that place—the camp that enjoyed the classical title of 'Bull Pen.'

Both pen and time would fail me were I to attempt to describe it. Language cannot do justice to the subject, so I pass it in silence, only asking the old soldiers who with me passed a few days in that camp to remember with me for a moment all the discomforts of that filthy place. At length the order came for all the men who belonged to the Fifth corps to march out through the gate of the high picket fence that enclosed the camp. It was the most joyous summons I received during the three years of my service.

I hastened to my bunk, from which I had been absent but a few moments, and found that in my absence someone had stolen my overcoat. It was no use to endeavour to find stolen property in a place like that, but it would not answer for me to go to the front at that season of the year without an overcoat. There was only one method of redress. My nearest neighbour was sound asleep. He had a new overcoat folded under his head for a pillow. I gently raised his head, removed the coat, and went on my way rejoicing, leaving the brave soldier boy to dream of 'home and mother.'

For several miles we rode on the military railroad the army had constructed from City Point up near Petersburgh. Then a short march across the country brought me near the locality where our regiment must be encamped. 'Where is the camp of the Twentieth Maine?' I yelled to a fellow who was passing in my front, with a dozen canteens hanging over his shoulder.

'Over there,' and he pointed to a cluster of white tents standing upon the plain some thirty rods away.

The sun was just setting at the close of day. I felt strangely happy. I wanted to see the boys. I felt like one returning home after a long absence. The old flag was unfurled in front of the colonel's tent. Our orderly sergeant was standing in the street of Company H, making a picket detail for the following day. He saw me approaching under the weight of a well-filled knapsack, and calling me by name, said, 'You will report for picket tomorrow.' I was quickly surrounded by old comrades, from whom I received such a welcome. But, alas, how many forms had vanished! How many voices had been hushed! Horton, Merriam, Davis, York, and a score of other brave fellows had been taken from us since we entered the Wilderness, but Clark, Winslow, Morrison, Tarbell, Gilmore, and a few others remained, while the depleted ranks of the company had been filled with recruits whom I had never seen.

The boys were bronzed with sun and storm; they were hardy and rugged, but the same grand old fellows whose society I had missed so much. With the liberty always exercised by old soldiers, they quickly made themselves familiar with the contents of my knapsack, and the fine woollen underclothing and stockings that I had purchased in Maine were quickly appropriated to their use. I never gave my consent to this, because it was never asked, but I do know that it gave me much more satisfaction to thus supply their wants than it did them to have their wants supplied. It was late that night before I went to sleep. I had to tell the boys about Maine, and of their friends whom I had met, and they told me of Laurel hill, Cold Harbor, Peeble's farm, and many other bloody fields where our brave men had fought and died. It was a sad, and yet a joyous evening.

One laughable event occurred at the evening roll call. When my name was called, and I answered to it, a number of recruits who had joined the company after I left, and who now fancied they were old soldiers, supposing I was a recruit, gathered around me to initiate me into the mysteries of a soldier's life. I thought of the recruits the winter before at Rappahannock station, of the jokes we then played upon them, and as I thus found myself mistaken for one of that unfortunate class, and almost made a victim of the same jokes I had helped to originate, I felt that for the recruits 'time had brought its revenge.' I found the boys all in excellent spirits. They were determined, like their great commander, 'To fight it out on that line.' The re-election of President Lincoln had been a source of gratification to the army, and every man was determined that no compromise should be made with treason.

Our regiment was only encamped at that place for a few weeks, and the quarters were not nearly as comfortable as they had been at Rappahannock station, but we made life enjoyable. We told stories, sang songs, went out on picket, foraged what we could, and played many games which I think that it would be better not to name, as it is not fair to tell tales out of school. The days passed very rapidly, and those few weeks spent on the banks of Hatcher's Run will be pleasantly remembered by the surviving members of our regiment. The weather was unusually fine, the bands played their most delicious strains of music, and the men were all anxious for the forward movement to be made.

Each day we saw new indications of the fearful struggle so soon to open. Slowly and surely the cords of death were drawn around the gallant army of General Lee. We knew, although the coming campaign might be brief, that it would be one of the most desperate and bloody of the war. Notwithstanding all the joy and mirth in our regiment, there were some anxious hours in those days of active preparations. Some had been with the regiment every day since it had been mustered into the service, had suffered in all its fatigue, endured all its hardships, and fought in all its battles, and only six months of their three years of service remained unserved. It is not strange that these soldiers were a little anxious about the future, and wondered if they had been spared through all the past, to fall in that last campaign of the war.

One of the bravest men in our regiment was Morrison, of Company H. He had been twice wounded, the last time receiving a severe injury in his hip, from which he could never fully recover. The surgeon informed him that he was not in a condition to endure the hardships of a march, and that he had better go back to the hospital and receive a discharge. Lieutenant Bickford, commanding our company, although disliking to lose so valuable a soldier, seconded the surgeon's advice. We all urged him to go back, but the brave fellow could not find it in his heart to leave the regiment on the eve of battle.

We were under marching orders; tomorrow we were to march under Sheridan, to make a movement upon our extreme left; that morning would be his last opportunity to go back. We slept in the same tent, under the same blanket; we talked over the scenes of our childhood, for we had been boys together. I urged him to go back, told him that he had done his part of the fighting, and that he should leave the rest to be done by those who were more able. When I had concluded, he made known his decision in these words:

> Whether I live or die it shall never be said that Morrison went to the rear when his regiment was marching to the front.

The results of that decision will soon be narrated.

One little incident, showing the desperate courage of one Southern soldier, is worthy of mention. While we were encamped at Hatcher's Run, our picket line was established near the battlefield of the same name. In a little fort on the bank of the stream, which we had captured from the rebels was the grave of the soldier to whom I referred above. He was a sergeant in a South Carolina regiment. When our line of battle advanced it was obliged to cross Hatcher's Run before it could reach this fort. But when the rebels saw our line forming on the opposite bank, they deserted the fort in a most cowardly manner.

All fled but this sergeant; he gathered up a pile of rifles that his comrades had thrown away, and took his stand in an angle of the fort, behind a tree. The stream was deep, and our only means of crossing was on the trunk of a fallen tree. A Union soldier sprang upon the log. There was the flash of a rifle in the fort, and the soldier fell a corpse. Another followed, and fell in like manner. Another, and yet another, went down before the same unerring aim, until seven of our men were dead, and not a rifle in the line could be brought to bear upon him.

The advance of the whole line was checked, and no one volunteered to step forth to certain death. But in this moment of uncertainty, a sharpshooter from a treetop some little distance in the rear saw the rebel sergeant. He took careful aim; a bullet went singing through the air, and he was dead. Our men kindly sent his effects to his friends in South Carolina, gave him a good burial in the fort where he fell, marked his grave, and on the wooden slab above his remains wrote the story of his daring deed.

On the twenty-ninth of March, we broke camp, and moved in the direction of Dinwiddie Court House. It was a rough country through which we passed, and our advance was necessarily slow. Our regiment was commanded by Colonel Walter G. Merrill. A dense forest covered a large portion of the country, broken here and there by small clearings. There were many ridges of land, broken and ragged with rocks and deep ravines, through which rushed and roared deep streams of water.

Soon after we broke camp a detail was made for men to go out as flankers, and I was named as one of them. We penetrated the thick forest, and formed our line some eighty rods from the column of troops, and moved in a parallel line with them. We had not gone far, before we came in contact with the enemy's skirmish line, which we were ordered to drive back upon their line of battle. This was an exciting and somewhat dangerous task. We advanced on a double-quick through the woods, across fields and ravines in which wild grape vines, thorn bushes, and a thousand obstacles impeded our way. Our clothes were torn into shreds, and blood flowed freely from our lacerated flesh. The enemy would occasionally make a stand and fight, and the minie-balls would fly back and forth in a lively manner. A number of men on both sides were killed and wounded.

We followed them for a mile, and halted on the edge of a large field. It was now past noon. Heavy firing was heard on our right, both musketry and artillery. It was but a short distance from us, and we knew that our division had encountered the enemy. For an hour we listened with much anxiety, and then the order came for us to advance. We crossed the field, and found the rebels in the woods, on the other side. The roar of battle on our right inspired us, and we rushed upon them. They gave us a heavy skirmish fire, and then fell back for a half mile, we following them very closely. Suddenly there was a sheet of flame in our front. *Whiz, crash, bang*, went a dozen shells above our heads. We had reached the enemy's line of battle, and a heavy infantry fire was also opened upon us. It was of course impossible to advance further. It would be folly to remain where we were, and so we fell rapidly back.

Many of our men were wounded before we got out of the range of the enemy's guns. One, a brave young fellow from Massachusetts, fell, shot through both legs. We would not leave him in the hands of the rebels, and laid him upon a blanket, to carry him back. He was much excited, and was determined not to be carried off the field. He called us miserable cowards for falling back from the enemy, and pleaded with us to put him down, and with our little skirmish line charge upon the rebels' line of battle.

We were soon relieved, and returned to our command. We found that our brigade had not been engaged, but that General Chamberlain with his brigade had fought a severe battle with the enemy on the Boydston Plank road, and had carried their position with heavy loss. General Chamberlain had gallantly led his troops in their charge, had been slightly wounded, and had received nearly a dozen bullets through his clothes. Our brigade was sent to relieve his, and we advanced across the field of battle. Many dead were lying upon the ground. The rebels had evidently fallen back upon a stronger line of works, in the rear of those carried by Chamberlain. We advanced cautiously along the narrow road. Soon there was a fearful roar in the woods, just in our front, and a score of shells came screaming through the air, just above our heads. The enemy had an excellent range of our position. We halted while our officers endeavoured to ascertain the strength of the enemy's position, which they soon discovered was very great, and could only be carried with great loss of life, and, after dark, we were withdrawn.

I remember one very sad event that occurred while we were lying there under the enemy's fire. A gray-haired soldier came down along the road where our dead men were scattered upon the ground. He was evidently in search of something. At last, with a heartrending groan, he sat down beside a dead body, and wept as if his heart would break. It was a father mourning for his son. They were both members of a Massachusetts regiment, and the son had been killed in the brilliant charge they had so recently made.

We returned a short distance to the rear, and then marched to a position upon the right of the fortifications from which we had just fallen back, and halted in an open field. Our regiment formed a part of a line drawn up beside some farm buildings. It was now ten o'clock at night. Great masses of black clouds obscured the sky, and the darkness was intense. "Throw up fortifications," was the order given, and quickly obeyed. The huge barn and out-buildings, built of hewn logs, were torn down and piled up, and upon these we threw an enormous quantity of earth, and soon had a comparatively strong line of defence. We were all very tired, but had a jolly time in building these works.

Near the barn there was a deep well partially filled with water, which in the darkness we had not noticed. Two of us were carrying a great stick of timber upon our shoulders; my chum carrying the foremost end, while I was staggering along in the rear. Suddenly, without a word of warning, the forward end of the timber came to the ground. It was so dark that I could not see my companion. I loudly called his name, and to my surprise, when his voice came back in reply, it came from the depths of the earth. I quickly made my way to the scene of disaster, and found him in a well twenty feet deep, and up to his ears in water. An alarm was given, assistance quickly arrived, and we at last succeeded in fishing him out.

At two o'clock in the morning the line of works was completed. The rain was now pouring down in torrents. We spread our blankets upon the driest spots we could find, and lay down to sleep. Daylight dawned, cold, wet, and cheerless. As the thick, heavy mists gradually cleared away we saw the rebels' advanced line intrenched upon the field in our front, some eighty rods distant. Theirs were light defences, and evidently covered stronger ones in their rear.

The rain continued to fall in great quantities, but there was no firing between the hostile lines, and so we sat in the mud and looked at each other until late in the afternoon. At four o'clock we advanced, and carried the enemy's works by assault, they falling back to the woods beyond. We then moved to the right flank, for a short distance, and formed our line, to charge upon the rebel works, a skirmish line being thrown out in advance. The rebels opened upon us with artillery, and shells fell all around us. It was evident that the enemy was prepared to receive us. The charge was not made, and we returned to the rebel earthworks we had just captured, and these we made as strong as possible.

Before dark our skirmishers were driven in by the rebel line of battle, which was advancing to recapture the line of works. A battery was sent out to support our regiment. The guns were placed right in the line of battle, and were heavily charged with grape and canister. On came the rebels with a deafening cheer. It was fun to see them advance. Our infantry and artillery opened upon them, but only for a few moments. Their columns were not heavy enough to withstand our fire, and they were driven back, leaving a number of prisoners in our hands. We presented a singular appearance at that time, as we had been lying flat upon our faces in red coloured mud, that now covered our uniforms, our hands and faces being black with burning powder, and our clothes torn. We did not much resemble the regiment that had moved out of camp at Hatcher's Run only two days before.

We remained in those works, that cold, damp, frosty night. Our wet blankets were spread upon the muddy ground, and we soon forgot all hardships and danger in a glorious, restful sleep. In the morning we were relieved, and marched a mile or more to the left, and stacked our guns in a small field surrounded by the dense forest. The storm had passed away, and the sun shone down warm and bright through the broken clouds. Our blankets were spread upon the ground to dry. We kindled fires and cooked our coffee. As we were enjoying our dinner, there was a fearful roar in our front, less than a mile away,—cannons, musketry and cheering, all mingling in one terrible roar,—and to our dismay we found that the awful tide was rolling toward us. We instantly understood its meaning; the rebels had charged upon our line, and were driving it back.

An orderly came dashing back to General Griffin, with orders for him to take his division in, on the double-quick, and fill the gap made in our line by the falling back of the third division. The bugle notes rang out, "Fall in," "Fall in"; the officers shouted their commands; the weary men sprang into line; we caught our guns from the stacks, and by the right flank rushed toward the scene of conflict. We soon encountered the broken fragments of the retreating division, closely pursued by the rebels, but reached a crest of land overlooking Gravelly Run. It was a good position. The rebels must descend a hill in our front, cross Gravelly Run, and then climb the hill upon which our line would be formed.

Our colonel gave the order, "By battalion into line!" and we quickly formed upon the crest of the hill. It was an exciting moment. The rebel line was advancing, in plain view, down the hill on the other side of the stream. Artillery had gone into position, and was throwing shells over our heads; the bands played; the cannons roared; our muskets crashed with awful force; the hill itself shivered as if with fear.

The rebel line came to the stream, but could come no further, and was thrown back. General Chamberlain's brigade, on our right, gallantly advanced, and occupied the position from which Crawford's division had been driven, and the fortunes of the day were restored. Our wounded men were cared for, the dead were buried, and we were soon preparing for the startling events that were to transpire within the next few hours—events that were destined to be death blows to the Southern Confederacy, and also to perpetuate the union of the stars and stripes.

It is four o'clock in the afternoon of March 31st, 1865, and the battle of Gravelly Run has been fought and won, but a fearful conflict is raging elsewhere. Away beyond us, far down on our extreme left, we can hear the roar of battle, the booming of cannon, and the heavy crash of musketry. We have no infantry at that point, and it must be Sheridan and his cavalry coping with the enemy, down near the Southside railroad. How intently we listened! The battle tides were receding, and it was evident that Sheridan's force was being borne back by the enemy.

General Warren, commanding our corps, became nervous and

restless; his mission is to support Sheridan's movement, and he has already led his troops through many obstacles, and is now awaiting further orders. His black eyes flash forth the intensity of his thought, and his classic features become pale, as he listens to the sounds of battle growing each moment more indistinct. At last he exclaimed, "I can endure this no longer, and without orders I will endeavour to send aid to Sheridan; Bartlett's old brigade must endeavour to make its way to Sheridan's relief."

A staff officer dashed away to Bartlett, and soon our lines were formed, and we marched in the direction of the distant battle. The narrow road along which we marched was lined on either hand with a dense growth of pine trees; the sun was sinking from view, and the tall trees cast their lengthening shadows across our pathway. It was to us a time of thrilling interest, as we all understood the situation. Our brigade was detached from the army, and was marching through that great forest to meet an enemy of whose strength and location we knew nothing. The sounds of battle in our front died away. The darkness became so intense that it was not prudent to proceed further, especially as nothing was to be gained by such a course.

The pickets were sent out, and we lay down to sleep and rest. At midnight we were aroused with the information that our pickets had discovered the enemy, who was in great force in our immediate front, so near that they could easily listen to the conversation of their pickets, and also of the soldiers behind their breastworks. Silently we fell into line, and retracing our steps along the way we came for several miles, encamped for the remainder of the night.

The morning of April 1st was clear, but cold and frosty. We were early on the march, moving to the left of the point from which we had fallen back the previous night. The whole corps had arrived. We were moving in a direction that would bring us to a place known as Five Forks, near which Sheridan had fought the day before. About ten o'clock in the forenoon we halted in the edge of an oak wood, and there remained until two o'clock in the afternoon. The Southside railroad was of great importance to General Lee, because over that road he brought all the provisions for his army in Richmond and Petersburgh; it was the life line that connected the Confederacy and its capital. If that line of connection was cut, Richmond must be abandoned.

To guard this road, General Lee had sent a large force of troops, which had constructed a long line of breastworks running parallel with the road for its defence. The centre of this line of defences was at a point known as Five Forks, so named from the five roads that centred there. Sheridan had advanced upon these works, on the 31st, but not being supported by infantry, had been crowded back for several miles. But General Warren had now arrived, and Sheridan's plan was to advance with his cavalry in front of the works, and, while thus attracting the enemy's attention, cause the Fifth corps to advance to their rear and take them by surprise.

At two o'clock our corps was formed for the advance, in two lines of battle, our regiment being in the second line. We were to advance over a rough, broken country filled with ravines and covered with a thick growth of forest trees. Having marched for some two or three miles, the lines were so changed while we were marching, that we soon found we were in the front line. Our regiment and the First Michigan were under the command of Colonel Walter G. Morrill, and in all our previous experience we had never been led by a braver or more skilful commander. We climbed a hill, looked down through the trees, and saw the breastworks but a short distance in our front. We had advanced so quietly that the enemy was not aware of our presence. Our lines were reformed, and then with a yell we charged.

Before the enemy had time to recover from their surprise, we were upon them, so that they threw down their guns without firing a shot, and surrendered. The number of prisoners embarrassed us, and we sent them to the rear as fast as we could, but they must have had ten men to our one. They soon discovered the superiority of their numbers, and the mistake they had made in surrendering.

A large portion of our men had gone to the rear with prisoners, when a rebel officer came dashing down the line, calling upon them to rally. A rebel who had surrendered was standing near Colonel Morrill, and catching up from the ground a loaded rifle, yelled with an oath, "We can whip you yet," and deliberately shot a captain of the First Michigan regiment who stood beside him.

At the same moment a private of Company D in our regiment thrust his bayonet through the breast of the treacherous rebel, who fell dead at his feet. In a moment's time the battle was raging all along our line. It was hot work, and in many places, it was a hand-to-hand fight. Men deliberately pointed their rifles in each other's faces, and fired. Clubbed muskets came crushing down in deadly force upon human skulls. Men were bayoneted in cold blood. Feats of individual bravery were performed on that afternoon, which, if recorded, would fill a volume. I can only refer to a portion of them.

On the right of Company H were four men; one of them was Morrison, whose name I have mentioned before, a man of gigantic strength and remarkable bravery. Another of the four was Gilmore; he was equal to Morrison in bravery, and nearly his match in physical strength. The third was Hickey, a man of Scotch-Irish descent, who had served in the regular army of England, and who had deserted and come to our country, and enlisted in our regiment. He was tall and robust, a perfect mass of bone and muscle. The fourth was younger in years, and more slender in form than his companions.

When we reached the rebel breast works, they threw down their arms and surrendered. They were densely packed in our front, as men gather in a crowd upon a public square. Some ten rods from the breastworks upon which we stood, we saw a rebel flag leaning against a tree; to reach it we would have to pass through this great crowd of men. Morrison saw the flag, and waving his hat, called, "Come on, boys, and we will capture the flag!" and suiting his action to his words, he sprang over among the rebels, and was quickly followed by the three men above described. There was evidently no danger, as the rebels were not disposed to fight, and the four men easily made their way through the crowd that opened to receive them, until they had passed over one-half the distance b tween the breastworks and the flag.

At least four hundred rebels were packed between them and their comrades. It was at this moment that the enemy rallied, and these four men found themselves surrounded on every hand, cut off from their comrades, and all hope of escape destroyed. But Morrison cried: "We will fight our way back to the regiment!" and the others turned to obey his command. A rebel officer sprang at Morrison's throat, and called upon him to surrender. The brave soldier brought the heavy stock of his rifle down with such crushing force upon the officer's head that he fell dead at his feet. It was now a most desperate fight. They were in such close quarters that neither party could well shoot. On one side it was half a hundred men striking and surging back and forth, thinking only of revenge and victory, on the other, four men, single-handed, pounding their way through all opposition.

The contest was as unequal as it was desperate. The most fearful blows were given and returned, but the four men, standing side by side, managed to stand upon their feet, slowly advancing as they fought, until bleeding, bruised, and stunned, they sprang from the rebel crowd, and reached an open space of ground between their comrades and the rebels. At that moment the baffled enemy poured a deadly volley upon the escaping soldiers. Morrison sprang high in the air, and fell with a deathly groan. Gilmore sank upon the ground as if dead, Hickey reeled and staggered, while the other received a rifle ball in the left arm, but succeeded in reaching the breastworks, and rejoined the regiment.

This was the supreme moment of the conflict; the rebels would climb up on one side of the breastworks, and our men on the other side would knock them back. We heard bugles in our front, and out from a piece of woods some eighty rods away came dashing squadrons of cavalry. With a cheer our men sprang over the works, and upon the rebels, who reeled and staggered before us. Colonel Merrill was in the thickest of the fight; Captain Fernald dashed among the enemy and captured a flag; Bickford, Fogler, and a score of other officers in our regiment led on their men. It was becoming too hot for the Johnnies, and they turned to ran.

It was too late; Sheridan threw his lines around them like a girdle of death, and five thousand prisoners were captured. While our regiment was thus engaged, General Ayers, with the first division, and General Chamberlain, with a brigade of our division, were fighting on our left, and, when the rebels broke before our advance, their whole line was in our possession, save one position on our right. We all rushed with wild enthusiasm in that direction; Sheridan went dashing past us, wild with the excitement of victory, shouting, as he swung his clenched hand through the air, "Smash 'em! Smash 'em! We have a record to make before the sun goes down; we must have the Southside road."

An open field was in front of the last position the rebels held. General Warren caught the corps flag from the hand of the man who carried it, and dashed across this field, leading on a column of soldiers he had hastily formed for the charge. It was the most gallant deed of the whole day's battle, and the whole rebel line was now in our possession.

The sun was low in the western sky, but there was no rest. Sheridan, like a madman, dashed here and there urging on his men; the cavalry followed the retreating foe, capturing prisoners by hundreds, while the infantry pressed on after them, and so we soon reached the desired point. The Southside railroad was in our hands and enormous quantities of property were destroyed. The intelligence fell like a knell of death upon the ears of General Lee that his last line of communication was in the hands of his foes, and that he must evacuate Petersburgh and Richmond.

Our bugles sounded the recall, and we were to march back to the battlefield and reform our lines. Slowly we retraced our steps, joyous over the great victory won, but sorrowful over the loss of our brave men. The battlefield was reached, and we encamped for the night, but we could not think of rest or sleep; the dead were to be buried; the wounded were to be cared for. I secured a short piece of candle and a small spade, and with a comrade to assist me, went in search of the bodies of Morrison and Gilmore. It was a lonely search in that hour of midnight, dark and damp; the silence was only broken by the groans of the wounded and the low conversation of the soldiers who were caring for them.

After a long search in the darkness, carrying the lighted candle in my hand, our quest was rewarded by finding the looked-for bodies; they lay as they had fallen. Morrison was shot through the body, and had evidently lived a few moments; Gilmore had received two balls through his heart, and of course had died instantly; Hickey had escaped with a slight injury. We dug two shallow graves under the shadow of a great, oak tree, and buried them side by side. We placed boards at their heads, telling their names, company and regiment, and there left the remains of two men as brave and fearless as any whoever breathed the air of patriotism and liberty.

Chapter 15

The Surrender

From April 1st to the ninth of the same month was an exciting time in the Army of the Potomac, especially so with the Fifth corps, whose duty it was to support Sheridan's cavalry. At two o'clock in the afternoon of April 2nd, we marched from the battlefield of the preceding day and soon crossed the Southside railroad. The boys were in high spirits. The cavalry was in the advance, and we laughed, talked, joked and ran, to keep up with the cavalry. We knew that we had gained an important advantage over the rebels, and, with such leaders as Grant and Sheridan, we knew that Lee would be hard pushed.

A staff officer came dashing back along the line, swinging his hat and shouting, "Petersburgh and Richmond are evacuated, and General Lee is in full retreat!"

The news was too good to believe. As old soldiers we remembered how often we had been told of great victories that never had been won, when they wanted us to make some great exertion at critical points in the campaigns through which we had passed. So, we shouted back in reply, "That's played out!" "Tell it to the recruits!" "Put him in a canteen!" "Put him out!" "Give him a hard tack!" Thus, the first intelligence of the glorious victory fell upon sceptical ears. But Colonel Morrill soon rode back along our line, and told us that the news was true. In a moment we were wild with excitement. We forgot all the disappointments and hardships of the past years, in that moment of extreme satisfaction. Our caps went up in the air, we shook each other's hands, and cheered until we were hoarse; and all the time our line was sweeping on in swift pursuit of the flying foe. What days those were! They can never be forgotten by the survivors of that army.

The situation of the two armies at that time is so well known that I will not dwell upon it. General Lee, with his brave army, was making a last retreat, but was pursued by a leader of remorseless energy. The rebel chieftain was endeavouring to reach North Carolina, where he could effect a junction with the troops of Johnson, and thus hoped to prolong the conflict. Doubtless, by skilful manoeuvring and swift movements, he expected to escape from the dreaded clutches of his old enemy, but Grant threw his army corps upon the rear of Lee. with such force that the retreat soon became a rout. There was incessant firing, and prisoners were captured by thousands.

While Grant was thus pressing the rebel army in its rear, Phil Sheridan, with his cavalry and the Fifth corps, was sweeping along Lee's flank like a tornado, thus preventing him from reaching North Carolina. I wish I could picture Sheridan as we used to see him. I have carefully examined many pictures of Sheridan, which I suppose are lifelike, but somehow, I have always been disappointed. Not one of them does justice to this peerless Union leader.

This is how he appeared on the field: A short, thick set man, with very short legs, his broad shoulders a little stooping as he sat upon his horse, having a very large head, with hair clipped close, a short, thick moustache; his uniform being usually the worse for wear and spotted with mud; wearing a soft felt hat, at least two sizes too small, and for safe keeping, usually pressed down upon a portion of the back of his head. He rode a splendid horse, usually went at a round gallop, and rolled and bounced upon the back of his steed much as an old salt does, when walking up the aisle of a church after a four years' cruise at sea. Some of his surroundings were also of a singular character.

At his side usually rode a party of a dozen scouts clad in the neat gray uniform of rebel officers, and ranking from captains to colonels. They were evidently brave, jolly, reckless fellows, and theirs was a most dangerous occupation—one that required skill, tact, and cool, deliberate daring. Entering the rebel lines and making themselves familiar with all their movements, dashing from one brigade to another, they would claim to be on one general's staff, and then on that of another, to suit the situation; they would give orders that purported to come from rebel commanders, to colonels, quartermasters, and officers in charge of wagon trains, and these being obeyed, would add to the confusion of the rebel army, and hastened its destruction.

A huge rebel wagon train was toiling through a long piece of woods, and the drivers were lashing their hungry mules to make them go as fast as possible, to escape from Sheridan's cavalry, when an officer in the uniform of a rebel colonel rode up to the quartermaster who had charge of the train, and said, "General —— (naming the one who commanded that division) presents his compliments, and orders you to pack your train in that field yonder," and then rode swiftly away. The order was obeyed, and soon the long train was packed in the field surrounded on all sides by the dense forest. Just as the last wagon was taking its position, there was a yell as if five thousand Comanche Indians were on the warpath, and Sheridan's cavalry came dashing out from among the trees, and the whole train was captured and destroyed in a few moment's time.

Brigadier-General —— was at the head of a rebel brigade, leading them in their hasty retreat. He was met one afternoon, a day or two before Lee surrendered, by a rebel staff officer as he supposed, who accosted him thus:

"General —— commands you to take your men out into the open field yonder, and halt there for a short rest."

"In what direction is the field?" questioned the general.

The staff officer pointed his hand, and then remarked, "If you will ride with me a few steps I can show it to you."

The general motioned for his staff to remain, and then followed his guide. They passed around a clump of small trees not over a dozen rods from his staff and escort, when two other men in rebel uniforms made their appearance, seized the general's horse by the reins, and bore him a prisoner to the Union Army. As he rode past our regiment, to say that he was a disgusted looking man would be a mild way of putting it.

Success made these scouts reckless, and quite a number were captured, and some, I believe, were executed before Lee surrendered. One of them rode up to a rebel general, and gave an order as to the disposition of the general's troops.

"Whose staff are you on, sir?" demanded the general.

"General ——'s," answered the unabashed scout.

"That is too thin, sir," replied the other, "for I am General ——, and do not recognise you as belonging to my staff."

The poor fellow had made a mistake. He was instantly captured, and if Lee had not surrendered on the following day, his blunder would have cost him his life.

Another singular feature in Sheridan's procession was, at least, twenty captured battle-flags, which were borne unfurled as trophies of the campaign. His staff officers and bodyguard were all as rash and daring as Sheridan himself, and whenever they went dashing past us, it would stir the boys up to the wildest enthusiasm, while they would cheer as if a pandemonium had broken loose.

On every hand we could see indications that Lee's army would soon melt away. Prisoners were pouring into our lines by thousands; baggage wagons, artillery, mortars, and baggage of all kinds, lined the roads along which the rebels were fleeing. We never endured such marching before, as it was not an unusual thing for us to march thirty-five miles a day. We grew tired and prostrated, but we wanted to be there when the rebels found the last ditch of which they had talked so much. Some sections of the country through which we passed had seen nothing of the war, and, there, foraging was good. Tobacco, molasses, bacon, cattle, sheep, pigs and poultry, were occasionally found, and were quickly appropriated to our use.

One morning our regiment was passing a house in which was discovered a large cask of excellent syrup. Of course, a crowd quickly gathered; men pushed and fought, each endeavouring to obtain a portion of the coveted article. In Company H was a little fellow, slim and pale, not over sixteen years old, who was known as "Sis." On this occasion he was in the midst of the crowd, endeavouring to make his way to the syrup; the stronger men crowding against him soon raised him from his feet, and in the scramble, he found himself upon their shoulders; the next moment he was thrown headlong into the half-filled cask of syrup. He was quickly fished out, but concluded that he needed no more syrup on that day. Thus, the whole route from Five Forks to Appomattox was filled with incidents never to be forgotten.

On the eighth of April we had a tedious march of thirty-five miles. The sun sunk from view, but there were no indications of halting. Our regiment chanced that day to be marching in the rear of our whole division a position which all soldiers will remember is the hardest in the whole line. Just at dark we entered a forest, through which was a single road, narrow and crooked. This road was filled with artillery, cavalry, infantry, baggage wagons, all pushing for the front. The night was dark, and in this blockade our regiment became separated from the division, and was left far in the rear.

At ten o'clock the situation had become much worse, so that it was every one for himself. The artillery, each gun and caisson being drawn by six horses, crashed and thundered along the narrow road, and by the right of superior strength claimed the "right of way."

We marched on as best we could, tired, hungry and mad. If the artillery horses came too near, we would hammer them over their heads with our guns. This, of course, would enrage their riders, and in the midst of all the uproar there was a fierce warfare of words and oaths and threats. We were descending a hill, when a gun came crashing down upon us; it was almost a case of life or death; one of our boys brought the heavy stock of his rifle down upon the head of one of the leading horses, and the animal staggered and fell.

The sergeant who had command of the gun, rode up to a lieutenant commanding a company, and ordered the man's arrest; the officer chanced to have a rifle in his hands, that he was carrying for one of his men, and with a half-muttered exclamation he dealt the sergeant's horse such a blow that horse and rider went down together, and we rushed on our way. That was a memorable night.

At two o'clock in the morning we overtook the division; they had been resting for two hours, and were just falling into line as we came up. We halted for twenty minutes, and then pushed on. Many fell out, and at daylight there could not have been over seventy-five men in our regiment. Just as the sun was rising, Sheridan sent back word that if we would rush on, Lee would be captured on that day. We forgot the long night's march, and pressed on with great rapidity.

Notice was also given that at nine o'clock we would draw rations. It is needless for me to say that, after that notice was given, I had no thought of falling out. It was a beautiful spring morning; the air was soft and balmy; the sun shone from a cloudless sky, and as he climbed in the eastern horizon he saw the two great armies in close proximity to each other, Lee standing at bay, with the broken fragments of a gallant army, Grant throwing the blue lines, like cords of death, around him. Nine o'clock came, but the rations we drew were not rations of food.

It was the ninth of April, 1865, and our long march was drawing to a close. But a few men were in Company H, at nine o'clock that morning, and perhaps a portion of these, like the writer, were there because they promised us rations. Our column halted in a field, and our guns were stacked as if we were to remain for a time. The firing in our front which we had heard at intervals that morning seemed to have died away. We broke ranks, and a portion of the boys ran in search of water, and others for wood. I started on a double-quick, hoping to secure a fence rail for fuel, so that we could make coffee after our rations were issued. A thousand men were in the same field, and on the same business.

I ran with all possible speed for a half mile, before I could secure one, and that, a huge oak rail, heavy enough for four men to carry. I managed to get the smaller end upon my shoulder, dragging the heavier, and slowly made my way to the regiment. It was all I could stagger under, and when I reached the company, great drops of perspiration were running down my cheeks. With an exclamation of triumph, I threw down my load beside my comrades, but just at that moment the bugle blew "Fall in!" "Fall in!" The boys laughed loudly at my adventure, and advised me to take the rail along with me. To say that I was slightly disgusted does not express the situation.

Heavy firing was heard in our front, not over half a mile distant. Orders were given to double-quick. We dashed through a thick belt of woods, and met cavalrymen riding back, badly broken up and demoralised. They told us they had been fighting all night, and holding the rebels in check until we should arrive, and this explained why we had marched all night. We passed through the woods, and came out into a field some forty rods in width. For a fourth of a mile in our front there was flat and level ground, and then a ridge of land, on whose crest there was a house, barn, and numerous outbuildings. The field on either side, up to this hill, was bordered with a forest, while beyond, there was—we knew not what. In that field we halted.

A group of Union generals were sitting upon their horses near us—Sheridan, Griffin, Chamberlain, and others. Sheridan was evidently much excited, and was talking rapidly, and adding emphasis to his words, by bringing his clenched right hand down on the open palm of his left. It was evident to all that some enterprise of importance was on foot. At that time, we had but one man in Company H, who had any claims to piety,—a grand fellow, quiet and beloved by all. He had marched all night, bound to keep up, but was so weak and footsore that he could hardly step.

When the company halted, and he saw Sheridan, he sank upon the ground with a comical groan of despair, and remarked, "The devil is to pay, sure!" And over beyond the hill, at about the same time, I think General Lee was cherishing the same opinion. Our brigade was quickly formed in two lines of battle to make a charge. Our regiment was in the front line, and General Sheridan formed a cavalry skirmish line in our front. The enemy's lines of battle were evidently over beyond the hill in our front, as some of their batteries opened upon us, and threw shot and shell very carelessly around.

The skirmishers advanced at a round gallop, Sheridan leading them on. When they reached the crest of the hill, and entered the forest on our right, we advanced rapidly across the plain and climbed the hill. Just before we reached its top, a shell exploded in the barn, and in a moment, it was in flames. In the confusion hens and chickens ran from the barn in every direction. By this time the enemy was pouring a very heavy artillery fire upon us, but it always requires something more than shot or shells to prevent hungry soldiers from chasing chickens, and so after the fowls we ran. Shells were crashing, officers were shouting for the men to keep in the ranks, the boys were screaming and laughing as they ran after the chickens, the flames roared and swept through the air, and the hens squalled in their most pathetic manner, as they were overtaken and captured.

Altogether it was a most remarkable medley. When the poultry excitement subsided, and we all got back into the rapidly advancing line, and looked out in our front, our mirth quickly subsided.

It was a desperate situation—one in which the most careless and indifferent would be brought to his senses. For three-fourths of a mile, an open field lay before us. A few rods of this distance was descending ground, then a level plain, and beyond that a ridge of land. At the foot of that ridge was the enemy's skirmish line. We could distinctly see the little rifle-pits in which they were intrenched. Beyond their skirmish line, and higher on the side of the hill, was their line of battle, behind breastworks, and back of this was their artillery, all in plain view. Their infantry had not opened fire upon us, but their artillery was firing rapidly and with good execution. We saw all this plainly, although advancing at a rapid rate.

We well understood what our mission was—to assault their position and silence their batteries. We thought of our comrades who had fallen out in the night, and who were then quietly sleeping back in the woods, and were angry with ourselves to think that for the hope of drawing rations we had been foolish enough to keep up, and by doing so, get in such a scrape. But it was then too late to fall out, and all we could do was to pull our hats down over our eyes as far as possible, keep up with the line, and endeavour to appear brave. We did not fear the artillery very much, for they fired over our heads, but dreaded the moment when the infantry should open on us.

We descended the hill and advanced across the plain, and were not far from their skirmish line. Not many words were spoken, but every mind was busy. Like a flash we thought of all the past three years, so many dangers passed through, and here, after all these hardships and narrow escapes, just as the war was about to close, our regiment reduced to a hundred men, was hurled into this desperate position, where nearly all must be slaughtered. It did seem hard, but not a man in that little band flinched, and as coolly as we had ever marched upon the parade ground, we marched up to what we supposed was the gates of death. We saw a white object flutter in an orchard up in the rear of their line of battle. A signal for their infantry to open fire, growled the boys, as they saw it. Then we expected to see their line of battle mantled in fire and smoke as they poured volleys of death upon us; but a moment passed, and not a gun had been fired.

We looked again; we saw the object we had supposed to be a signal flag, but it had changed its position. It was advancing almost down to their line of battle. It continued to advance, and passed their battle line. Three men accompanied it. What could it mean? It was a white flag. We could not believe our eyes. At a brisk gallop the officers rode to within twenty rods of our line, then turned down to our right where Sheridan had disappeared; and on we advanced. A staff officer came out from the woods; his spurs were pressed hard against the smoking flanks of his noble horse. He was swinging his hat like a madman, and yelling—"Lee has surrendered! Lee has surrendered!" "Halt, halt, halt!" came the order, and the last charge was over.

But such a scene! I cannot describe it. Seventeen years have passed, but the blood tingles in my fingertips now, as I think of it. There was such a change in the situation, such a transition in our experience! Men laughed and shouted, shook hands and actually wept for joy. Could it be possible? It seemed more like a dream. Had Lee actually surrendered, and was the war about to close?

The joy of that hour will never be forgotten. We forgot the long, weary marches, the hours of suffering, the countless exposures, and many sacrifices, and for the time, even forgot our disappointment in not drawing rations at nine o'clock that morning. Many of the boys were even then sceptical as to the actual surrender of Lee, and contended that he only sent in the flag of truce to gain time, and thus steal a march upon us; but in the afternoon, all doubts were removed. The advanced lines of the enemy had been withdrawn soon after the white flag came within our lines, and now large numbers of the rebel soldiers came over to us. We were glad to see them. They had fought bravely, and were as glad as we that the war was over.

They told us of the fearful condition General Lee's army was in, and we only wondered that they endured the hardships so long as they did. We received them kindly, and exchanged pocket knives and sundry trinkets, that each could have something to carry home as a reminiscence of the great event. To our division was assigned the honour of staying to receive the remainder of the arms, while the rest of the army moved back toward Richmond. We had three days' rations of food in our baggage wagons, and this was divided with our prisoners; and thus, for the day or two intervening between the surrender and the final stacking of their arms, we camped on the same hillside, ate the same hard-tack, and almost drank from the same canteen.

The rebels were all loud in their praise of General Grant, for the generous terms of the surrender, and pledged themselves to go home, and live and die under the shadow of the old flag. They had fought for four years, been completely whipped, were sadly disappointed, but, like men, were determined to go home and work to regain the fortunes they had lost. For two days after the flag of truce came in, and hostilities ceased, we were making preparations for the formal surrender. We were very thankful that it was our privilege, at the close of the war, to witness this most important event, while all the army, save our division, marched back in the direction of Richmond.

The twelfth day of April, 1865, was a memorable one to the First division of the old Fifth army corps, for upon that day the army of General Lee stacked its arms, and the above-named division was the one designated by General Grant to receive the surrender. The morning dawned clear and warm. At an early hour the regiments were prepared to fall into line. Major-General J. L. Chamberlain was in command of the brigade. Before nine o'clock the troops were in line, our brigade, consisting of nine old regiments, being in the advance. Anxiously we waited for the appearance of the rebel army. Soon we saw a gray column of troops advancing through the valley at our right. A thrill of excitement ran along the line, and exclamations like the following: "There they are," "The Johnnies are coming," "The Confederacy has found its last ditch," were whispered among the men.

Before their advanced line reached our column, every man was in his proper position, and we stood like a blue wall at a "shoulder arms," as they marched in our front. There was a space of some four rods between us. When their column had advanced the length of our line, they halted, "front faced," and there we stood—two hostile armies in well-formed lines, with only that narrow space between us. Our commander, with the true courtesy of a chivalrous spirit, gave the command "Shoulder arms," and we thus saluted our fallen enemies. They returned the salute, then "Ordered arms," "Fixed bayonets," "Stacked arms," placed their colours and equipments, upon the stacks thus made, moved by the "right flank," and marched sadly away.

And thus, they came and went, until all that remained of the grand old army of northern Virginia had stacked their arms. We had a most excellent opportunity to review these Southern troops, and notice their peculiar traits. As a rule, they were tall, thin, spare men, with long hair and beard of a tawny red colour. They were all clad in the uniform of Southern gray; nearly all were very ragged and dirty, while their broad-brimmed, slouching gray hats gave them anything but a soldierly appearance. A little fellow on my left, seeing how thin and lean they were, muttered, "No wonder we didn't kill more of them; either one of them would split a minie-ball if it should strike him."

Some of the brigades seemed to be well-disciplined, and marched in a very commendable manner. General Longstreet's corps seemed to be in the best state of discipline of any in the army, while many of the regiments and brigades marched in as irregular a manner as if they had never been drilled for a single hour. Their arms were of all designs and patterns; many of them were of English make, and had been doubtless smuggled through the blockade by the English blockade runners. Their colours were all stained by storm, and many of them were torn to shreds; some were elegantly mounted upon richly ornamented staffs, while others were fastened to rough poles.

It was quite an affecting scene to see some of the various colour guards, as they were about to leave the old flags they had carried so long and defended so bravely, turn and tear small pieces from the old banner, and hastily put them in their pockets as if fearing our officers would forbid their doing it, if they saw them. Many a brave Southern soldier turned that day with tearful eyes from the old colours they had loved so well, and for which they had sacrificed so much. No conversation was allowed between the two armies as the surrender was being made, but occasionally a pleasant word would be exchanged. One division that we had encountered an several different fields of battle, halted in our front, and as they were stacking their arms they learned to what division we belonged, while one of them cried in a jocose manner: "Well, old fellows, we have met you again." And thus, the day passed until they had all surrendered.

We had received them with every courtesy that could possibly be extended by a victorious army, and with a single exception not an uncivil word had been spoken to any officer or private in the whole army not a single word or act that could add to the humiliation of their position. That single exception was this: A brigadier-general came riding in at the head of his brigade, and attracted the attention of all. He was a small, thin man, with a red face, and shrill, sharp voice. The point of attraction was, that his uniform was all of the Confederate colour, with the exception of his coat, which was the Union blue, such as was worn by our own officers. He rode a large, powerful horse, and looked like a grim, soured, passionate man.

We quickly detected the fact that he was not admired by his men. They halted in our front, and the officer gave the necessary orders to have placed them in the proper position to receive our salute, but their lines not being "dressed up" as promptly as he desired, with much profanity he abused the men for being so tardy in their movements. I imagine they had borne much of this from him before, but now remembering that the war was over, and that the power of his authority was broken, the fire flashed from their eyes in response, as several of them in a most taunting manner replied to him, "Oh yes, you are brave enough now, but you was never so near the Yanks before in your life," while with this greeting, to which he could not well reply, he rode to the right of his command.

"Who is he? Who is he?" a hundred of the curious Yankees hastily asked.

"General Henry A. Wise," they answered.

For a moment we could hardly comprehend the truth. We thought of brave old John Brown and Harper's Ferry, of the imperious governor of the Old Dominion, that had ordered his execution, and here was the same old general surrendering his command to a Yankee Army. The mills of God may grind slowly, but always the work is done effectually. Our men could not let the opportunity pass without firing a few shots at the hot-headed old Virginian, and he was greeted with such exclamations as the following, which must have grated somewhat harshly upon his ears: "Who hanged John Brown?" "Where did you steal your coat?" "Hang him on a sour apple tree!" "Shoot him, shoot him, shoot him!" and if there was a disgusted looking man that rode from the surrender at Appomattox that day, it is safe to say that it was ex-Governor Wise.

When they stacked their arms, they marched to our headquarters, where they signed their parole of honour, and then rapidly departed to their homes, so that on the day following there was scarcely a rebel soldier to be found upon that historic field where General Lee had surrendered.

Much work remained for us to do after the rebels had left, in gathering up the stores and munitions of war. In the woods where the rebel army had encamped, rifles were scattered upon the ground in every direction. We found where whole battalions had stacked their arms and scattered for their homes, without taking any part in the surrender, or even signing their paroles. There is but little doubt that many thousands went in this manner, which, if added to those who marched in and stacked their arms, would have swelled Lee's army, in the aggregate, to more than fifty thousand men who actually surrendered on the ninth of April.

It was a wearisome and thankless task for us to gather up those guns, and carry them a long distance to a place where they could be transported to Washington, for we were tired and footsore, and had divided our rations with the rebels. The railroad bridges had been destroyed, so that trains could not run, while the condition of the roads made it almost impossible for wagon trains to reach us. Our rations had been exhausted, and we were almost famishing with hunger. Foraging expeditions were made, but the results were scanty.

A little beef was secured, but it was poor and tough, and also so tainted with garlic that it was almost impossible to eat it; but this supply was soon exhausted. Some were fortunate enough to find where corn had been fed to the horses and mules, and which had been trodden into the ground by their feet. These kernels were gathered up, washed, and then parched, and eaten with greedy appetites.

Many relics were carried from the field. Among these relics was the historic "apple tree," which was all appropriated. The first time that I saw this tree, the men had just cut it down. It was some twelve inches in diameter, had a straight, smooth trunk, and a large, wide-spreading top. The second time that I passed that way, the trunk had all disappeared, and a number of the boys were at work upon the branches. The third time, trunk, branches, and even the roots had all disappeared. Carbines, sabres, and pieces of rebel flags were also carried away, and many of them, I presume, are still preserved in the soldier's family as sacred reminders of that bloody war.

All of our associations with the rebels at Appomattox were of the most pleasant character. Great care was taken by our soldiers not to wound their feelings, and they exhibited their gratitude by many pleasant words. Generals Lee, Longstreet, and Gordon were all favourites in the rebel army, but Jefferson Davis was most bitterly denounced, and many of their disasters were attributed to him. Those Southern men were brave, patient, brilliant soldiers, and we hope that, if they or their descendants are again called to stand in the ranks of war, they will be marshalled under the Stars and Stripes.

If they display the same bravery in its defence that they showed under the "Stars and Bars," our country will be proud of its defenders. They had lost all by the war, but they accepted the situation gracefully, and have won success and prosperity by industry and toil. To all such, the survivors of the old Army of the Potomac wish a hearty Godspeed.

The day before we departed from Appomattox, the rain poured down in torrents; many of us had no tents; we had no rations; it was cold, wet and muddy. The picket line of our camp was maintained, and I was detailed for picket—my last detail for that purpose. It was a cheerless night, dark and drear, the rain falling in blinding sheets. The long hours wore gradually away, and at ten o'clock the next forenoon we were relieved, and returned to camp, to find that we were under marching orders to move at one o'clock.

I was famishing for food; my tent-mates Mac and Dick had captured about a pint of corn meal, and told me that if I would cook it they would divide. It was a godsend to me. I found an old fruit can, put in about a quart of muddy water, poured in the precious meal, and went forth to cook our dinner. A small fire of green pine limbs was smoking and sputtering in the rain, a short distance from our camp, and I quickly placed the can upon the fire, but I could not get heat enough to make it boil. I stirred and stirred the meal and water, and would occasionally taste of it to see. how it was progressing. The meal was sour and bitter, but it tasted good.

The temptation to eat was too strong to resist; I continued to eat until the last particle of the meal was consumed. I then took the can, which was supposed to contain pudding, to my comrades, who were under a shelter-tent, chuckling to themselves how fortunate they were in having their dinner cooked for them. The dish was placed upon the ground. We formed a circle around it, and made an assault upon the contents with a knife, spoon and stick, but to *our* surprise there was nothing but water. Dick looked up to me with a puzzled expression upon his face, and said, "Gerrish, where in —— is that meal?" and I could only innocently answer, "It must have dissolved in the water."

Our wet blankets were folded; our lines were formed; the order was given to move, forward. We turned our backs toward Appomattox, and bade farewell to our last battlefield.

CHAPTER 16

Appomattox to Richmond

Saturday, April 15th, at one o'clock in the afternoon, we began our march from Appomattox to Richmond. We have all heard much of the "Conquering armies," "Flying banners," and of their majestic appearance, but it was not so with our division on that day when we turned from the field upon which General Lee had surrendered. We had even marched from fields of defeat with more of a military display than we there made. It was raining very hard; the mud was ankle deep in the roads; our uniforms were ragged and covered with mud; the men were hungry and consequently savage.

There was no attempt made to keep in the ranks, but at a rapid pace we straggled along the muddy turnpike, each man picking his own way through the mud as best he could. "We were to draw rations" that night, the officers said, and with that thought to inspire us, we pushed bravely on. Darkness came that afternoon at an early hour, but no halt was ordered until at least an hour after dark. We then received the cheering intelligence that "someone had blundered," and that we had marched the last two miles in the wrong direction. With many expressions of anger, we retraced our weary steps, until we regained the turnpike from which by mistake we had departed.

Here we received the somewhat sarcastic order to break ranks, and make ourselves comfortable for the night. You can imagine the situation; we were on a low, boggy piece of ground that was covered by a stunted growth of scattering pine trees. The ground was so thoroughly soaked with water that it came up through the surface, and stood around our feet as we walked upon it. We had no means with which to build fires, and we could only spread our blankets upon the flooded marsh, and endeavour to sleep. My tent-mate at that time was a gallant son of the Emerald Isle, fresh from the home of his ancestors. His name was Matthew McElroy, and he was a brave, generous-hearted, full-blooded Irishman. He would always persist in doing the most ludicrous things in the most laughable manner, and on this evening, when we halted in the forest, wet and cold, he with much zeal declared that we must pitch a tent so that we could keep warm and dry.

In vain I expostulated with him. After I had exhausted my arguments, I rolled myself in my blanket and lay down across the roots of a tree, and tried to sleep. How the rain poured down! The water came from the branches of the pine tree in blinding sheets where I was lying, but I slept, and obtained a good night's rest. I have an indistinct recollection of Mac, as he stormed around nearly all that night in the mud and rain, ejaculating, in true Irish brogue, that "A Yankee would sleep if the divil sat at his head!"

The next morning was as cold and raw as a November day, the clouds were thick and black, the plunging rain was so cold that it seemed to have glanced from an iceberg, on its way to the earth. The depth of the mud had increased at least several inches during the night, and the roads looked like well-filled mortar beds. Of course, there were no rations to eat, and we were faint with hunger. I obtained a small piece of beef weighing perhaps one-half a pound, that had been taken from the neck of a creature several days before, bloody, tough and so tainted with garlic that it was uneatable. It had been carried in a dirty haversack, which to say the least, had not added to its excellence, but I was grateful to receive it.

A small fire was gasping for life by the roadside, upon the coals of which the meat was roasted, being seasoned with ashes and the falling rain. When it was cooked, I sat upon an old log, and ate my morning meal with a ravenous appetite, and was soon again upon the march. The roads were nearly impassable, but with heroic fortitude we pressed on our way.

At noon we crossed the Appomattox river upon a temporary bridge, and soon reached the little village of Farmville. The rain had ceased to fall, the clouds had cleared away, and the warm sunshine was pouring down upon us. We marched to the top of a little hill which overlooked the village. The scene spread out before us was a most beautiful one, while to our great joy we saw our wagon train, and so knew that we were soon to have rations. That was a very pleasant afternoon, for we received our rations, and also letters from home. We lay upon the green grass, and for the first time seemed to comprehend the fact that the war was over. There had been so much confusion and excitement thus far, that we had hardly realised this before.

We also walked through the pretty village, which, for neatness and enterprise, resembled a New England town. The people were all very quiet, but met us kindly, and were undoubtedly glad that the war had ended. We visited the little cemetery on the hillside, and found that many Confederate soldiers had been buried there, a number of them within a few days, the victims of a skirmish that had taken place near that village.

On our return to our regiment we found that a great cloud of sorrow had settled down upon the encampment in our absence. A dispatch had been received by our officers, bringing the intelligence of the assassination of President Lincoln. At first, we did not believe the report, but when we were compelled to do so, we supposed that he had been shot by some of the rebels made desperate by their recent defeats. I never saw men so deeply moved as were those soldiers. It was a fortunate affair for both sides that the rebel army had been paroled before that deed of assassination took place, for with the intense feeling that existed when that intelligence reached us, there would have been a conflict of the most deadly character. But soon we learned who the assassin was, and were grateful to know that it was none of those who had received such generous treatment from our hands at the surrender of Lee.

It is impossible for me to describe the feeling that existed. We had all loved Abraham Lincoln so much, and in all those years had never doubted his integrity for a moment, even when we were obliged to confess that we had been mistaken in many men whom we had learned to love. No cloud had ever for a moment obscured the beloved form of the noble Lincoln. "Too bad, too bad, that spoils it all; I wish Lee had not surrendered"; "I would like to fight it longer"; "I do not want to go home now," and a hundred similar expressions, could be heard as with sorrowful countenances the men sat and discussed the situation. Nowhere in the Union was there more genuine sorrow for the martyred President than in the army. It was a sad Sabbath evening for us all.

On Monday morning we broke camp and marched to Burksville, and then proceeded in the direction of North Carolina, along the line of the Danville railroad. On the following morning we learned that someone had made a mistake, and that we were to return to Burksville, and, so, near that place we encamped for the night, and remained there all the following day. From this point we proceeded in a leisurely manner in the direction of Petersburgh, and on Sunday, April 23rd, we went into camp at Sutherland station, a few miles from the city of Petersburgh.

An amusing incident occurred here. Our line halted in its march, but we supposed that it was only for the purpose of resting a few moments, our regiment being near a regiment of coloured cavalry, which hailed from Massachusetts, and had reached the field just as the war closed. The commissioned officers of this regiment were white, the others were all black. Several of our boys went up to the tent of their regimental sutler, and found that he had a very large stock of such goods as army sutlers usually sell. The coloured soldiers had not seen much service, but put on many airs, being, evidently, quite proud of their new uniforms.

Our boys were ragged, rough, and ready for any kind of a skirmish that might arise. They stood up very near to the sutler's goods, and the coloured soldiers, who were guarding the tent, ordered them to fall back, but they did not feel disposed to obey the peremptory order, and remained as they were. The corporal of the guard, a huge, black fellow, evidently wishing to magnify his office, came up and undertook to arrest our men for disobeying orders. The result was that one of our boys struck out from the shoulder and landed the poor corporal upon his head in the ditch.

In a moment all was excitement and confusion. The officers of the coloured regiment evidently knew but little more than their men, and rushed down with drawn swords to arrest the offenders, but, by the time they arrived on the battle ground, there were at least fifty of our regiment in the melee. I cannot write without laughing, as I think of the charge those officers made upon that crowd; their swords went flying through the air, their new hats, with bands and tassels of golden cords, were kicked like footballs among the men. In the struggle some of the boys managed to get hold of the sutler's canvas tent, a terrific yell, and the whole institution was upset, and barrels of apples and cakes, boxes of butter, cheese, tobacco, and raisins went flying among the men until all were captured or destroyed. Then our men withdrew in good order and returned to the regiment.

If the cavalry officers had been wise, they would have let the matter rest there, but to our surprise we heard their bugle sound the call to "boot and saddle," and saw the colonel, with two or three squadrons of his men well mounted, come dashing down to our regiment. That officer in a loud voice asked for the commander of our regiment. Major ―――― stepped to the front, and said that he was the senior officer in the regiment, present, and asked what was wanted. The colonel stated his case, and demanded that those men be arrested and punished, and added the threat that, if they were not, he would arrest them himself. Suiting his action to his word, he pressed his line forward until the horses stood between our stacks of guns.

By this time the boys were all on tiptoe, ready for the fun, and when the orders were given to take arms and charge bayonets, it did not require many moments to put them in execution. The result was, the cavalry was most handsomely repulsed with the loss of half a dozen horses, including the colonel's, all of which were injured by our bayonets, and had to be shot, to end their sufferings. I presume, if any of the members of that regiment are living now, they will remember the Twentieth Maine.

Here, at this station, we went into camp, and remained until May 2nd. While we were stopping at this place, soldiers were stationed at all the houses, as safeguards, to protect the property from foragers of either army. At these houses we usually had very enjoyable times. I was detailed to go to a large plantation down upon the bank of the Appomattox River, which had formerly been the home of a wealthy planter, who became a colonel in the rebel army. This property had been seized and confiscated by our government, and was then leased to a large number of contrabands, who were engaged in planting corn. Of these there were nearly one hundred, of all ages, colours, and of both sexes. They had a number of horses and mules, which they had captured, and several cows, which they had, by some means, obtained.

I wish I could truthfully picture those days to you,—the only period in all my life when I undertook to be aristocratic. "I was monarch of all I surveyed," and those hundred negroes all obeyed my orders. I selected the mansion for my headquarters, and the common people occupied the outbuildings and sheds. If I wanted a drink of cool water from the spring that boiled and bubbled underneath the oak trees in front of the house, I only had to speak the word, and it was brought to me. My meals were always prepared and brought to me in royal state, none of the coloured people thinking of eating until I had finished.

Pitch-pine knots were gathered, and in the evenings a bright fire flamed in the open fireplace of my home. The choicest hoe cakes and the most luscious piece of bacon were selected for my use, and I had plenty of good, rich milk. It is needless to say that this detail was a red-letter period in my soldier's experience. Having invited a number of the boys out to dine with me, I told "Aunty," the old coloured cook, that she must do her best in order to maintain the respectability of the institution; and didn't the old lady cook and work! The table was loaded down with steaming hoe cakes; we had coffee, milk and bacon in abundance, and we Yankee soldiers put our legs beneath the old rebel's mahogany table, and had a grand time. We ate, talked, laughed and sang, until "not a wave of trouble rolled across our peaceful breasts."

An old crippled negro, who had been on the plantation for years, told us that, just before our advance, that spring, General Lee and his staff had been invited out to a house in that neighbourhood to dine, and that as they were taking their leave, some of the ladies present having expressed a fear that the Yankees would soon advance, the gallant General Lee had quieted their fears by telling them there was no danger, and adding, that when the Union Army entered Richmond, it would be over his dead body.

When Lee's army retreated, a portion of it crossed this plantation. We were much amused, as the old negro described it to us in his own graphic manner. The rebels were retreating very rapidly, and had thrown away everything, even to their guns. They rushed down over the steep bank of the river, and a number of them were drowned as they were crossing. Soon after they passed, a group of rebel officers rode up, and began to question the old man, and we knew at once that they were Sheridan's scouts. They asked him if he had seen any of our men, and he, supposing them to be rebels, answered, that some of them had just passed.

"Where did they go? "asked an officer.

The old man shook his head dolefully, and replied, "To the debble, I guess, by the way they went past here," and, to his surprise, the officers loudly laughed at his reply.

But there was one mystery the old coloured gentleman could not solve, *viz*.: while the officers were thus talking with him, a squad of Union cavalrymen came out of the woods, and all went off together. All this he told, with his queer sentences and gestures, much to the pleasure of his listeners. The boys voted that I was the prince of hosts, and returned to camp.

On May 2nd I was ordered to join my regiment, and bade farewell to my coloured colony. On the day following we marched through the city of Petersburgh, and a very interesting day's march it was to us. For several miles before we reached the city our line of march was inside the rebel defences, and there we saw the lines of forts and breastworks which had so long defied our advance. In the distance we could see the long line of fortifications behind which we lay so long, and also the high signal tower our engineers had erected near Hatcher's Run.

As we passed through Petersburgh we had the pleasure of seeing our old beloved commander, General Warren, who had been relieved from his command by the order of General Sheridan, at Five Forks. The corps had not been satisfied with his removal, considering it both cruel and unjust, and his appearance was the signal for the wildest enthusiasm. There was cheering all along the line, as the Fifth corps passed that point, and it must have been gratifying to the heart of the gallant soldier to know that his men honoured him in the moments of his unjust punishment and disgrace.

Our thoughts were so absorbed in the person of General Warren, that I have but an indefinite impression of the size, condition and general appearance of this town. We were soon upon the turnpike that connects Petersburg!! and Richmond. It was a broad pike, and in good condition, with stone mile posts standing by its side. Strange emotions filled our minds as we marched along this road, and recalled its past history, away back before the war, when the wealthy, aristocratic inhabitants of the beautiful capital of the Old Dominion used to ride in their luxury over it, little dreaming that a Yankee Army of invasion would ever march along the same way. Through the war how often the brave Southern soldiers had marched and countermarched along that road in their heroic defence of the Confederate capital.

At night we halted within ten miles of Manchester, a small city situated upon the bank of the James River, directly opposite Richmond. The next day we marched to the former town, and encamped just at its edge, where we had a fine view of the late rebel capital. We remained there two days, and as we had been striving to reach that place for three years, it can easily be supposed that now we had much anxiety to see all that was to be seen. There were some names in and around Richmond with which the people of the North had become strangely familiar through the last two years of the war; among them was Belle Isle, Libby Prison, and Castle Thunder.

There was no phrase in the English language that contained more horror, through that period, for the Union soldier, than the expression, "rebel prisons." As soon as permission could be obtained, after we encamped at Manchester, we went to gratify our curiosity in looking at the prisons where our brave comrades had suffered so much, and where so many of them had died. We visited Belle Isle first. We found it to be a small island in the James River, containing several acres, near the famous Tredegar Iron Works. The river's current ran very swiftly on either side of the island.

The upper portion of this island was a grassy bluff, covered with trees, while the lower part was a low, sandy plain, nearly on a level with the water of the river in times of freshet. The island was connected with Richmond by a bridge. The prisoners were never allowed to go upon the green hillside, and sit under the shade of the trees, even in the hottest of the weather. That plain was a hell spot of suffering and anguish, and the green, shady hillside must have seemed to the sufferers like a heaven whose pleasures they were not allowed to enjoy. This sandy plain was surrounded by a line of breastworks some four feet high, and on each side of these earthworks was a deep ditch. Along the outer ditch guards were stationed about forty feet apart, who kept watch day and night. There was no shelter for the men.

At first some miserable shelter tents were furnished, but these were soon taken away, and, in that country so abundantly supplied with lumber, no attempt was made to build a single barrack or shed, to protect that mass of suffering humanity from the weather. At one time there was not less than eleven thousand men crowded upon that plain, that did not contain over five acres. Their sufferings can never be estimated, but we can obtain some conception of them, when we consider their situation, five thousand of them crowded together in that mass. Each man had only a space of three feet by seven to occupy, by actual measurement, with nothing but the thin and ragged uniforms in which they were captured, to protect them from the winter's cold.

At times the snow lay deep upon the ground around Richmond; ice formed in the James River, frequently, and flowed down the stream in thick masses upon either side of the island; water left in buckets on the island froze two or three inches deep in a single night. The poor fellows, coatless, hatless, and often shoeless, did all in their power to protect themselves from the awful cold. If the material had been furnished them, they would gladly have constructed their own shelter, but this godsend was denied them. At nights they lay in the ditch, as the most protected place, heaped one upon another, and lying as closely together as possible, and taking turns as to who should lie in the outside row, which was the most exposed.

In the morning, all along that row, there would be the forms of those who were sleeping their last sleep, men who had frozen to death during the night; and all the while they were starving for food. One writer says:

> The cold froze them because they were hungry, the hunger consumed them because they were cold. These two vultures fed upon their vitals, and no one in the Southern Confederacy had the mercy or pity to drive them away.

When winter gave way to summer, the situation became worse; the sun poured his intense heat upon those unprotected men; they were not allowed to use the running water of the river, and diseases multiplied in the heat until Belle Isle became almost a pest-house. The poor fellows digged holes in the sand, hoping to find cool moisture there, but even that was hot and dry. No wonder they died by thousands.; I only wonder that any escaped from that horrible place. In our visit we found evidences on every hand, showing us for what purpose the island had been used. The earthworks, ditches and pits all remained; rags and filth covered the ground, and a sickly sensation crept over us as we viewed the scene. As the sand grated under our feet, we could almost imagine that we could hear the groans of anguish that once filled the air.

It is a fearful comment upon the Christian sympathy of the ladies in the South, that, while Northern ladies were so kindly caring for the rebel prisoners in Northern hospitals and prisons, not one Southern lady was seen upon Belle Isle, during all the time our men were suffering there. I do not wonder that our passions were stirred as we beheld the situation in which our men had been placed, and I think, if at that moment Jefferson Davis or any other of the Confederate leaders had stood in the midst of that squad of twenty men, that they would have been hanged upon one of those trees, whose shelter they would not allow our men to enjoy.

We recrossed the bridge, entered the city, passed down to Carey street, where Libby Prison was located. This prison had formerly been used as a tobacco warehouse; it was a large, brick building, some four or five stories in height; it looked black, dirty and grim; a board was nailed upon one corner, and upon this was printed, in large letters, LIBBY PRISON. The building contained six rooms, each one hundred feet long and forty feet wide. At one time these rooms contained twelve hundred Union officers of all grades. The rooms were low; the walls and ceilings were very black; the ventilation was very poor; they were allowed no other rooms in which to eat, sleep, cook, wash, dry clothes, or take exercise; all these must be done in that space, so crowded that each man was only allowed a space ten feet by two.

The glass in the windows was nearly all broken out, so that in the winter the men must have suffered much with the cold, while in summer the rooms were warm to suffocation. The captives were not permitted to go within three feet of the windows, and if they crossed that dead line by either accident or design, they were deliberately shot by the guards. The only satisfaction that we derived from the inspection of Libby Prison was to see its rooms filled with rebel prisoners. We did rejoice to see them there, that they might understand something of the situation in which our men were placed, although the officer in charge, who kindly showed us the prison, informed us that the government furnished them with plenty of food and fresh water, and also permitted the citizens to do the same.

Castle Thunder was on a much smaller scale than either of the other prisons I have named, but it had its full proportion of horrors. The building had originally been a slave pen—a place in which runaway slaves were confined when captured, while awaiting their master's orders. Slaves, when taken from the plantation to be sold in the Richmond market for the Southern cotton trade, would be thrown into this building, so filthy that a Northern farmer would not confine his animals in it, until they were placed upon the auction block. The same men who took delight in imprisoning their human cattle there, took equal delight in imprisoning within the same miserable walls the captive soldiers of the Union. In either case the air was filled with groans of anguish wrung from tortured human hearts, but in neither case, did they awaken sympathy in the hearts of the "Southern Chivalry."

But the question we asked ourselves as we examined those prisons was, who was responsible for all this suffering and death? and that question repeats itself now. An attempt has been made, since the war, to throw the blame all upon Winder, Turner, Wirtz, and a few other Confederates who held subordinate positions under their government. I have no doubt that these men were guilty enough, and that the government was justified in hanging, at least, a portion of them, as it did, but these men were only the instruments or creatures of the government under whose orders they acted, and whose hellish malice they exhibited in their treatment of our men. The terrible responsibility of murdering these thousands of Union soldiers must rest upon the representative men of the Southern Confederacy, two of the most prominent of whom were Jefferson Davis and Robert E. Lee.

For the first named person I think no excuse has been offered, and he must bear upon the pages of history the burden of his guilt, without a word being spoken in his defence. General Lee did speak in his own defence before the Joint Committee of Reconstruction, in February, 1866, testifying that he was not aware of any bad treatment suffered by Union prisoners, was not aware that any of them died of cold and starvation; that no report was ever made to him of the sad condition of Union prisoners anywhere; that he never knew who was in command of the rebel prisons at Andersonville, Salisbury, and elsewhere, until the close of the war; and that he knew nothing of the alleged cruelties about which complaints had been made.

Better would it have been for the memory of General Lee, as Commander-in-Chief of the Confederate Army, to have lived in history without any defence for the great wrongs he inspired or allowed, than to have plead ignorance to that which, from the position he occupied, he must have well understood. "Did not know of their condition:"—What a defence for the "brilliant soldier" and "Christian gentleman" to make in his own behalf! Why, upon any of those days when he visited his family in his elegant brick mansion on Franklin street, he could have stepped out upon its upper gallery to the south, and with his field-glass have looked into the ghastly faces of the starved and freezing captives on Belle Isle.

Eight minutes' walk from the same elegant home would have taken him to Libby Prison, where he could have learned the condition of those officers who were his prisoners by the fortunes of war. The treatment of those men was discussed upon the floor of the Confederate Congress, and in the columns of the rebel newspapers; the civilized world stood horrified at such devilish cruelties, but the unsuspecting mind of General Lee was in blissful ignorance of it all!

It may be unkind to speak of these things, so long after the war has closed, but lapse of time has not permitted us to forget the wrongs poured upon the heads of our noble comrades, and in that day when the slain and the slayer shall stand before the Judge, those wrongs must be righted.

From the city we passed down the James River, and viewed the rebel fortifications upon its banks below the town. As we inspected these, we were not surprised that our gunboats were unable to ascend the river, the previous year. In many places the banks rose almost perpendicular, to a height of one hundred feet above the water, and upon these banks, much in the form of terraces, were the rebel fortifications.

Many of the huge guns which manned these fortifications were pointed almost directly downward, and so were able, from this great height, to hurl their shells upon our boats, while our men found it impossible, in the narrow channel of the river, to elevate their guns sufficiently to reach the enemy. It was an interesting tour, to inspect those defences which the most skilful Confederate engineers had constructed, but it was to us a source of deep regret to remember that their skill had been acquired in the military schools, and at the expense of the nation whose life they were now endeavouring to destroy. The old adage that "republics are ungrateful," can often be applied to individuals.

CHAPTER 17

Marching through Richmond

This, which to us was a memorable event, took place on the sixth day of May. After three years of bloody strife and many defeats and disappointments, it was some satisfaction to march through the streets of this city. "On to Richmond" had been our battle cry for three years, but not until nearly thirty days after Lee's surrender did we have the privilege of marching through its streets. We were to march through, in review at battalion front.

The city, notwithstanding the ravages and desolations of war, was a pleasant and beautiful town. The lower portion of it was in ruins, and the huge piles of smouldering bricks and crumbling granite served to remind the citizens of the last act of courtesy they had received from the rebel army, who determined that when they could no longer defend the city, they would burn it, regardless of the sufferings that the great conflagration would cause the inhabitants of the town. The State Capitol, which had also served as the Confederate Capitol, was a large edifice, quite imposing in its architecture, and was situated on a wide, beautiful street, well shaded with trees. Almost opposite the Capitol was a noble statue of General Washington, which was situated in a beautiful public park. There were many other pleasant and beautiful buildings in the town, some of the latter being elaborate in design and elegant in finish.

As we marched through the town, the inhabitants, especially the coloured population, gave us quite a cordial reception, the sidewalks being covered with people, many of whom were white. Our bands played national airs, but there was not much cheering by the spectators in the way of response. Our boys were placed on their good behaviour, and marched in a quiet, dignified and soldierly manner. The ladies came forth from their homes in large numbers, in the intense heat, and kindly supplied us with cool water to drink, an act of courtesy that will be long remembered by our soldiers. Many of the citizens spoke kindly of the late President Lincoln, and expressed sorrow at his assassination; they were also loud in their praises of the manner in which General Grant had treated the Confederate soldiers. Our uniforms were torn and ragged, and our flags hung in shreds from their staffs, but our columns were inspected with much interest by the citizens of Richmond.

Before noon, our corps had all marched through the town, and as we bade farewell to its inhabitants, we turned and took a last view of the city for whose possession so many lives had been lost. From Richmond we were to march to Washington, by the way of Fredericksburgh. On the first night we camped at Hanover Court House, twenty miles from Richmond. Our marching for the few following days was severe. General Griffin, who was in command of our corps, seemed to have forgotten the great interest that he had always manifested for his men, and on this march, where there was no possible reason for haste, we were rushed along almost beyond the power of human endurance, so that that last march was one of the most severe of the whole war.

We crossed the rivers whose names had become familiar to us in the great campaign of the previous year, and occasionally came upon lines of earthworks which the rebels had thrown up at different times, to check the advances of the Union armies. As we passed over the plains, crossed the rivers, and climbed the hills which were once crowned with hostile forces, we could hardly make ourselves believe that the war had ended; so that, at moments when lost to the present in the reflections of the past, we would find ourselves listening for the roar of battle.

On the ninth of May, late in the afternoon, we crossed the Rappahannock River, about four miles below the city of Fredericksburgh, and went into camp for the night, nearly opposite that town. We were now upon ground made familiar to us by past campaigns. There had not been many changes in the intervening months. Above us were the hills where General Burnside had massed his troops, prior to his crossing to fight that fatal and disastrous battle; beyond the river from our tents was Fredericksburgh, encircled by those heights from which the troops of Burnside had been hurled back in defeat, but which General Sedgwick so gallantly carried in the following May, while the Battle of Chancellorsville was being fought. In the dim twilight of that evening hour I obeyed a strange impulse, crossed the river, passed through the city, and up the heights, as I have related in a previous chapter.

Early the following morning we were again on the march. Every step of the way was familiar to us, and awakened many sad thoughts in our minds. We passed near the old camp-ground at Stoneman's Switch, but there had been many changes in its surroundings since we left it. A few of us turned aside from the regiment, walked along what had been our parade ground, visited the cemetery on the hillside, and bade farewell to the graves of our old comrades. We marched through Stafford Court House, and again camped for the night.

On the morning of the tenth, just as we were breaking camp, a very sad event occurred, that cast a deep gloom over the whole regiment. Lieutenant Wood, a brave soldier who had been at the front for three years, and who had escaped a thousand dangers, when rising to leave his tent, was fatally wounded, as follows: A wagoner having discharged a carbine accidentally, some twenty rods distant, the bullet passed through several tents, and entered the body of the gallant soldier, who suffered much pain, and died on the following day. It did seem very hard that one who had fought so bravely and for so long a time should be killed after the war was ended, and on the eve of his departure for home.

The night of May 11th was a most memorable one in the history of our regiment, as the last night on which we marched, and its history must have a place in this volume. At four o'clock in the afternoon there was a very heavy shower that continued until six; the rain came pouring down in blinding sheets, but we continued our march, and, of course, when the rain ceased falling, we were all thoroughly drenched. The road was made muddy and slippery, and the marching was very heavy, but our column continued its advance at a rapid rate. Many of the men became disgusted with the folly of our officers, in thus pressing us on, and fell out of the ranks, and pitched their tents for the night in the woods by the roadside, so that but a few of us remained.

At dark we entered a forest, and began marching over a Virginia corduroy road. The pine logs of which this road-bed was composed were made slippery with the rain, as the bark had fallen from them. In many places the logs had been removed by either men or floods, so that deep, muddy holes abounded in the way. The night was very dark, and great drops of water fell from the tree tops. The darkness was so intense that we could not see where we were to place our feet, and could scarcely see each other. The column was moving rapidly, and we ran, jumped, slipped, stumbled, fell, growled, swore, and vowed vengeance upon the heads of the officers, as we made our way through that forest.

That night's treatment was the most scandalous usage we received during our term of service. At one o'clock in the morning we came out upon a floating bog, so wet that the thick sods on its surface would settle many inches in the water at each step we took, and frequently the water would be nearly to our knees. Upon that marsh we were ordered to camp for the night. If we had halted in the afternoon, we could have had a most excellent camping ground, but now we were to camp upon the place I have described. There was no wood that we could obtain for building fires, and the men reeking with perspiration, after the rapid march, spread their blankets upon the wet ground, and with the water standing in deep pools around and beneath their bodies, tried to sleep.

No wonder that several of the men in our division perished before the morning dawned. I determined to find wood, and build a fire if possible, and marched out into the darkness for that purpose. I walked a great distance before I could find anything in the shape of wood. At last I stumbled upon the trunk of a small pine tree that had been turned up by its roots in a gale of wind and was lying upon the ground. The trunk was short, and the top was large and bushy. With great difficulty I lifted the end of the trunk with the roots upon it upon my shoulder; it was all that I could possibly stand up under, and the huge top must be dragged. I made several ineffectual attempts to move it, but at last my efforts were crowned with success, and I started for the regiment with my prize.

The way was long, the tree grew heavy as I advanced, and it was with much difficulty that I determined where the regiment was, as the darkness completely screened it from my view. There was only one incident of interest that occurred on the route, and that was a source of much gratification to me. There was in our regiment at that time an officer who was much disliked by the boys in the ranks; there were several reasons why we disliked him, which I will not mention here. At this time, he wore white pants. As I was approaching the regiment, and had nearly reached my destination, I saw those white pants, and supposed the officer was not far away. I saw at a glance that, if I did not change my course, I would come in contact with the white pants.

As, in the darkness he did not see me, or the pine top that was so near him, I was in the right frame of mind to do something ugly, so I turned not to the right hand or the left, but when the pine top was about four feet from the pants, I increased my rate of speed about one hundred *per cent*; there was a slight shock, and I knew that the pine limbs and the white pants had formed a connection. A savage oath from the officer served as an inspiration for a greater effort on my part, and I made a most desperate advance. The result was, that the officer was caught up in the dried brush, and borne onward a few feet, while, in his efforts to escape from something, he knew not what, he turned one or two hand springs, and fell upon the wet marsh, in a most dilapidated condition. He never knew the source of his misfortune.

As he mounted his horse, on the following morning, those pants looked as if a hundred pound shell had exploded in the immediate vicinity of their owner. I reached the company with my fuel; we broke up the dried limbs as best we could, and built a small fire in front of our shelter tent, so near that our feet would almost reach the fire as we lay in the tent. Our blankets were spread upon the wet ground, and we retired for the night. The wind blew almost a gale, and swept great masses of black clouds through the air; the water was cold beneath us; the little fire snapped and crackled at our feet; I was tired and fell asleep.

Sometime before daylight I awoke and found that I was nearly dead with severe cramps in all parts of my body; I felt a strange and unnatural pressure on my feet, and found that half-a-dozen fellows from other regiments had camped around our fire, and that three or four of them had deliberately lain down upon our feet and legs. It is no fiction that I write, when I say that, for the next five minutes, our feet flew lively and with vigour; and I can imagine that the sleeping Pennsylvania Dutchmen, upon whom our kicks were falling, dreamed that they were once more under fire, and that rebel shells were exploding around them. In the morning it was very cold, and we were nearly frozen.

I think that all my old comrades will say, with me, that the last night's march of our old regiment was the most uncomfortable one of our three years' campaign. Quite early in the morning we were ordered to "fall in," and soon marched away. We passed by Fairfax Court House, and knew that we were rapidly nearing our destination, the city of Washington. This afforded us new inspiration, and as we thought how soon our marches were to be over, we unconsciously increased our speed; rapidly we crossed fields, climbed hills, and descended into valleys. We began to climb another steep ascent it was Arlington Heights and we knew that from its top we could see the city of Washington. We remembered when our regiment saw it the last time, in those dark days between the disastrous campaign on the Peninsula and the Battle of Antietam, when we had joined the army.

Then the booming of the Confederate guns was distinctly heard in the streets of the national capital; but now the rebels were disarmed and treason was crushed. We reached the crest of the heights, and looked in the direction of Washington, but to our disappointment a bank of fog obscured it from our view; but as we continued to gaze with a longing look, the fog began to scatter beneath the rays of the sun, and indistinctly we began to see the outlines of the city. Soon we saw it in all its beauty; and as we stood and surveyed that scene, we understood something of the feelings that filled the hearts of the crusaders, when, after their long, weary marches and bloody battles, they stood upon the hills that encircled Jerusalem, and for the first time obtained a view of the holy city.

We soon went into camp upon Arlington Heights; our company streets were made, and for the last time we pitched our shelter tents on the soil of Virginia. That camp was but a short distance from Fort Craig, where we had passed our first night upon the sacred soil of the South. As we connected the two dates in our minds, and surveyed the period of time between them, as we thought of the many dangers through which we had passed, of the twenty battlefields on which our regiment had fought, and the wonderful manner in which our lives had been preserved, our hearts were filled with gratitude and thanksgiving. The days we passed in that encampment were very pleasant. The peach orchards were in bloom; fields were carpeted with grass and flowers; and we visited many points of interest in and around Washington.

The great army of General Sherman arrived at Washington, and we had the pleasure of becoming acquainted with those heroes who marched from Atlanta to the sea. There was, of course, much rivalry between the two armies, and occasional skirmishes between some of the men, but the associations were very pleasant and much enjoyed by both armies. The days passed rapidly away. We knew that preparations were being rapidly made to muster us out, and that we would soon be at home.

CHAPTER 18

"The Great Review"

It was decided by the government that, before its gallant armies should be disbanded, their great victories should be commemorated by the greatest military display that was ever witnessed on the continent,—a review in which the two great armies of the Potomac and the Southwest should take a part,—and elaborate preparations were made for it in the city of Washington. Along the route where the procession was to pass, tiers of seats were constructed, huge stands of observation were erected, and the buildings which had so recently been draped in mourning at the death of President Lincoln, were now robed in the national colours, while mottoes of welcome on every hand were to greet the conquering heroes.

Thousands of citizens from all parts of the United States (save, perhaps, the South), hastened to the capital to behold the wonderful procession, the equal of which would probably never be seen again in the history of the United States. Two days were to be consumed in this vast military display, and the twenty-second and twenty-third days of May was the appointed time. We were tired and worn from the long, weary marches we had made, but it was not a difficult task to get up considerable enthusiasm over the coming review. The thoughts of it reminded us of the histories we had studied in our school days, about the armies of Rome marching in grand processions and carrying the sacred eagles through the Eternal City, amidst all the beauty and luxury of the great Roman capital, and we looked forward with considerable anxiety for the day to arrive when, in like manner, we should march through the streets of the capital of the great Western Republic, amid scenes as magnificent, and with step as haughty, as those of the old Roman soldiers in the days of their pride and power.

There was, evidently, a determination on the part of our officers that the Army of the Potomac, which was to be reviewed on the first day, should make as fine an appearance as the army of General Sherman, which was to be reviewed on the following day. Many articles of new clothing were dealt out to the men; white gloves were provided for a large portion of them; we took great pains to have our uniforms, guns and equipments all in excellent order; and when we fell into line that morning, we were as fine a looking body of troops as were ever mustered upon the continent.

It is impossible for me to describe that royal scene; the buildings were all draped in national colours; flags were flying in every direction; the sidewalks were packed with spectators; every square and yard was thronged with the vast multitude; the windows, balconies and roofs of buildings were filled and covered with human beings; the great stands erected were occupied by officers of high rank in both civil and military life; the tiers of seats were filled with thousands of school children, all dressed in white, who hurled hundreds of beautiful bouquets of flowers upon us as we passed; we marched with columns closed to half distance, with thirty men abreast; the artillery posted around Washington thundered forth a grand welcome; the bands all played the national airs; the people cheered until they were hoarse; banners waved and handkerchiefs fluttered. When a regimental colour made its appearance in the procession, that was torn and tattered, it was a signal for the most uproarious applause; and thus, through the day, the nation welcomed its defenders.

We marched through Pennsylvania avenue, and up to the edge of Georgetown, recrossed the Potomac River, and reached our camping ground early in the evening. It had been a very severe day's march, but I imagine it will always be remembered with much pleasure by every soldier who participated in it.

On the following day we had the pleasure of seeing Sherman's veterans as they marched along the same route. The contrast in the two armies was. a most ludicrous one. As I have already stated, our officers had shown much anxiety to have us present a very soldierly appearance as we marched in review, and, much to our disgust, had insisted upon our drawing new caps and wearing white gloves, but Sherman's men went to the other extreme. One would have supposed, as he observed them, that they were making their renowned march through Georgia, instead of marching in review through the streets of Washington.

Such an appearance as they made! There were evidently no attempts made to keep their lines closed up and well-dressed as they advanced, but each man marched to suit his own convenience. Their uniforms were a cross between the regulation blue and the Southern gray. The men were sunburned, while their hair and beards were uncut and uncombed; they were clad in blue, gray, black and brown; huge slouched hats, black and gray, adorned their heads; their boots were covered with the mud they had brought up from Georgia; their guns were of all designs, from the Springfield rifle to a cavalry carbine, which each man carried as he pleased, whether it was at "a shoulder," "a trail," or a "right shoulder shift"; and thus ragged, dirty, and independently demoralised, that great army, whose wonderful campaigns had astonished the world, swept along through the streets of the capital, whose honour they had so bravely defended.

The great chieftain, Sherman, rode at its head, tall, spare, bronzed; grimly he rode, in a plain uniform, as if utterly indifferent to all the honours a grateful country was pouring upon its honoured son. The men chatted, laughed and cheered, just as they pleased, all along the route of their march. Our men enjoyed this all very much, and many of them muttered, "Sherman is the man after all." The two armies encamped near each other for several days, and soon quite a bitter rivalry sprang up between them. Sherman's men regarded the Army of the Potomac with considerable contempt, and thought that, although we understood all about "reviews" and "dress parades," we knew nothing of great campaigns and desperate battles.

On the other hand the Army of the Potomac stoutly contended that if Sherman had encountered the army of General Lee, in Georgia, instead of a small force of "bushwhackers," his army would never have "marched down to the sea." These discussions soon became warm, and resulted in frequent skirmishes between the two armies. But one day some of Sherman's men unexpectedly "caught a tartar." They chanced to come in collision with the remnant of that gallant body of men known as "The Irish Brigade." Sherman's men entered the encampment of this old brigade, and with their usual coolness and audacity, began to stir things up. The brave Irish men were perfectly at home in that kind of work, and a fierce struggle was soon raging. It was a square stand-up and knock-down affair, with the success all upon the side of the Irishmen.

For once the gallant men from the Southwest had found their match; for a time, they fought desperately, but were at last obliged to retreat to their own camp, with bloody faces and in wild disorder, while the wild cheers of the victors would have done credit to "Donnybrook Fair." From that time Sherman's men had more respect for the Army of the Potomac, so that when any of them came to our regiment, and began to boast in an offensive manner of their prowess, we had only to ask them if they had ever heard of the old Irish Brigade, and Sherman stock would depreciate a hundred *per cent* at the bare mention of that name.

Many amusing events occurred during the few weeks we were encamped on Arlington Heights, awaiting our discharge. The forts around Washington were then garrisoned by men who had never been to the front, and who knew but little about war, and of course there was very much red tape among both officers and men. A squad of our boys went over to visit one of these forts, and of course had much curiosity to look it over. It had been constructed upon the crest of a hill, so that, in its front, the ground descended quite rapidly for a long distance.

Some of the boys had climbed up on the side of the fort, to inspect one of the guns that was mounted there, when a little fussy, bandbox sort of an officer, who apparently did not know much about "the stern realities of war," came out of the fort, and commanded them to get down. They evidently did not like the tone of authority in which the officer spoke, and so did not obey him, while he, flaming with anger, drew his sword, and dashed in among them. The men caught him up in their hands, as they would a child, and then looked around to see what innocent punishment they could inflict upon him; fortune favoured them; near where they stood, a huge cask was sitting; it had been emptied of its contents in the sutler's shop, and had been carelessly placed outside the fort; only a portion of one of the heads had been removed; this was just what they wanted, and they hastily squeezed the officer through the small opening, until he was safely caged, then with derisive shouts they placed the cask upon its side, and sent it rolling rapidly down the steep hillside, and scampered away just in time to elude the guard of soldiers who had heard the alarm, and were now rapidly advancing.

I presume the officer was soon liberated from his novel place of confinement, but, if he is living, I will venture to declare that he still remembers the ride he enjoyed in that great cask, as it rolled, bounded and bumped for twenty rods down that memorable hillside.

Many other incidents of a similar character could be narrated, if space permitted, many of which would be condemned by those who know nothing of army life, but they were all done thoughtlessly, and without malice. The boys had been at the front for three years; the war had ended, and the country was saved; as a matter of course, they were all in excellent spirits, and these episodes were but the safety-valves through which escaped the excessive amount of their animal nature.

We visited all the points of interest in and around Washington. We found much to interest us while visiting the late home of the rebel general, Robert E. Lee, a magnificent residence, beautifully situated, commanding a fine view of Washington and the surrounding country. It had been confiscated by the government, by whom it was henceforth to be owned and used. A beautiful national cemetery has been constructed there, that contains the remains of several thousand Union soldiers, who gave their lives to put down the rebellion that the owner of that princely estate helped inaugurate. We also exchanged visits with many of our old friends who were members of other regiments, whom we had not met for years, and talked of old times when we were boys together, and fought once more the battles of the great campaigns through which we had passed; and thus, the days passed rapidly, and the time soon came when we were to be mustered out of the United States service, and return to our homes.

Chapter 19

Homeward Bound

Sunday, June 4th, was a beautiful day; the deep blue sky was not flecked with a single cloud; the sun rose majestically, and rode up the eastern horizon in a chariot of gold. It was ten o'clock in the morning, the church bells in the distant city were summoning the people to assemble for worship, and the invitations thus pouring forth from their brazen throats came booming faintly over the hillside where we were encamped, but we listened not to their music, for other events of greater importance to us were transpiring. The regimental bugle sounded the call to "Fall in"; our regiment was soon in line, and we marched to our parade ground, near the colonel's headquarters, and there we were mustered out of the United States service,—an event for which we had been looking with much interest for three years,— an event for which many of our comrades looked in vain.

On the following day we marched to Washington. I still remember my own feelings as we marched down Arlington Heights for the last time, and the feeling of relief I experienced when we stepped upon the long bridge, and knew that we had bade farewell to the Old Dominion. No more weary tramps for us through the mud of Virginia's sacred soil! We remained in Washington for several hours; the city was filled with troops who were departing for their respective states, and every train of cars was loaded with the bronzed veterans. At six o'clock in the afternoon we left Washington, by rail, for Philadelphia, and reached that city the following day, soon after noon.

The Philadelphians gave us a royal welcome, no other people in the Union exhibiting greater generosity for the soldiers than did the inhabitants of the city of "brotherly love." They never thought to inquire of a soldier, or a regiment of soldiers, as to what state they were from; it was enough for them to know that they were soldiers in the service of the Republic, and all their wants were supplied by a most generous hand. We marched to an elegant refreshment saloon, where a fine dinner was served to us, "without money and without price." We gave three ringing, hearty cheers for our generous hosts, and, amid the cheers of the thousands of spectators, we departed for New York, and reached that city early in the morning of the seventh.

We camped for several hours at the battery, near Castle Garden, and in the afternoon, we marched to embark upon one of the steamers of the Stonington line for Boston. Our line of march for a considerable distance was along Broadway, and I wish I could describe the scene. The people poured from their houses and places of business by thousands; the great thoroughfare was literally packed with humanity; every sidewalk, yard, lawn, square, park, window, balcony and roof was covered and filled with people; the street was filled with teams of every description, all locked in together, and it appeared to us as if they could never escape from such a deadlock; our band played, and the people cheered.

The New Yorkers have a cheer that is peculiar to themselves, about halfway between the yell of a Comanche Indian, and the cheer of a rebel soldier, with the howl of a wolf thrown in for variations. A brawny truckman would mount his dray, and yell hi, hi, hi! a hackman off in another part of the crowd would catch it up, and add to its quantity by giving several yells peculiar to himself, and then ten thousand voices would come in on the chorus—hurrah! hurrah! hurrah! We were never received anywhere with greater enthusiasm than in the city of New York. Early in the morning of June 8th we arrived in Boston. We were to remain there until eleven o'clock, and the boys quickly scattered through the town, and all that was left to remind us of the existence of our regiment, were the guns, and the men detailed to guard the regimental property.

At ten and a half o'clock, Joe Tyler, the bugler, blew the old call, "Dan, Dan, Dan, Butterfield, Butterfield, Butterfield," and our boys came dashing along the streets of Boston, with as much zeal to assemble on the colours, as they had displayed on the fields of the South, when surrounded by the scenes of war. We were quickly on board the cars, and at four o'clock that afternoon we arrived in Portland. We waited for a few moments at the depot, when the train bearing the gallant Seventeenth Maine regiment arrived, and then, forming a procession with them, we marched through the principal streets of the beautiful city. The citizens were out in great numbers, and gave us a hearty welcome.

Early in the evening we stacked our guns in the City Hall, and sat down to a sumptuous repast the ladies had provided for us. That evening was a very enjoyable one, and at its close our regiment marched to its old encampment on Cape Elizabeth. It was past midnight when we reached the gloomy old barracks; we were tired and sleepy, and quickly climbed into the dirty bunks and were soon asleep. We dreamed of peace and home and friends, but to our great surprise, when we awoke in the morning, we were surrounded by reminders of war. The encampment was enclosed by a fence too high for even old soldiers to scale, and the only passages out were by the way of huge gates, and these were guarded by a detachment of the Invalid corps. We were informed that no one could pass out without obtaining passes from the officer who was in command of the camp.

A squad of us quickly went to the headquarters of that important functionary, and asked for passes. He very coolly informed us that he had decided not to give any passes at present, but that if he changed his mind, our regiment would be notified of the fact. Just at that moment the breakfast call was heard, and with much indignation we made our way to the cook-house, where we were to receive our rations. A cup of black coffee, without sugar, and half-a-dozen mouldy "hard-tacks" were handed to each man as his rations for the day. The indications of war that had been visible for the last hour now became more apparent. To receive such usage in our own state, after a three years' service at the front, we had not expected.

The gallant commander of the camp saw that a storm was brewing, and wisely decided to crush it at its birth, and so, in "full regimentals," he soon made his appearance among the men, and ordered them to go to their barracks, and there remain until they received orders from him permitting them to come out. At that, our men were beside themselves with rage. They caught up the contents of the hard-bread box, and opened a brisk fire upon the portly form of the officer, who began to make a rapid retreat across the parade ground, toward his headquarters. It was a ludicrous spectacle, the intrepid major under fire, perhaps for the first time, puffing along on the double-quick, dodging to escape the sheets of hard-bread which his merciless pursuers were throwing at him.

When this officer had made good his escape, we held a council of war, and it was unanimously decided that the safety of the country demanded the destruction of the gates, and a storming party was quickly formed to make the assault. The officers in command of the camp were busily at work, and quickly had a double line of guards from the Invalid corps formed between us and the great gates. While our assaulting column was forming, we could see the lines of guards as they deliberately loaded their guns, and heard their officers command them to open fire upon us if we made any attempt to pass out. The officers were so angry that I think they would have been glad if one-half of our regiment had been shot, but many of those guards were old soldiers, and we did not believe that they would shoot; and when all was ready, with a loud cheer, we threw ourselves upon the lines of guards.

They did not have time to fire, even if they had been disposed to do so, and before they recovered from the panic, the gates were broken into pieces, and heaped upon the parade ground, thus making excellent material for the bonfire we built as a signal of our victory. For this little skirmish our discharge was delayed, so that it was several weeks before we received our pay and took our departure; but a large portion of the regiment refused to remain in camp, and found more comfortable quarters in the city, at their own expense. I recollect that a small squad of us were accustomed to place our feet, three times a day, beneath the mahogany of a first-class hotel, at the rate of twenty-one dollars a week for each individual.

But the day at length arrived when we were to march down to the city, and turn our guns and equipments over to the government. It was the last march of our gallant regiment, but how unlike the regiment that was mustered there, three years before! We had been terribly smitten by the storm of war, and there was but a remnant left to tell the story of our adventures.

In a street near the arsenal we stacked our guns, and upon their bayonets we hung for the last time our equipments. It was a sad moment; we had not realized before how it would seem to separate. Colonel Morrill called for three cheers for the old rifles that had done us such excellent service, and they were given with a will; then three more were given for the colours under which we had fought, and then three more for the "Land we love the best." When these cheers had all been given, the boys voluntarily gave three more for gallant Colonel Merrill, a man whose "Courage was only excelled by his modesty." Then came the last handshakings and goodbyes. Eyes grew moist, cheeks that had been unblanched amid the horrors of the battlefield became pale and sad in these moments of separation. The ties that bound us together were of the most sacred nature; they had been begotten in hardships and baptised in blood.

Men who lived together in the little shelter tent, slept beneath the same blanket, had divided the scanty ration, and "drank from the same canteen," were now to be separated forever. The last goodbye was said, our ranks were broken for the last time, and we turned our faces homeward. For us there were to be no more weary marches, no more midnight alarms. The strife, dangers, and deaths of a soldier's life were no more to follow our footsteps, but in the more peaceful pursuits of civil life we were to move. No matter how humble the positions we were destined to fill, we were always to derive infinite satisfaction from the thought that in the hour of the country's peril we had not been found wanting, but had cheerfully rendered what little service we could, to defend its honour and preserve its life. Thus, we separated; many of us have never met each other since; I presume we never shall in this world; but in that day when the reveille of God shall awaken the slumbering hosts of humanity, may we reform our ranks upon the parade ground of eternity, as the soldiers of the great Prince of Peace.

CHAPTER 20

Hospital Life

Was an experience in itself to the soldiers, an experience that was determined largely by the location of the hospitals, and character of those men who were in charge of them. In the field hospital, of course, the experience was of a stern, harsh, rugged nature; it was a place where sick men received but little care, where wounds were carelessly dressed, and limbs were recklessly amputated. The associations of those places cling to one much like the indistinct memories of a nightmare, and many a maimed hero will shudder at the thought of his experience in the field hospital. But those located at a greater distance from the front, of course afforded many more conveniences and comforts than those of which I have spoken.

In Washington the hospitals were admirably conducted, and the "Sisters of Charity," who kindly acted as nurses, conveyed much sunshine to the suffering soldiers. But the climate was so unfavourable, and the hospitals were usually so over crowded, that there was much sickness and death at the best. The kind Sisters of Charity, who came from their homes of peaceful seclusion, to minister unto the wants of the suffering and dying, deserve much gratitude for their noble work. As they moved among the wounded in their quiet way, they seemed like angels of mercy sent in the providence of God to do His work for suffering humanity.

One of my comrades related his experience to me in something like the following language:

> You remember I was shot in the Battle of the Wilderness; the Johnnies winged me just as our division was falling back, on the afternoon of the first day's fight; the minies shattered the bones of my leg, but with the assistance of my chums I managed to

escape from the Johnnies, and reach the division hospital, about a mile in rear of the line of battle. My wound was not dressed until I reached Lincoln Hospital, in Washington; it was after dark when I arrived, the surgeons held a consultation, and decided that my leg must come off. They put a sponge to my face, and all became indistinct. When I awoke, everything around me looked dim and ghostlike.

At first, I thought I had been mustered out for good, and was becoming acquainted with the other world, but as objects became more distinct, I saw that I was in a long, narrow room, with a row of beds on each side. Then I remembered that I had reached the hospital before I fell asleep.

My injured leg was feeling very singularly, and my ankle, foot and toes were all paining me severely. I raised my head, and to my great surprise found that my leg had disappeared; it had been amputated, and carried away, but was as painful as ever. I groaned, and fell back upon my pillow. At that moment a form that I had not before noticed arose from a seat at the head of my bed, and stooped down over me.

I wish I could describe that person to you; it was a woman dressed in curious black garments, with an odd, white gear upon her head; but I forgot all that when I glanced at her face. I never expect to see the like again until I see the angels; her face was pale, sad, and plain, but there was much tenderness and sympathy expressed in it; her voice was so gentle and pleasant, and the touch of her hand upon my head was so soothing, that somehow, I fancied that I was a little child once more, and that mother was soothing me to sleep.

When I awoke, she had vanished, and I asked the fellow in the bed next to mine, who on earth that woman was in the black dress and white head-gear. He replied, 'One of the Sisters of Charity; they are inmates of some Catholic institution uptown, but volunteer to assist in taking care of the wounded soldiers.' She soon made her appearance again, and for three weeks, day and night, when my life was given up by all the surgeons, that woman stood over me, and by her skilful nursing my life was saved.

I tell you, Gerrish, I have always heard terrible yarns about the Catholics, how wicked they are, but when I think of the treatment there given me, I have about made up my mind that being a Catholic does not prevent one from being a Christian.

I presume many of my old comrades will remember a similar experience, and will agree with the verdict given above.

But of all the hospitals in the country, those in and around Philadelphia, for comfort, convenience and kind treatment bestowed, excelled all others. The citizens, with a measureless generosity, used to bear large quantities of delicacies and luxuries to the patients. The surgeons were nearly all civilians, and many of them belonged to the Society of Friends, kind, generous, noble-hearted men. They were thoroughly honest themselves, and expected everyone else to be the same. The boys used to take many advantages of them, and play many deceptions and practical jokes upon them, but when they discovered it, in the kindness of their hearts, it was generally overlooked.

I well remember the reception that a large squad of us received when we entered the McClellan hospital. This hospital was located between the cities of Philadelphia and Germantown, upon a beautiful plain that stretched its fertile acres for a great distance in every direction. There were beautiful orchards, magnificent dwellings, and grand old shade trees, and in the midst of them was the hospital, a great clump of buildings capable of accommodating two thousand patients. We had been wounded several weeks before, and were now being transferred from the Lincoln Hospital at Washington to this place.

It was a lovely summer's day when the train stopped at the little village of Nicetown, and, with wounds unhealed, we walked across the beautiful field that intervened between the depot and entrance to the hospital. The sentinels stepped back from the gates as we approached them, and we passed through those openings in the high board fence that enclosed all the buildings. We quickly observed that all parts of the hospital were in a very neat, tidy condition. The gravelled walks between the wards, and the little parks in the centre of the grounds, were lined and covered with beautiful plants and flowers that filled the atmosphere with a delicious odour, and in their blushing beauty seemed to give us a hearty though silent welcome.

We were conducted to the reception room, where our wounds were to be examined, and where we would also be assigned to our respective wards, and our squad of two hundred men were soon seated upon the clean benches, awaiting further orders. The doors were soon opened, and a delegation of waiters entered, bearing large kettles of hot coffee, loaves of bread, and delicious lumps of yellow butter; these they quickly distributed among the men. This was a new experience to us, that reminded us of home, and as we ate with ravenous appetites, many eyes in the company were moist with tears of gratitude that we could not find words to express.

Before the repast was finished, the surgeon in charge of the hospital arrived, and quickly introduced himself to us. He was evidently a fine, genial gentleman, and his countenance beamed with benevolence, but his appearance was a most ludicrous one,—a short, stout man, full formed, bald-headed, with small legs that seemed to bend under the weight that was placed upon them; his eyes were screened with green glasses, and all the apology he wore for a government uniform was the green sash worn outside his ill-fitting suit of dark gray; his face was round, and reminded one of the moon at its full. He waddled to the centre of the room, and doubtless recognising the importance of the occasion, bowed, and made what he designed to be a military salute with his hand, and addressed us as follows:—

Well, boys, you are now in my care, and I can tell you that you are in clover, provided, of course, you obey all the rules and regulations of the hospital. This is a government institution, and the discipline, you will find, is very severe.

Here he stopped to wipe the perspiration from his face, but as we saw his countenance beaming with sympathy and kindness, we had no serious fears as to the discipline of which he spoke. He continued:—

I have had thousands of the boys here under my care, and not one of them has ever transgressed a single law; if they had, their punishment would have been most severe, and I shall expect the same behaviour from you.

We were quickly assigned to our wards; I was placed in ward number one; clean clothes were issued to us all; we had nice beds, with fresh, white linen, and everything was as neat and tidy as we could desire. What pleasant weeks those were! Our ward, containing sixty patients, was a long, narrow building; the beds were all single, and placed with the heads next to the walls, leaving a broad aisle some ten feet wide in the centre of the room, between the two rows of beds. At one end of the ward were the bathrooms, and at the other, the dining-hall.

What stories we used to tell, and what practical jokes we used to play upon each other! I fear that at times we used to take advantage of the unsuspecting physicians and attendants, and do many things which their regulations forbade. I have an indistinct recollection that some of the boys used to climb out of the back window, and that there were certain pickets in the fence that could be easily taken from their places, so as to allow us to pass through, and then be replaced so as to conceal our tracks. Many of those little beds were vacant at night, when the authorities supposed that the patients were all in.

Ten passes were issued in the ward each day, and upon these, ten men could pass through the guard, and visit the city; so that at least once a week we were permitted to go free; but many plans were devised to increase our visits, so that scarcely a day passed in which we did not enjoy all the liberty we could desire. Our old friend, the surgeon in charge, visited us each day, always kind and pleasant, but so honest and unsuspecting that we took great delight in playing practical jokes upon him,—jokes that did him no actual harm, but were a source of great amusement to us.

I remember that one day he visited us, and stood in the centre of our ward, and made us a little speech,—making those little speeches was a favourite pastime with him;—he told us that he was then on his way to the gates, where he was to meet a large delegation of ladies who had come down from Harrisburgh to visit the hospital, and that he was to escort them through all the wards, beginning with ours. They were ladies of high social rank, and of course we would all be gentlemen while they were passing through the ward.

The physician was an unmarried man, some forty years of age, and was, this morning, clad in a fine new suit of clothes that he had put on for the occasion; but most unfortunately for him, when he was speaking, he stood with his back near the bed of Jack Wright, a wounded soldier hailing from the state of Delaware. The latter was always ready for fun, and was very skilful in carrying out any plan for mischief that his fertile brain conceived. On that morning, Jack was playing with two small flags; just as the physician entered the ward, he succeeded in fastening them together, in a crossed position, with a large brass pin surmounted with a huge bronzed eagle.

While the physician was speaking, Jack, with great dexterity, pinned these flags upon the back of the officer's coat, just below his waist, who soon hurried from the room, with the national colour surmounted by the American Eagle flying at his coat tails. As the door closed behind him, a volcano of laughter shook the ward.

"What a patriotic old saint he is," roared Jack Wright, and then another burst of laughter rolled along the two rows of beds.

All we feared was, that the flags would be discovered by the victim of our joke before the ladies saw him, but we were soon relieved by the sounds of voices, and approaching footsteps. The door opened, and down along the broad aisle came the physician, followed by a score of ladies. This was the moment and occasion of his life, and I never saw him put on so many airs before; his face was wreathed with smiles; his small, crooked legs did heroic service to support the portly form that bobbed and rolled along between the two rows of beds; the little flags flapped and fluttered as if with pride; and the great eagle seemed as if about to give a scream of national defiance and independence.

We viewed the display, and endeavoured not to laugh. The elderly ladies, who followed next to the physician, evidently supposed that this ornamentation was a badge or insignia of the officer's rank, and so they surveyed, with becoming awe, these emblems of American greatness; but the younger members of the party, who followed after their seniors, saw the mirth sparkling in the eyes and shining upon the countenances of the soldiers, and mistrusted that some joke was being played; and as they peered over the shoulders of those who were in front of them, and saw the patriotic display pinned upon the coat tails of their escort, they could only refrain from laughing outright, by placing their handkerchiefs to their faces. The procession soon after left our ward, and then such fun as we had over the brilliant success of the whole affair!

Early the next morning the physician came to our ward. It was the only time we ever saw that face clouded with a frown. He was in a state of great excitement, and in a trembling voice told us of the outrage that had been perpetrated upon him. There were two questions that he proposed to ask, and we must answer them truthfully. Had any man in that ward had any knowledge of the party who performed the act? If so, he must state what he knew, since to remain silent would be an offense so great as to receive the most severe punishment. Every boy in the room was silent, which of course was positive proof that we knew nothing about it. Had any man in the ward noticed the flags or the eagle, as he passed through with the ladies? Not a man spoke, thus giving the encouraging thought that the flags were not so conspicuous as the victim had feared.

Jack Wright here arose, with deep regret pictured on each feature, and inquired how long he had worn them before he discovered the outrage. The officer informed us that it was after the ladies departed, and he had returned to his own room. In a few well-chosen words,

Jack, the graceless scamp, expressed regret that such an unpleasant event had occurred, and called for all those in the ward, who were in sympathy with his remarks, and who would pledge themselves to endeavour to ascertain who the offender was, to manifest it by standing up. It is needless to add, that every man in the ward stood upon his feet, and that the unsuspecting victim left us, after expressing his gratitude for our sympathy and manly conduct. I do not think that the physician ever learned who the culprit was, and I suppose it was a mean joke for us to play upon one who was so kind to us, but it was such fun to us, that I hope it was excusable.

A gentleman in the city, who was the proprietor of a large eating establishment, had a brother who commanded the Second division of the Sixth corps, and naturally had a great interest in the men who belonged to his brother's command. Their corps badge was a white Roman cross, and whenever this gentleman saw a soldier wearing that badge, he would invite him to eat, and never charge him any price for his refreshments. We soon learned that fact, and white Roman crosses became very plenty, and almost every soldier hailed from that division. Several weeks passed before the gentleman became aware of the fraud being practiced upon him, and for those few weeks his tables were well filled.

But through all those years of war, while thousands of sick and wounded soldiers were being cared for in that beautiful city, the generous, kind hearted, patriotic citizens forgave all the misdemeanours of their guests, and treated them with royal kindness until the war was over. Other Northern cities honoured themselves in showering many acts of kind generosity upon the soldiers in the hospitals, but Philadelphia stands far above them all.

We had much rare sport while in the hospital at Augusta, in our own state, for a few weeks, and I presume that, if any of the farmers on those fertile hills around that city read these pages, they will re member how we used to make raids upon their apples, sweet corn, and beehives; how they used to endeavour to frighten us away by firing guns directly up into the air, and trying to make us believe that the watch dogs were coming to devour us; and how we sat on the fences, ate the best apples, and laughed at their anger. I suppose it was enough to make a man angry, to see us behave in such a manner, and take so much liberty with things we did not own, but anger is not always the most effective weapon of defence.

I well remember that, one pleasant afternoon, four of us went out from the hospital to the hill, some three miles upon the road leading to Winthrop. There was a magnificent orchard in view, and we were determined to have some fruit; we climbed the fence, and entered an orchard which was very near the large farmhouse. We had just begun to pick and test some of the apples, when a pleasant gentleman appeared, and, to our great confusion, told us that those apples were not as good as he wished us to have, that he had gathered his best fruit, and if we would follow him to the shed, he would give us some better ones. We could not refuse the polite invitation, but it was a severe punishment for us to follow him.

While passing through the shed, the call for supper was made, and our host insisted upon our becoming his guests at the supper table. In vain we made a dozen excuses, but with our faces mantled in shame, we sat down at the well loaded table and ate. As we arose to depart, the gentleman informed us that, while we remained in Augusta, he wanted us to come to his home as frequently as we could, and that his fruit and food were at our disposal at all times. It was a relief to us when we passed out of his home. From that hour his property was sacred in our sight, his kind words and generous act had done more to overcome us, than all the angry threats made to us by his neighbours.

In this description of hospital life, I have omitted the scenes of suffering that were daily witnessed; how the brave men, whose bodies and limbs were broken and mangled by shot and shell, heroically endured the long hours of intense agony, until their wounds were healed, or their gallant spirits were mustered out by the grim messenger—death.

Many there suffered with sickness, and death was a daily visitor that came and bore some gallant soul away to its eternal reward. No other nation on the globe ever provided such elaborate hospitals for their soldiers as did ours, and, as we remember how the government has always stood by its defenders, it inspires our hearts with a new determination to always stand by the government.

CHAPTER 21

Pen Pictures of Union Generals

ULYSSES S. GRANT

The form and features of this officer are too familiar to all our American people, to require a description from my pen. That he was the pre-eminent general of the Union Army is a fact now accepted by all. Whoever may be assigned to the second position, the first must always be given to the subject of this sketch. After the beginning of his brilliant career in the Southwest, we had always wished that he might be transferred to Virginia, and be placed in command of the Army of the Potomac; but he did not arrive until after we had lost much of our boyish enthusiasm for our commanders, and consequently he was never received, when riding along the lines, with that overwhelming amount of cheering that always greeted General McClellan.

General Grant was a fighter, and took much more pleasure in drilling his men to shoot, than he did in teaching them to cheer. His military creed was brief and rigorous; it was made up of bullets, blows and battles, and he never displayed a great taste for reviews, parades and receptions. There was nothing dashing in his appearance, but when the "old man" rode out among us, we always gave him a respectable amount of cheering. We always had great confidence in his ability, and never doubted that he would crush the army of General Lee.

Our losses were enormous while he was in command, but we derived much satisfaction from the thought that, at last, the Army of the Potomac had a commander who would not retreat at the close of every battle, and that the Confederacy was reeling under the heavy blows that were falling from his mailed hand. In his personal appearance he was very unassuming. Anyone gazing at the plain looking man, clad in blue pants and blouse, black slouched hat, and heavy top boots well spattered with mud, would hardly suppose that he was the distinguished Lieutenant-General of the Union Armies. His face was unshaved, and was usually covered with a bristling, clipped beard of a reddish colour, about one inch in length. The only insignia of rank that he wore were the small glittering stars upon his shoulders, while there were many lieutenants in the army who sported much more gold lace than he.

He always looked the same, in camp, on the march, or in the battle, where he was carrying responsibilities that would have crushed a giant. In all the emergencies that arose around him, he was the same cool, sagacious, grim, silent commander. He met the most skilful general of the Confederacy, Robert E. Lee, for the first time, in the Wilderness, where he grasped the rebellion by the throat, and never relinquished his hold, until treason gasped in death. No man was ever more cruelly slandered arid criticised than was General Grant, from the opening of the Wilderness campaign, unto its close.

But through that storm of censure, which would have swept a less resolute man from such a prominent position, General Grant remained firm, and, through those long, bitter months, the most perilous that this country ever saw, his massive brain, rugged will and powerful arm were the bulwarks that preserved our national life from the tides of deathly influence that were poured in upon it by the rebels and their traitorous sympathizers.

But when the Southern Confederacy lay in broken fragments at the feet of the gallant army that Grant had led on to such glorious conquests, for a brief time all parties forgot their prejudices, and rendered unto this hero the honour he so justly deserved. Many years have passed since then, but the survivors of those battles love to think of their old commander, and the great work he did in preserving the nation's life. It has been quite fashionable, for a few years, for certain classes of politicians to declare that the only way to save the country from certain calamities that threaten it, is to abuse the character and motives of General Grant.

The boys in blue have not taken an active part in such discussions, but as they have listened to those men who are so warlike in times of peace, but who were so peaceful in the days of war, they can but think that, if it had not been for the "old man" whom they now abuse, perhaps we should now have no country to save.

So then, in the midst of all this criticism, let us remember that the services rendered by this distinguished officer in a single campaign did more to maintain the institutions of our country than all the so-called brilliant public services rendered to it by the persons and press who have come in collision with him.

George G. Meade.

Of all the commanders of the Army of the Potomac, General George G. Meade was the most successful, and of that small group of men who stand forth as the pre-eminent leaders of the Union Armies, no one deserves a warmer place in the affections of the American people than he. His bravery and ability have been universally acknowledged and appreciated, and it has remained for General Doubleday, nearly twenty years after the close of the war, and ten years after the death of his old commander, to win the unenviable notoriety of making grave charges of incompetency against him, charges which were made in February, 1864, but which then carried no weight, because the government, to whom they were made, was familiar with the facts, and also acquainted with the two officers.

The book written by General Doubleday, and just issued from the press of Charles Scribner's Sons, comes to us as a history of the Chancellorsville and Gettysburgh campaign. History should be a calm, impartial statement of facts, and can only properly be written by an unprejudiced author. Now the value of General Doubleday's production as an impartial statement of facts, may be estimated from certain testimony that he gave before the congressional committee on the conduct of the war, in February, 1864. Being asked why, in his opinion, he had been relieved of his command on the first day of July, and why General Hancock was ordered by General Meade to assume command of the troops of General Howard, who was Hancock's superior officer in point of rank, General Doubleday answered as follows:

> I think that General Meade thought a couple of scapegoats necessary, in case the next day's battle turned out unfavourably. General Meade is in the habit of violating the organic law of the army, to place his own personal friends in power. No man who is an anti-slavery man, or an anti-McClellan man, can expect decent treatment in the army as it is now constituted.

A man who would make such bitter and ground less charges in 1864, is hardly the one to select as the impartial historian of the same events, twenty years later.

As to General Doubleday's charge that General Meade designed to retreat from Gettysburgh at the close of the first day's battle, let us listen for a moment to the testimony of the dead,—the words of our old commander, as spoken under oath before the above-named committee, in February, 1864:

> I utterly deny, under the full solemnity and sanctity of my oath, and in the firm conviction that the day will come when the secrets of all men shall be made known; I utterly deny ever having intended or thought for one instant to withdraw that army, unless the military contingencies which the future should develop during the course of the day might render it a matter of necessity that the army should be withdrawn. I base this denial, not only upon my own assertion and my own veracity, but I shall also show to the committee from documentary evidence, the dispatches and orders issued by me at different periods during that day, that, if I did intend any such operation, I was at the same time doing things totally inconsistent with any such intention.
>
> I refer you to General Hunt, chief of artillery, and who had artillery occupying a space from four to five miles, drawn out on the road, and who, if I had intended to have withdrawn the army, should have been told to get his trains out of the way, the very first thing, because the troops could not move until the artillery moved. I would also ask you to call upon General Ingalls, my chief quartermaster, who had charge of the trains; also, General Warren, my chief engineer, who will tell you that he was with me the whole of that day, in constant intercourse and communication with me, and that instead of intending to withdraw my army, I was talking about other matters.

I think that, with these scraps of history before them, the public will not be at a loss to decide as to which testimony is the most reliable, and will also place a proper estimate upon the book of General Doubleday. But if these were not in existence—fortunately for the memory of General Meade, and unfortunately for General Doubleday, the selfish, egotistic I stands forth so prominently in the work referred to, that it will not endanger the reputation of General Meade, or preserve that of his critic.

We remember General Meade as a tall, spare man, with broad, stooping shoulders, high forehead, and prominent features. He had not the dashing appearance of many other generals, but when we saw that tall, bowed form, enveloped in a great brown over coat, riding to the front, we always felt safe. He was conservative and moderate, cool and sagacious, patient and brave. On the peninsula, at Antietam, Fredericksburgh and Chancellorsville, he displayed such qualities that the Government was justified in giving him command of its principal army, in the most critical hour of the civil war. That the honour of the victory at Gettysburgh is not largely due to him, the country will never believe; and the fact that he retained the command of that army through the succeeding campaigns, possessing to the fullest extent the confidence of General Grant, is proof enough of his ability as a commanding officer.

GEORGE B. McCLELLAN

Was the most popular commander in the armies of the United States. Bonaparte was never a greater favourite in the armies of France than was General McClellan in the Army of the Potomac. In appearance, at least, "he was every inch a soldier." He possessed a fine form, was always clad in a rich, neat uniform of dark blue, was a magnificent horseman, and was as fine a looking officer as the Union Armies ever saw. No Union general has been more severely criticised than he; many have charged him with cowardice, and others with treason; both classes display much more prejudice than good sense in their accusations. That he was neither a coward or a traitor does not need to be argued for a single moment. If we desire to find causes for his disastrous failures while in command of the Army of the Potomac, we can easily trace them to other causes than these.

First. It cannot be denied that his superiors at Washington, by the skilful and excessive use of "red tape," successfully paralyzed many of the movements he undertook to make. The victories of the past century have been won by commanding generals in the field, not by those cooped up within the walls of a war department scores of miles from the fields of battle.

Second. For the first two years the civil war on the Union side was largely an experiment; we were learning how to fight, and the information thus gained, the wisdom thus dearly earned, had much to do in moulding the successes of the last two years of the war.

Third. The most ardent admirers of General McClellan cannot deny the fact that he lacked many elements of character essential to success, even under the most favourable circumstances. His bravery and loyalty are not to be questioned for a moment; his skill as an organiser and as a civil engineer is admitted; but that he was conservative, fault-finding, un decided, hesitating, and fatally slow, must also be confessed. He lacked the determined zeal and resist less energy that a great leader must always possess.

The great mistake of his life—the one his old soldiers can never forget—was that, when they were fighting in the trenches to preserve the life of the nation, he turned his back upon them, by accepting the presidential nomination of a party whose platform declared the war a failure. But, notwithstanding that, so long as there are survivors of the old Army of the Potomac, so long will Little Mac be kindly remembered.

Ambrose E. Burnside

Possessed certain elements of character that have made him the target, for many years, of those who see no beauty in such qualifications. He was a very modest, unassuming man,—one who never pressed his own interests or boasted of a superior greatness. Promotion came to him unsought, and at times, if his own preferences had been followed, honours would not have been accepted. He always assumed the disgrace of his own failures. When, after consultation with his brother officers, a movement was made which ended in a disastrous defeat, he did not attempt to make a scapegoat of some subordinate officer, but had the rare manliness to declare: "I alone am responsible for the failure."

As an individual, he was noble, generous, brave and beloved. As a corps commander, he was effective and successful. At Antietam it was the desperate charge of his corps at the Stone Bridge, that turned the tide of battle, and thrilled the nation with the bravery of our troops. As a commander of the army, he was not alone responsible for the disastrous failure. Fredericksburgh came immediately after Antietam. The assault made upon St. Mary's Heights, at the former, was not more desperate than that made across the Stone Bridge, at the latter; it was simply on a larger scale.

The success of either must be decided by the fortunes of war. One was a brilliant success, the other a sorrowful defeat. The country that honoured him for the desperate chances taken at Antietam, must not crucify him for taking the same chances at Fredericksburgh. From a private's point of observation, I remember him as a noble, dignified officer, brave, kind, and sagacious, but a victim to a threefold power that would crush any man.

First. He was promoted, against his own wishes, to a position he knew he was not capable of filling.

Second. Circumstances which he could not control seemed to be all combined against him.

Third. His subordinate officers refused to give him their warm, cordial support, without which no commander can hope to succeed.

The rank and file of the army knew him well, and his form was familiar to every common soldier. We knew of his kindness, his generous nature, his bravery, and his ability. The survivors of that old army will denounce any attempt to assassinate the memory of their beloved commander, since his eloquent voice can no longer speak in his own defence.

Joseph Hooker.

At the mention of this name we seem to see the old veteran once more,—not the helpless paralytic that he was the last few years of his life, made such by the injuries received at Chancellorsville,—not the vain, shallow, boastful man in a gilt uniform that his critics would make us believe,—but the brave, dashing, brilliant leader, one who could plan as wisely and battle as bravely as the most eminent of those who criticise him. Tall, erect, commanding in appearance, he was one of the most brilliant commanders upon the Potomac. As a subordinate officer he was perhaps proud, ambitious, and disposed to have his own way; but all that was overshadowed by his skilful management of troops, and by his heroic bravery.

As a commander of the Army of the Potomac, he was its most skilful organiser, and its most rigid disciplinarian. All admit that the Battle of Chancellorsville was as wisely planned as any battle of the war; but it ended in defeat, and there is a disposition on the part of some to place the responsibility of that defeat upon General Hooker. It is a very easy task to sit in an elegantly furnished room, fight battles, and decide the fortunes of war, twenty years after the struggle has ceased. A few strokes of a gifted but prejudiced pen measures the commanding general's ability, and decides the place he must fill in history.

I have no fault to find with those who are striving to give the American people an impartial history of the civil war, even though it censures the officers we learned to love. But of the critic who condemns General Hooker for not bringing all his troops into action before he retreated across the river, I only ask, as he writes his lines of condemnation, to remember that Hooker was a wounded and disabled soldier hours before that retreat was made. He sustained injuries from that cannon-shot at the Chancellorsville House, from which he never recovered, and therefore, for confusion, delay, and subsequent mismanagement, if there was any, he was not responsible. He retained the command for hours after the injury was received, but it was not Joe Hooker, with his keen sagacity and unerring skill, but a stunned, bewildered and disabled man.

In relation to the Battle of Chancellorsville, the causes of our defeat, Hooker's subsequent resignation, and the criticisms upon his conduct, the Congressional committee upon the conduct of the war, of which Hon. B. F. Wade of Ohio was chairman, after carefully reviewing all the testimony in the case, utter the following significant words:

> It would appear that there were three, perhaps four, reasons which contributed to render this campaign unsuccessful, after it had been so successfully begun, *viz.*:—the stampede of the Eleventh corps, the injury received by General Hooker at the Chancellorsville House, the failure of General Sedgwick to carry out the orders he had received from the commanding general, and the entire failure of General Stoneman to carry out his part of the programme.
>
> Your committee would observe that they consider it to have been extremely unfortunate that General Hooker was not permitted to have the use of such troops as he deemed necessary to carry out his plans for destroying the rebel army. That these troops were disposable, is shown from the fact that his successor was immediately authorised to use them. Nor can the committee doubt that, had General Hooker been clothed with the power immediately conferred upon his successor, the result of the campaign might have been far more decisive than it was.

As to the charges of his being intoxicated on the battlefield, the following items from the same report are interesting reading:

> Your committee have examined such officers, as from their position and opportunities would be presumed to have the most accurate knowledge upon the subject, and all, without exception, have testified that the charge was entirely unfounded. This examination would not have been pressed further, but for one fact. There had appeared, in the public press of England, and also in leading journals in this country, what purported to be a statement of some remarks made by Rev. Henry Ward Beecher,

on July 5, 1863, at a breakfast given by the National Temperance League in England. The *New York Independent* copied that statement from an English paper, the *Alliance*, with editorial comments. The extract is as follows:

> If it were fit, he (Mr. Beecher) could name several great misfortunes which had befallen the North on the field, owing entirely to the drunkenness of officers. The Battle of Chancellorsville was lost from this cause; but he heard it from almost direct authority, that the general thus implicated, knowing his weakness, had been previously abstaining, but that having received a severe contusion, he had been prescribed whisky medicinally, and it was taking it for that purpose, that the old appetite had been revived, and overcame him.

The *Independent* commented as follows:

> Mr. Beecher stated this as a private communication, but the case of intemperance referred to is no secret here. That General Hooker was drunk, and thereby lost the Battle of Chancellorsville, has been published wherever the English language is read. And it is due to the inculpated general that the explanation made by Mr. Beecher should be made known.

On the eighteenth of March, 1864, the chairman of the committee was instructed to address a communication to Mr. Beecher, asking him for his authority for the grave charges thus made, and the names of reliable witnesses to substantiate the same. On the fourth of April following, no answer having been received from Mr. Beecher, a second communication of the same character was addressed to him, and on the sixth of the same month Mr. Beecher forwarded the committee this somewhat remarkable answer:

> Brooklyn, April 6, 1864.
> Dear Sir: I did not make any public remarks about General Hooker, while in England. At a temperance breakfast strictly confidential, and pledged to make no report of proceedings, I alluded to Hooker's condition. My remarks were published in violation of confidence. As to my evidence, it was such as to produce moral conviction, but not to establish the fact legally, that during the last part of the Battle of Chancellorsville, Hooker was under the influence of liquor. I do not feel

at liberty to mention my informant, until I see him and get his permission.

I am very truly yours,

H. W. Beecher.

I think that the committee, after receiving this statement as the only excuse or proof for uttering and printing such baseless charges, commented in a very mild manner, when they say:

> Your committee regret to state that, although Mr. Beecher's attention was twice called to the subject, and he was explicitly asked each time to give his authority, with the names of reliable witnesses to substantiate the charge he had circulated, he has made no reply to them but the one above quoted.

In closing this sketch, I would say to the literary vultures who are endeavouring to destroy the character and fame of the gallant dead, the old soldiers around you are not disinterested spectators of events now transpiring, and I know they will join with me in saying, sleep on, brave old commander! your fame was recorded with the point of your own good sword, and it will require more than the false slanders of your foes, or the pen of a prejudiced critic and historian to tarnish it.

OLIVER O. HOWARD

No officer in the United States Army has been more severely censured than General Howard. His courage, ability and character have all been repeatedly assailed. Many investigations have been held with reference to the charges made against him, but, thus far, the only fact that has been proved against him is, "That he is a Christian." The readers of the last volume of the *Campaigns of the Civil War*, written by General Doubleday, and just issued from the press of Charles Scribner's Sons, will not be surprised to find the religious element in General Howard's character sneered at wherever it can be done. It may not be for me to say whether all this abuse arises because the United States Army is not the proper place for a Christian gentleman, or whether the moral tastes of his accusers render them incapable of appreciating the virtues of a Christian character.

But as to the first, I do not believe that the English Army was ever disgraced by the prayerful devotion of the saintly Havelock, and I do not think the United States Army will ever be disgraced by such Christian character as that of General Howard. But leaving him to reply to his own critics, I must only speak of him as he was seen by a private soldier,—a quiet, unassuming, and yet a noble and dignified officer, having a genial countenance, pale, but very expressive, an eye that could flash as brightly as the gleam of battle, or beam with the tenderness of a woman.

The empty sleeve pinned to his shoulder tells of devotion and sufferings for his country's life. When we looked at him, it always reminded us of friends at home. As an individual he was kind, generous and sympathetic; as an officer he was beloved by his men, was cool, skilful and successful. Except by some of the German troops in the Eleventh corps, his skill and ability was never doubted. He was a man among men. I once sat on the picket line, at the Rappahannock, with a large squad of soldiers who were members of different regiments, and hailed from different states, while General Howard was being discussed. Some of the soldiers, with much profanity, were abusing him. After many remarks had been made, one man, a tall, muscular fellow, hailing from Ohio, spoke:

> Boys, I will tell you what I know of General Howard. Just before Chancellorsville, my only brother, a mere boy, was sick and dying; we were together in a little tent; Jimmy knew that he must soon be mustered out. One dark, stormy night, I sat down by his side, and took hold of his thin hands, while he talked of home; he sent little messages of love to the old folks and the girls, gave me some good advice, but I saw he was uneasy like; something seemed to trouble him.
>
> After a while he told me he was sort of uneasy about the future; he kind of thought there was to be a general inspection over there, and he was not ready for it; he wanted someone to pray for him. I never took much stock in those things, but he looked so pitiful like, I made up my mind that I would find someone to help the poor fellow to prepare for the future, and so through the rain and mud I ran; it was awful dark, but I soon found the chaplain's tent, but he was sick, and not able to go out. What to do I didn't know; I never could go back to the poor boy alone. I happened to think of Howard; I had heard the officers laugh about his prayers; and so, without stopping to think what I was doing, I ran across the field, half a mile, to his headquarters. The guard had been removed, and I knocked at the door of the general's tent. When he came, I blurted out my errand. He caught up his hat, and hurried with me to my tent. Poor Jimmy

was very low, and breathing hard, but he knew me; and when I told him who the general was, his pale cheeks flushed with joy. Howard got down by the poor boy's side, and how he prayed! My own eyes were so dim that I could not see much, for a few moments, when I did look, Jimmy had passed away. He had one hand on the general's shoulder, and there was a sweet smile on his face. Howard spoke lots of encouraging words to me, before he left, and when Jimmy was buried, he came down to the grave, spoke a few words of sympathy, and kindly shook my hand. Now, boys, you had better change the subject.

It is needless for me to write that there was no more abuse of General Howard on that picket post.

John Sedgwick.

No corps commander in the Army of the Potomac was more dearly beloved by his men than the subject of this sketch, who was known among them as "Uncle John." His history is an unbroken record of faithful and gallant service rendered to the government. He was a man that looked to be fifty years old, broad-shouldered, heavy-framed, with a full, brown, tangled beard. When in camp he always manifested much interest in his men, and was careful to do all in his power to add to their convenience and comfort. He was a plain, common-sense, practical man, who despised all appearance of "red tape."

When on the march, had it not been for his military surroundings, he would have been mistaken for a rough backwoodsman, wearing, as he did, an old slouched black hat, a loose-fitting blouse, blue pants, a woollen shirt of a reddish colour, muddy boots, and having a general appearance of untidiness that you would hardly expect to see in a corps commander. And yet under his kind training and skilful leadership, the gallant Sixth corps reached a degree of discipline that made it one of the most brilliant corps of the whole army. He was a kind, brave, generous officer. There was little danger of any disaster to our arms, when General Sedgwick, with the Sixth corps, was at the front. The men all loved him, and had the fullest confidence in his ability. When he rode along the lines, they always cheered until he passed from their view. His death at Spotsylvania was a national calamity, and cast a deep gloom over the whole army.

Winfield S. Hancock.

Two years have passed since our last presidential campaign made this name so familiar to the American people. We will not speak of him as a candidate for the presidency of the United States, but as the clean cut, neatly clad, soldierly commander of the Second army corps. It does no injustice to other generals to say that no corps commander in the army was regarded by his men as the equal of W. S. Hancock. His troops were always prepared for a fight, and he usually fought to win. His military history was brilliant and successful. No man rendered more faithful service than he, and if he had been elected president of the United States, he would undoubtedly have honoured the country that had thus honoured him. In the days of the civil war, he was tall and erect,—a soldier in every respect. His men had such confidence in him that they would follow him wherever he led the way.

The survivors of his old corps will bear testimony, with me, that whoever followed Hancock through a battle would at least encounter all the dangers that the battle afforded. Many harsh and unjust things have been said about him, when our blood was stirred with passions, but so long as the nation remembers Gettysburgh as the turning-point of the war, we must not forget that, to General Hancock, as much as to any other man, are we indebted for that great victory. Howard and Hancock were the men who selected the position for our lines of battle,—a position saved to our country by the bravery and blood of the gallant Reynolds with his First corps.

We must also remember that the brilliant and successful charge of Hancock, at Spotsylvania, was the brightest page in all that campaign from the Rapidan to the James. All the old soldiers, and especially those of the Second corps, earnestly hope that the regular army may long bear on its rolls the honoured name of General W. S. Hancock.

Gouverneur K. Warren.

This skilful engineer, brilliant soldier, and successful general was in command of the Fifth corps, from the opening of the Wilderness campaign, until the first of the following April. Previous to that he had been in command of the Second corps, and also chief engineer of the Army of the Potomac. He was a slight-built man, thin, wiry, and nervous, but possessing great powers of endurance; he had a dark, swarthy complexion, straight black hair, Grecian features, and large expressive eyes that could beam in tenderness or flash with the wild light of conflict. His uniform of dark blue neatly fitted his fine form. In company with any party of men, he would always be selected as a person of superior ability. He was quiet and retiring in his manner, but his men all loved him, and had great faith in his ability.

He was reckless and daring to a fault, sparing himself neither exposure or fatigue. No sacrifice was too great for him to make, no danger too great for him to face, if it would only bring success to the Union cause. He was a successful general, and won a reputation as a soldier of which any man might be proud. We always regarded the act of General Sheridan in removing him from the command of our corps, at the Battle of Five Forks, as a serious mistake, and one that should have been righted long before this date. Warren had encountered dangers, and had fought bravely and with success, through the war. Five Forks was the decisive battle that closed it.

Warren had done all that a man could do in getting his corps into the battle. We had fought like heroes, and had captured the enemy that had driven Sheridan and his cavalry from the field. Sheridan, brave, rash, impulsive, excited as a madman by the bloody victory we had gained, received an impression that Warren had not done enough, and ordered General Griffin to relieve him of his command upon the field of victory, in the midst of the thousands of prisoners he had captured. Before Griffin could reach the side of General Warren, to assume the command, Warren had stormed the last position of the foe, leading a column of troops across an open field, under a deadly fire, with his corps flag in his hand,—a feat of reckless and gallant bravery which would have honoured General Sheridan himself.

We can forgive Sheridan for the injustice of an act performed in a moment of excitement, but to persist in it for seventeen long years, preferring to crush a brother officer rather than acknowledge an error he had committed, is not an honourable course for a brave man to pursue. The old Fifth corps will stand by their commander, and whether he receives tardy justice or not, he has the sympathy and love of the men he once led to battle.

John F. Reynolds

Was a tall, thin, fine looking officer, who, for many months, was in command of the First corps. He possessed the confidence of all who knew him. Wise in council, skilful in the execution of a movement, fearless as a lion in battle, he was a leader whom the men loved to follow to battle. The government had great confidence in him, and had it not been for his untimely death, he would undoubtedly have been promoted to a larger field of usefulness. He was a native of Pennsylvania, and was born in 1820, not far from the spot where he fell in death, in 1863.

In his zeal to hurl the enemy from the soil of his native state, he led his men against fearful odds, and fell in the advanced lines, at an early hour on the first day of the great Battle of Gettysburgh. His death was deeply mourned by the whole army; and the State, whose soil was moistened with his life's blood, points with much pride to the military record of this gallant son. A beautiful monument has been erected to his memory, in the National Cemetery at Gettysburgh.

Daniel E. Sickles

The form of this officer was at one time familiar in the Army of the Potomac. He was a short, thick-set man, of heavy build, broad shoulders, large head, and full, round face, the moustache and goatee that he usually wore giving him a military appearance. He was a brave officer, whose courage no one disputed, but we thought he lacked in judgment, and that the disposition of his troops when preparing for battle was not always fortunate. At Chancellorsville and Gettysburgh he greatly distinguished himself, the Third corps doing grand service on both occasions. At the last-named battle, he lost a leg, and so the army lost one of its most fearless leaders. The last time I saw him was in the autumn of 1863; he was then walking with crutches, but received a most enthusiastic reception from the hundreds of old soldiers who gathered around him.

Charles Griffin

Was the popular and brilliant commander of the First division of the Fifth corps, until the removal of General Warren, when he assumed command of the corps. No officer in the army could have been more dearly beloved by his men than was General Griffin. At one time he was absent from us for several weeks, on account of sickness; on his return, when he met his old division, the men rushed from the ranks, and pressed around him by hundreds, and actually removed him from his horse and carried him for several rods upon their shoulders. With tearful eyes he exclaimed, "Boys, I will never leave you again."

He was a tall, slim, well-built man, and rode very erect, with his head well thrown back, and with his long, sharp chin well advanced to the front. His uniform was always neat and well fitted to his form; he usually wore a soldier's cap upon his head; his face was shaved smooth, while his lip was adorned with a heavy moustache. General Griffin was one of the finest looking officers in the army. Always kind, pleasant and cheerful, his presence even in defeat always seemed like a sunbeam.

He was as fearless as a tiger, and would lead his division anywhere. He had formerly been an artillery officer, and consequently had great faith in that branch of the service, and would run his batteries out anywhere on the skirmish lines, if by so doing he could get the enemy under fire. When "Old Griff" was in command, we did not care much where we were ordered to go. The last time that we ever saw him, was when our regiment was marching from Arlington Heights to Washington, where we were to take the cars for Maine; we met him as he was riding from the city, and gave him three rousing cheers, he taking off his hat and sitting with uncovered head until we had passed. We all mourned when his death was announced, several years after the close of the war. He died of yellow fever, in Texas. There were but few officers in the Union Army more worthy of praise than was General Charles Griffin.

Joshua L. Chamberlain

This officer, so intimately connected with our regiment and State, requires no introduction to the people of Maine. We saw much of him during the three years we were in the army, but we always saw him the same kind-hearted gentleman that he had been before he entered the service. Rapid promotions and the many honours he received did not change him in the least degree. A brave, brilliant, dashing officer, one whom we were always proud to point out as a soldier from Maine. There were but few officers who displayed greater bravery, faced more dangers, and shed their blood on more battlefields than did General J. L. Chamberlain. His history is as brilliant as that of any officer who entered the army from New England. Tall, slim, erect, he was an officer who, when once seen, was always remembered.

But this little group of Union officers, whose once familiar features are here so imperfectly sketched, would be incomplete, if I did not add two other generals, who by their brilliant daring became the favourites of the army and the nation. The first one is

Phillip H. Sheridan

Who was the great cavalry commander,—brave, brilliant, energetic, competent, desperate. It seemed that all the necessary elements of success were combined in this wonderful man. In a previous chapter I attempted to describe his personal appearance. He always fought to win, and on the battlefield seemed transformed to a demon, whose only demand was for more blood. He bore a charmed life, riding fearlessly into the thickest of the conflict, where his men were falling by hundreds. When in pursuit of a retreating foe he was as remorseless as fate itself, always pressing them hard. On those great raids through the enemy's country, he sent terror to the heart of the foe, by the enormous quantities of property he destroyed, so that I think that the last Yankee soldier to be forgiven by the Southern chivalry for the imagined wrongs they suffered from our hands, will, undoubtedly, be Phil. Sheridan.

He possessed a wonderful magnetic influence over his men, and they would undertake any enterprise if he ordered it. I once heard a veteran officer remark, as he saw them follow Sheridan in one of those desperate charges upon the enemy's lines, "Those fellows would follow Sheridan if he rode through the gates of hell." His exploit at Cedar Creek, where he arrived from Winchester, reorganising his army on the field of battle, and changing a disastrous defeat to a decisive victory, stands without a parallel in the military campaigns of the past century. Long may he live and enjoy the fruits of his bravery!

George A. Custer

How vividly we all remember that slim, boyish figure, the long flowing locks of golden hair, and the blue uniform profusely decorated with gold lace! He was a mere youth, having graduated at West Point in 1861, when twenty-one years old. What a brave fellow he was, and how fearlessly he would lead his cavalry upon the enemy! He was reckless to a fault, and yet he passed through all those baptisms of fire unharmed. Idolised by his men, his character and history are as romantic as romance itself. How strange that a man should pass through all those dangers, only to die, as he did, far out upon the Western frontier!

I shall never forget how heavy my heart was, when I read the telegrams that our gallant Custer had fallen on that memorable battlefield far out on the Rose Bud River. He did not die amid the booming artillery and wild cheers of his men,—sounds with which he was once so familiar,—but amid the wild savage whoops of his uncivilised foes, as his brave men went down in bloody death. The name of Custer will always be an inspiration in the army, and his successful career will be a worthy example for young soldiers to imitate.

Chapter 22

A Review

It is fitting that one chapter in this volume should be devoted to a review of the record that our soldiers made through those eventful years of the war. This is of special importance, as we are living in an age that is concentrating its thoughts and energies in the present and the future, and is too rapidly for getting the events of the past, while, consequently, the rising generation is but very imperfectly informed as to the great events of the civil war, of the situation in which the government was placed at its outbreak, and the sacrifices that were made to preserve its life.

The Nation's Peril

Twenty-one years have passed, (as at 1882), since the country was aroused from the security of peace, to face the stern realities of war. It is a most difficult task to describe the perilous situation of the country at that time. Our gallant little army was divided into fragments, and stationed in the United States forts within the southern states, where they could be easily overpowered by the Confederate forces; our arms and munitions of war were also deposited within the southern territory, where they would easily become the prize of the traitors; our navy was scattered on distant seas; there was no money in our treasury, and we had little credit at home or abroad. It was a most perilous hour in the history of the country, when Abraham Lincoln, America's foremost son, stepped from his western home, and placed his honest hand upon the helm of our ship of state.

We had the utmost confidence in his integrity, but was it not then too late to prevent the destruction of the Republic? A number of states had already seceded; great armies had been marshalled; a hostile Confederacy had been organised; treason walked in defiance along the streets of Washington, and uttered its voice fearlessly upon the floors of Congress, and loyal men hardly dared to hope; the storm that had been gathering for a long period of years had burst upon us in all its fury; the clouds came swirling down so thickly that not one gleam of light fell athwart the pathway of the nation. It was under these circumstances that the first call of our government was made for troops to defend the nation's life. How like a keen bugle's blast the call of our President rang through the North, asking for seventy-five thousand men to volunteer as soldiers to maintain the laws of the government! How would the people respond? It was a perilous experiment to ask men to volunteer under such circumstances, for the rebels were all prepared for war, and from a human standpoint the odds were all against the North.

Jefferson Davis and his cabinet were in session at the city of Montgomery, Alabama, when the information reached them that President Lincoln had called for seventy-five thousand volunteers. These arch traitors laughed in derision at the idea of seventy-five thousand men being found in the great cowardly North, who would volunteer to face the gallant sons of the rebellious South upon the field of battle. Many of the empires across the sea looked on with smiles, and prophesied that the boasted republic on the western continent had come to the hour of its death. But there were many loyal men in the North who had been waiting with anxious hearts to hear the first call for help, and who, when the sound of that call fell upon their ears, sprang to arms. Their answer to the call rang out distinctly from the mad, tumbling waters of the great Penobscot, to the rocky ramparts of the nation beyond the western plains. That answer was: "THE UNION, IT MUST AND SHALL BE PRESERVED."

THE SOLDIERS' SACRIFICES.

Nearly a generation has passed away since the breaking out of the war, and many of those now living know but little of the soldiers' sacrifices. These should not be forgotten; the nation cannot afford to have them blotted out, and for that reason I shall endeavour to enumerate a few of them. They sacrificed for a time all the domestic relations of life. This may appear to some as a very small sacrifice to make. But ask that man who, on that eventful morning, kissed his wife goodbye, and pressed his little child to his breast for the last time, as he shouldered his knapsack and marched away, or ask the smooth faced lad who went forth to battle, with his mother's kiss damp upon his brow, and they will tell you of a fearful experience that raged within their hearts. This was one of the greatest sacrifices that men can be called upon to make for the country, and none but patriotic men can make it. They sacrificed the conveniences and comforts of home for the inconveniences and sufferings of the field. No army was ever marshalled upon the globe, that left such homes of comfort and luxury as did the Union Army, in the war of the rebellion.

They exchanged the mansion of comfort for the miserable shelter tent; the soft, clean bed for a soldier's blanket spread upon the hard ground; good, wholesome food for the scanty rations of a soldier; lives of ease and healthy labour for the exhaustion and weariness of forced marches; they threw aside for a period of years the personal liberty so dear to every American citizen, and took upon themselves a species of slavery, to be commanded by other men who were frequently their inferiors in all save military rank; they exchanged a life of comparative safety for one impregnated with a thousand dangers; they stepped forth from the peaceful circles of safety, within which so many remained, and boldly stood forth in the way where death passed by, and there bravely battled for the principles of liberty and justice. All these sacrifices were made for the salvation of the Republic.

Their Sufferings

These men suffered without complaint. What a lesson may be learned from their example! We often hear men murmur about the burdens they bear for the government; complain bitterly about the war taxes that they are obliged to pay,—a tax levied upon the property which they accumulated when the country was passing through the throes of war. I wonder if those men ever stop and think how much their soldiers suffered, sleeping on the hard, frozen ground, the cold winds sweeping over them, with nothing but their thin, ragged clothing to protect them from the elements, marching barefooted over the rough roads where their tracks were stained with blood that flowed from their lacerated feet, weary and exhausted, famishing with hunger when the government had no bread to give them; lying for days on the battlefields between the contending lines, with broken limbs and mangled bodies, the sun pouring its deadly rays upon them, without food, their lips and throat parching with, thirst, no medical aid, and their gaping wounds festering in the intense heat.

All this they endured without murmuring, to preserve the union of states. What an example they have set for us to follow! How grandly their characters compare with those who murmur at imaginary burdens, and revile the government that those men died to save! The patient sufferings of our soldiers through those four years of war should be held up as object lessons before our American youth, for all the years to come, that their hearts may be moulded in the same patriotic love and devotion for the country's welfare.

Loyal to the Flag

Our soldiers were always loyal to their flag, and determined that the rebellion should be crushed. Amidst all the disasters of that war they never faltered for a moment in that heroic determination. When victory rested upon their banners, and the rebels were hurled back in defeat, they smiled in the confidence they possessed that right would prevail; but when defeat came, and we were pressed back with broken columns and bleeding battalions, they would turn and defiantly face a triumphant foe, and, with words strangely prophetic, declare that they would continue the struggle until the rebel flag was in the dust, and treason should lie dead at their feet. Never for a single moment would they entertain the thought of allowing the South to secede.

But it was not so at all times with our loyal men at home. There were times when disasters came so rapidly that they became discouraged, when their vision became so dimmed with disappointment that they could not see a single ray of hope. I distinctly remember passing through the State of Maine, with a shattered leg, in the darkest period of the war; I was passing from the battlefield to my home, and tarried for a few weeks with friends in one of the principal cities of the state. General Grant was pounding away at the rebels without any apparent success. Our men were perishing by thousands. Each day the telegraph wires were throbbing with new tales of woe.

England and France were giving material aid to the rebels. Our national currency was almost worthless. Great political conventions throughout the North were declaring the war a failure, and demanding the withdrawal of our soldiers from the South. Men stood on the streets and boasted of the victories their rebel friends had won, and defiantly declared that they could never be compelled to remain within the Union. The loyal men were pale and sad. Appeals came for funds to provide means of comfort for the perishing heroes, and with nervous fingers men signed their checks, without stopping to think of the princely sums they gave. When these men endeavoured to arrange and balance the ledgers, as they had been doing for years, in the long columns of figures they seemed only to see wounded, groaning, dying men—brothers and sons in the winding sheets of death. With compressed lips and unsteady steps, they turned to their homes, and within those sacred retreats they breathed the words of despair: "The sacrifice is too great"; "We shall have to let them secede"; "We cannot conquer them."

But such words were never spoken by men in the trenches; they stood firm; there was not a moment when they would listen to the thought of permitting the rebels to destroy the Union; suffering seemed to increase their loyalty to the country; amid all the horrors of those prisons in the South, where they received treatment from their captors that would bring a blush of shame to the cheeks of uncivilized warriors, they all remained loyal and true. Not a single soldier, so far as I know, entered the rebel army from one of those prisons, to escape from the horrible situation in which he was placed. My heart has been strangely moved as the survivors from those prisons have told me of the intense loyalty to the country those men exhibited when dying.

In Andersonville, the most hellish in its character of all those prison pens, where our men died by thousands, when their forms became thin and weak, and they discovered that they were about to die, they would summon their comrades, and talk about home and friends, but more about the old regiment, the flag, and the country.

One of our regiment was dying there from the effects of hunger and festering wounds, a brave, noble youth from one of our country towns; he raised his thin, shadowy hand and motioned for a comrade to come; the comrade bowed down over the wasted form of the dying hero, and as he sent tender messages of love to parents, brothers, sisters, and friends, his voice became so weak that his comrade supposed that he was dead, when suddenly he raised his thin, weak arms, and clasped them around his comrade's neck, and bringing his ear close to his cold lips, exclaimed, in a voice that sounded like a whisper from the eternal shore, "Tell the boys to fight until the rebels are whipped, and take good care of the old flag." His head dropped back upon the ground, and he was at rest.

It is said that when Hannibal was a child, his mother carried him to a heathen temple, and there placing his little hand upon the sacred altar made him, in the presence of the gods, swear allegiance to his country. Men have thought that the impressions and oath of that hour had much to do in moulding the warlike character of that great chieftain. And it would seem that the mothers of these men of whom I write must have carried them, in the days of their infancy, to our beloved temple of freedom, and there consecrated them to their country's service, and that the inspiration of that consecration made them the loyal men of whom the nation is so proud.

Bravery

Our soldiers were brave men, and faced dangers fearlessly. The nation, I fear, is forgetting those deeds of bravery too rapidly. If we could only pass along those battle lines once more, and gather up those feats of individual daring, so many of which occurred in every regiment,—deeds, which if they had been performed in the Spartan wars, or in the days of the Crusaders, or of Napoleon the First, would have been recorded on the pages of history, and would thrill the passing generations as they read. I wish we could gather up the unwritten history of the war,—the deeds that were performed by heroes whose names were never known outside the ranks where they fought, or the beloved circle of friends at home, and which, if preserved, would fill volumes.

These soldiers were as modest as they were brave, and many of them have never spoken of the wild adventures through which they passed, or of the narrow escapes, the hand-to-hand encounters which they experienced, or of the shot and shells that went tearing past them, so near that the slightest deviation from their onward course would have caused their death. These events are locked up within their own breasts, cherished as sacred reminders of God's providence in preserving their lives. But some evening, as you sit beside some maimed hero, draw him forth from his seclusion, get him to unfold that secret chapter of his life, and as he proceeds with that wonderful narrative, you will decide that I have not exaggerated when I have claimed that my comrades were brave men.

Brilliant Soldiers.

In estimating the military character of our soldiers, we must always remember that there was a great contrast between those men and the soldiers of the nations of Europe. Their soldiers are trained for war; they know but little else; it becomes natural for them to fight. An old warrior, when surrounded by his comrades who wondered at his thirst for blood, and the reckless courage that he displayed upon the battlefield, replied:

It is not my fault; it has become my nature; I have never been taught anything else but war, (and with an outburst of eloquence continued), I was born on a helmet, cradled in a buckler, soothed to sleep by the music of the war dance; and there was nothing that gave so much joy to my boyish heart as when I saw the red flames of war leap forth from the signal tower in my native village.

So, with the soldiers of other lands; they are born and reared among the scenes and associations of war, and we must expect that they will become brilliant soldiers; but our soldiers were born amid the associations of peace; they were trained in the peaceful avocations of life; and when they went forth from the farms, the stores, the mills and the mines, to shoulder the knapsack and the musket, they had not taken the first lesson in the science of war. But, notwithstanding that great disadvantage, those men made a record as brilliant as that written by the soldiers of any nation in the present century.

It has been claimed by other nations that our American people are boastful and selfish; but in relation to this subject I fear we have passed to the other extreme. When we wish to speak of some remarkably brilliant feat of arms, we usually refer to some battle fought by the armies of England, France, or Germany. But our soldiers gave us a record of our own, of which either of those nations would be justly proud.

Do we love to behold the brilliant deeds of fearless men? then let us turn to the Battle of Antietam, down on the left of our line where Burnside's men assaulted the Stone Bridge, and carried the heights beyond, or up on the right of our line, where the gallant Hooker and his equally gallant men fought in the cornfield until the ground was wet and slippery with blood; let us turn to Fredericksburgh, where our solid columns charged repeatedly upon those fatal heights, when the men in the assaulting columns knew that it was impossible to capture them; let us go anywhere along the line at Gettysburgh, and see the desperate valour displayed on the first day of the battle, by the gallant First corps, Howard's defence on Cemetery Ridge, Sickles' bloody stand in the peach orchard; or view the ragged side of Little Round Top, where Chamberlain and his regiment so distinguished themselves.

And thus, it was through every campaign; at the storming of Missionary Ridge by the army of the Southwest, or where Hooker's men climbed so far up the bold, rugged sides of Lookout Mountain that they stood above the clouds, and so that the glare of their victorious guns shone down like lightning from the skies. With what admiration should the American people look upon that brilliant record! There were many individual deeds performed in that war, any one of which will give us a military reputation throughout the world, for ages. Let us for a moment review a small number of them.

Think of the grand old frigate *Cumberland*, in Hampton Roads, shot through and through by the rebel *Merrimac*, quivering in the throes of death; refusing to surrender, and firing her last broadside of defiance with the muzzles of her guns beneath the surface of the water as she went down to a watery grave. Think of the gray-haired old admiral lashing himself in the main-top of his flag ship in advance of all his fleet, ordering on a double head of steam, and dashing ahead into the fleet of the foe, like a crazed demon, smiting destruction on every hand as he disappeared amidst the dun clouds of war. Think of the great chieftain cutting loose from his base of supplies, at the head of a magnificent army sweeping from "Atlanta to the sea," leaving a trail of desolation forty miles wide as he advanced,—a man who wrote history with the point of his sword, and put in great victories as punctuation points.

Think of the solitary horseman dashing along the turnpike, to check the retreat of a defeated army, and to snatch a glorious victory from the bloody jaws of a disastrous defeat. Think of the grim, silent man, rising from dense obscurity by the prowess of his own arm, until he commanded all our armies with such skill that an astonished world cried out, "Behold the greatest captain of the nineteenth century!" It is a brilliant record that our soldiers left as a heritage to our country, and as such, may we cherish it in gratitude and patriotic love.

THE RESULTS

Gathered from the civil war are so many and of such importance that all must be convinced of the fact that the great sacrifice of human life was not made in vain. I will enumerate a few of them.

SLAVERY

That plague-spot upon the Republic, whose existence was a source of perpetual strife, an institution that was begotten in crime, and was nursed upon the most cruel and outrageous wrongs ever perpetrated by a civilized government upon human beings, perished in the home of its friends, struck dead by the blow that it had inspired its own devotees to strike against the government. Were this the only result derived from the war, all freemen would say that it was not in vain.

State Rights

This doctrine was a legitimate offspring of slavery, and received its death-blow from the hands of our soldiers. It is almost impossible for us to believe the written history of the past, with reference to the teachings and claims of this infamous doctrine,—that the old Union was simply a confederation of sovereign states, the authority of either being superior to that of the union of them all, and any state having the right at any time to repudiate the bond of union, and the other states having no right to object. It was the most dangerous political creed that was ever taught in America, but it was gloriously shattered in the civil war. When Father Abraham took the old Union whip, and deliberately compelled the thirteen unruly children to come back into the Union, this doctrine was at a discount; it was dead, never to be successfully resurrected.

A few political "Rip Van Winkles" may now and then dolefully declaim about the sacred doctrine of State Rights, but any political party that is simple enough to embody that doctrine within its platform of principles, is doomed to defeat. Such an organisation must crumble before the ballots of intelligent freemen, as the Confederacy crumbled before the bullets of our soldiers. We rolled this heresy in its winding-sheet, and laid it to rest upon the plains of Appomattox. "Peace to its ashes," and pity for its mourners.

The New South

Is rapidly coming to the front, and the old South is passing from view. "Mason and Dixon's" line is no longer an impassable barrier, over which the nervous energy and skilful lab or of the North is not allowed to pass. That line was blotted out in blood, and when the clouds of war passed, the South with its genial climate, fertile soil, magnificent water-powers, and undeveloped mines, lay at the feet of the nation, asking with mute lips for honest labour, skilful enterprise, accumulated capital, and the inspiration of a creative genius, and all were freely given; the rugged, healthy blood of the North was breathed through the enfeebled Southern system.

A score of years only have passed, but already the South is thrilled with new life, and is marching to the front. It is capable of becoming the most wealthy and influential section of our vast national domain, and we believe that such is its destiny,—that the land drenched so profusely with the blood of our brave men will pour a vast and magnificent stream of wealth into the treasury of our nation, that will bring to it many elements of strength, and add permanence to its institutions. Without the civil war, and the bloody victories gained by the "boys in blue," the new South would have been an impossibility.

"Our Brothers in Black"

There were some facts developed in regard to the negroes in that bloody strife which appear remarkable when we consider their moral condition and the positions in which they were placed. When our white brothers in the South look in haughty disdain upon the negroes, and question as to what rights they should expect to exercise under our government, I think it would be wise for "Uncle Sam" to whisper these facts, thus developed, in the ears of his proud spirited sons. In all those eventful years no negro was ever found in a traitor's uniform. The "stars and bars" had no beauty for them; they had not forgotten the old "stars and stripes."

There were plenty of white men in the South who were willing to shoot and starve Union prisoners, but no black man was found base enough to do such work, although slavery had kept them in ignorance and degradation, although, their virtues had been debauched to gratify the passions of their owners, although the government itself had allowed them to be placed on a level with the common animal. But notwithstanding all this, beneath each black skin there was a human heart that disdained to descend to depths of infamy that would permit them to so treat their fellow creatures.

They never misused a Union prisoner, but were to them angels of mercy, aiding them in their terrible flight for life from those prison pens, giving the last crumb of bread and meat in their possession, guiding them through the trackless forests and across the bayous and rivers, concealing them by skilful devices when the hoarse deep baying of the pursuing blood-hounds came too near.

They fought heroically when marshalled under the stars and stripes, so that, when the war closed; they had nobly earned the ballot that the government placed in their hands. With deep interest and much gratitude, the old soldiers have watched their struggles and rapid development in all the elements of good citizenship since the close of the war. As these two races march beside each other in the struggle of life, we only ask and demand that those who, in their poverty, did all they could to save the nation and assist its defenders, shall not be deprived of their sacred rights by those who fought to destroy the nation, and rejoiced in the death of its soldiers. Give the "brothers in black" an equal chance with other citizens. Let the general government protect the rights of every citizen, without regard to colour or race. That is all we ask, and that we have a right to demand.

Respect for the Flag

Was a lesson faithfully taught by the Union soldiers to all sections of the country. Prior to the war it was no unusual occurrence for men to talk about destroying the American flag. If every petty grievance, whether actual or fancied, was not immediately adjusted to their satisfaction, why, the old flag must perish, but a new principle in relation to the flag was begotten in the Civil War. General John A. Dix was the first man in authority who embodied that principle in words. When his subordinate officer in the South, at the outbreak of the rebellion, sent him a telegram of inquiry as to what course he should pursue if the rebels attempted to take possession of his position, the Spartan Dix replied: "*If any man haul down the American flag, shoot him on the spot*" and the soldiers all responded, Amen.

We rather liked that doctrine, and resolved that, for the country's good, we would perpetuate it. With long lines of bristling steel, we wrote that principle upon the escutcheon of the nation. Twenty years have passed, but that writing distinctly remains; it will never be blotted out; he who runs may read it. As a result, Americans have ceased to insult the flag. This flag floats in triumph above a united and patriotic people, unto whom it is an emblem of supreme authority, before which they bow in loyal devotion and loving obedience.

Our Republic is at the Front,

Among the nations of the earth; it was placed there by the heroism of our soldiers. That Europe had no faith in the permanence of our institutions, is shown from the fact that it was almost an impossible task for us to place a small government loan in their financial markets just before the breaking out of the rebellion. Those nations always sneered at our claims to national power, and some of them eagerly loaned their assistance to the Confederates, as they attempted to destroy the Union. But all that has changed; our national securities are considered among the best in the world; and the way we are grappling with our national debt is a marvel to all financiers.

The world recognises the fact, at last, that we are a powerful people, and even England learned a lesson as she listened to the roar of our guns, and for once in her history, in the court of nations, at Geneva, acknowledged that she was in the wrong. Immigration is pouring like an infinite tide upon our shores; our population is over fifty millions of people; our resources are being developed; and our national outlook is most hopeful. All this is a direct result, gathered as the fruit of the sacrifices made by our noble soldiers. Truly, as we thus enumerate the results of the war, we understand the importance of the principles for which they fought.

Our Dead

Are not forgotten. One day of each year is devoted to the sacred duty of scattering our tears and flowers upon their graves, a service which we cheer fully perform. The little mounds in the cemeteries that we decorate are becoming more numerous each year, as our comrades are transferred from the visible to the invisible ranks. But a great portion of our dead are not in these cemeteries; their dust is in the far South, where they fell, at Antietam, Fredericksburgh, the Wilderness, and in the wild mountain gorges around Chattanooga. A mother said to me recently:

> I wish my poor boy was buried here, so that I could put the flowers on his grave, sing hymns above his ashes, and stand as a guardian over his precious dust.

I presume many others have felt the same, as they have thought that there were no flowers or music above the ashes of their sons, and no one to care for their last resting-place. But that is not the case. God has not forgotten the brave men who went down in death, to preserve the institutions of liberty and right; and while you are decorating the graves in your cemeteries, the vines are creeping over the little mounds in the South, and those beautiful flowers are blushing in all their new-born beauty, as if our kind Heavenly Father had sent his angels down to plant them above the honoured dead, while the feathered songsters in those tangled thickets are making music more divine than any ever made by human voices.

I believe those remains are guarded. Sometimes, while the great storms are raging, my thoughts have gone forth to those scenes of strife and carnage, where we buried our men by thousands in the rough, rude ditches; I have thought that I would love to stand there in the solitude and darkness, and listen. There would be the sobbing of the storm, the moanings of the wind, the rustling of the boughs; and I fancy that I should almost hear the rustle and tramp of the unseen sentinels sent down to guard the ashes of the fallen hosts. They are safe, and when the bugle-call shall sound the last reveille, they will come forth in the glorious uniforms of immortality, form their ranks upon the parade ground of eternity, and salute the great Captain of the ages.

The Survivors

Are now a numerous company; we find some in almost every circle. We have not forgotten the old experiences of army life; we remember our duties to the memory of our fallen comrades, and their suffering families who survive them; we cherish the same love for the country that we had in the days when love for country was shown by sacrifices. We have not forgotten each other. Great changes are taking place within our ranks; time is leaving his imprint. Some of our comrades are now aged men, with furrowed brows and gray hair, and we, who then were mere lads, are now sweeping on beyond the point of middle age; our numbers are growing less each year; death is thinning our ranks.

We are now an army for which there are no recruits; the tide is bearing us on; we are facing the situation as manfully as we can; we cling to each other; earth knows but few ties more sacred than these which bind us together,—relations baptised in blood. We gather in our Grand Army Halls, to fight our battles over again, to sing the old patriotic songs once more, and under that inspiration, to reform our ranks, while we "shoulder arms," and awkwardly march to the music of the fife and drum. We derive satisfaction from that.

Many of those who were not soldiers wonder why we cling to each other as we do; they are surprised to see us so harmonious, regardless of race, creeds and politics, but it does not surprise us. We shall all soon be "mustered out," and it will seem very lonesome to those who are among the last to go. I do not want to be in that relief; it will be a lonely task for the last detail to stand all alone, after the great army has passed by, and hold the few scattering picket posts until they, too, are withdrawn. But we must make the best of our situation; we are all under marching orders, and while we await the final summons, let us obtain all the information we can about the country unto which we are ordered to march, have our equipments in excellent order, and be prepared to strike tents. Dear old comrades, may we be wise unto our salvation, and come into possession of the countersign while it is possible to obtain it.

Our Reward

Is to be sufficient to repay us for all we have suffered and sacrificed for the country. As we may honestly differ upon questions which relate to the future, I will only speak of the earthly reward we shall receive. Our conscience repays us each day for all we ever endured in the service of the government It is a great satisfaction to us, as we behold our magnificent Republic, to think that, when it was in peril, when the hand of the assassin was at its throat, and it called our name, we responded by doing all in our power to deliver it from its foe. It is a grand thing to know that we are worthy of the country in which we live, and that we are permitted to leave a rich legacy to our children. Many of us may not leave to our children much worldly wealth, or high social position, but we leave them something more precious than those.

I would rather have my boy stand by my grave and say, "My father was wounded in the Wilderness, and fought with Phil. Sheridan at Five Forks, and saw Lee surrender at Appomattox," than to have him say that I was a millionaire, or a member of the United States Senate.

The country itself loves and honours us for the service we rendered it. The soldiers are coming to the front, into the positions of trust and honour. When they are worthy of those places, the people love to put them into those positions, as a reward for their patriotism. Some few complain at this, but the powerful tide of public sentiment is against them, and other things being equal, the soldier candidate for position is bound to win. The country will always honour our memory, and not forget us when we have vanished from its sight. Our graves will not be neglected when there are no Grand Army comrades to scatter their floral offerings upon them. This ceremony is to be handed from one generation to another; it is to increase in interest and solemnity as the ages advance and recede.

Perhaps we may be permitted to view these ceremonies, looking down over the ramparts, a hundred years hence. What a spectacle, aged men and women, those in the vigour of middle life, young ladies and gentlemen, the children in white apparel gathering in the cemeteries, beneath the shadow of the soldiers' monument, with grateful hearts, hymns of praise and beautiful flowers to decorate the mounds that contain the ashes of the once great army of the Republic!

Our country will be a great nation then; its resources will be well developed; it will probably contain two hundred millions of people, and be the centre of the world. But those people, standing in the midst of all that national glory and power, will turn their tearful eyes heavenward, and devoutly thank God that, away back in the days of war and peril, there were men grand enough to sacrifice everything, if by so doing, they could save the nation from an untimely end. And as we survey it all, our reward will be sufficient, and we shall exclaim to each other, *SATISFIED, SATISFIED.*

A Brief History of the 20th Maine Regiment in the American Civil War

To give the full particulars of every march, encampment, skirmish and fight in the history of the Twentieth Regiment would fill volumes, and is not within the scope of an evening's address. I ask you, therefore, to overlook any seeming omissions or too brief representation of important events.

The Twentieth Maine Infantry was the last of the three years' regiments raised in pursuance of the requisition and authority of the President of the United States, dated July 2nd, 1862. The regiment appears to have been formed from detachments of men enlisted for the Sixteenth, Seventeenth, Eighteenth and Nineteenth, and afterwards found to have been unnecessary to complete those organisations. A large proportion of the men were enlisted before the order for the formation of the Twentieth Regiment was promulgated. The authority for the organisation was as follows:

Headquarters Adjutant General's Office,
Augusta, August 7, 1862

General Order No. 26.

The Secretary of War having requested that another regiment of Infantry be organised from the enlisted men of Maine's quota of an additional 300,000 volunteers, called for by the President, the Governor and Commander-in-Chief orders and directs that all companies already enlisted for new regiments under this call, and which shall be hereafter designated, the same not necessarily comprised in the organisation of the Sixteenth, Seventeenth, Eighteenth and Nineteenth regiments of Infantry, report to Col. E. K. Harding, Asst. Q. M. General, and go into camp at the rendezvous established for this regiment (the Twentieth of Maine Volunteers) at Island Park near Portland, on or before the 13th inst., where quarters and subsistence will be provided. The organisation of this regiment will be completed forthwith.

By order of the Commander-in-Chief,
John L. Hodsdon, Adjutant General.

On the 11th of August, in pursuance of this order, squads of recruits began to arrive in camp, afterwards known as "Camp Mason," and in a few days the ranks of the Twentieth regiment were full. Adelbert Ames, of Rockland, a graduate of West Point, who had already acquired a reputation for military skill and bravery, was commissioned Colonel; Joshua L. Chamberlain, of Brewer, Professor of Modern Languages in Bowdoin College, Lieut. Colonel; and Charles D. Gilmore, of Bangor, Captain of Company C, Seventh Maine, Major.

The Twentieth was supplied with an English arm, known as the Enfield Rifle Musket, with the regulation equipments, and the uniform consisted of the usual fatigue cap, blue frock coat, with the *unu*sual dark blue trowsers.

The men having received slight instruction in the "School of the Soldier," were mustered into the service of the United States by Capt. Bartlett, 12th U. S. Infantry, on the 29th, at which time the regiment numbered 965 officers and men. On the morning of the 2nd of September, the comfortable quarters at Camp Mason were abandoned, and the regiment quietly took its departure for Boston by rail, where it embarked on the steamer *Merrimac* and sailed the next morning for Alexandria, Virginia, arriving on the afternoon of the 6th.

Sunday, the 7th, the Twentieth proceeded to Washington by steamer and occupied grounds near the arsenal. Having been assigned to Butterfield's famous "Light Brigade" of Morrell's Division, Porter's Corps, the regiment moved about sunset on the 8th, crossed Aqueduct bridge over the Potomac and marched to Fort Craig, Arlington Heights. This moonlight march of four or five miles was our first experience, and the soldier's privilege of grumbling was freely indulged. Looking back through the *vista* of years, it does not strike us as at all surprising that Col. Ames, disgusted with the conduct of his command on that occasion, should have exclaimed:

> If you can't do any better than you have tonight, you better all desert and go home!

The brigade to which the Twentieth had been assigned was composed of the Twelfth, Seventeenth and Forty-Fourth New York, Eighty-Third Pennsylvania and Sixteenth Michigan, and was then under the command of Col. Stockton of the Sixteenth.

September 12th the brigade crossed the Potomac to Georgetown and started on the forced march to Antietam. That night, after a march of sixteen miles, scarcely a corporal's guard of the Twentieth stacked arms when the brigade went into camp. The stragglers, however, came up in a few hours and the regiment marched with full ranks the next morning. On that day a march of twenty-four miles was made, and, during the day, a majority heard the distant roar of battle for the first time. The regiment marched through Frederick on the morning of the 15th and bivouacked that night at Middletown, arriving near Sharpsburg the next evening. The next morning the Twentieth moved forward with the brigade and took a position in reserve near the centre, east of Antietam Creek.

During the afternoon of the 17th our brigade and another were ordered to the right to support troops in that quarter. The emergency having passed the Twentieth returned to the former position, and the men lay on their arms that night. The next morning the brigade took up a position in the rear of Burnside, on the left. The infantry of Porter's corps took no active part in the Battle of Antietam, but the position it held during that eventful day was a most important one.

On the 19th the command moved forward through Sharpsburg to Shepherdstown Ford, where the main body of the rebel army had crossed the Potomac. The next morning Morrell's division and a portion of Sykes' made an attempt to cross over and drive the enemy from their position. Sykes' division and the first and second brigades of our division, with a portion of the third, including the Twentieth, had crossed and pushed out a short distance, when the enemy developed such force that a retreat was ordered. During the recrossing of the ford under a sharp and severe fire from the rebels, who now lined the bank, the Twentieth was kept in excellent order and discipline, and the conduct of the regiment, for the first time under fire, was noticed and much praised. As soon as the regiment recrossed it was formed along the canal bank, and kept up a hot fire with the enemy across the river.

The Twentieth being a portion of the force left to guard the upper Potomac, remained near Shepherdstown three weeks. On the 7th of October the brigade moved to the Iron Works, near the mouth of Antietam Creek, where it remained till the 30th. Colonel Ames now found an opportunity to give the regiment a taste of discipline and drill which it so much needed. Company and battalion drill, dress parade and inspection kept the men from idleness, and the line officers were obliged to apply themselves to the study of tactics until they become proficient in the manual of arms and in all the evolutions of the company and battalion. Col. Ames was an educated soldier and a rigid disciplinarian, and although at times his orders were severe in the extreme, yet the soldierly bearing of the regiment soon became conspicuous, and without question much of the fame which the Twentieth Maine afterwards achieved, was due to the sense of subordination and attention to duty, instilled by the teachings of its first commander.

The hardships to which the men had been exposed, the forced march, the change of climate and above all the failure to supply the regiment with shelter tents, now began to show its results in the long list of sick borne upon the rolls. It is almost incredible but nevertheless true, that, when the advance was made into Virginia from Antietam, the Twentieth sent away three hundred invalids, and many of those who remained on duty were reduced to a condition from which they did not recover for months.

October 30th the regiment broke camp and marched in the direction of Harper's Ferry. The next day the Potomac and Shenandoah were crossed, and the column having wound around the base of Loudon Heights, continued the march down Loudon Valley. While the army was moving south through this beautiful valley, the enemy was moving up the Shenandoah on the other side of the Blue Ridge. November 2nd an advance corps had a fight with them at Snicker's Gap, and that night we camped near a village with the euphonious name of "Snickersville." On the 6th, marched through Middleburg, where eight months later the Twentieth and the Third Brigade had a spirited brush with the enemy.

The next day the march was interrupted by a snow storm, and the troops camped in the woods near White Plains. November 9th, we went into camp at Warrenton and remained till the 17th, during which time Gen. McClellan was superseded by Burnside, and a general reorganisation of the army followed. Continuing the march, the Acquia Creek Railroad was reached on the 24th, at a point three miles from Fredericksburg, afterwards well-known to you as "Stoneman's Switch," where the regiment settled down to the monotony of camp and picket duty for three weeks.

At daylight on the morning of December 11, we marched in the direction of Fredericksburg, but did not cross the river till 2 o'clock on the afternoon of the 13th. Passing through the town under a terrible fire of shot, shell and railroad iron, the Twentieth formed and advanced across the field, while the enemy poured upon them a terrific fire of musketry and artillery. With Colonel Ames gallantly leading in advance of the colours, the line moved in admirable order over fences and obstructions, through the ranks of troops lying down, until the extreme front was reached. Relieving those already engaged, Colonel Ames placed his men as much under cover as possible, and held his position for thirty-six hours, constantly under fire.

During the night of the 14th the brigade was withdrawn from the front and bivouacked on the pavements of the city. The next night they were again moved to the front, and it soon became known that the movement was designed to cover the retreat of the army. The men were kept in position until the troops were all over, when they too approached the pontoons, and just at dawn of day reached the north bank in safety. The small loss which the Twentieth suffered at Fredericksburg may be attributed largely to the skilful manner in which the regiment was handled by Colonel Ames.

With weary steps and thankful hearts, the Twentieth Maine found its way through mud and rain to their old campground and went into winter quarters. At Fredericksburg many of the men exchanged their Enfield for Springfield rifles, and in a short time the whole regiment was supplied with those muskets.

The duties of camp and picketing a few miles to the rear, were interrupted December 30th by a reconnoissance to Richard's Ford, and the celebrated "Mad March" January 24th, 1863. Towards spring by an egregious blunder, the men were inoculated with smallpox, and on that account the regiment was moved on the 22nd of April to isolated camp. On the 27th the Fifth Corps moved to Chancellorsville, and Colonel Ames volunteered as an aid on the staff of Gen. Meade. May 3rd the Twentieth was ordered to Banks' Ford to guard the telegraph, returning to its former camp after the battle.

May 21st the regiment moved with the brigade three miles to the right, and went into a pleasant camp. Colonel Ames having been promoted to Brigadier General, the command of the Twentieth devolved upon Lieut. Col. Chamberlain, who was soon after commissioned Colonel. About this time Col. Strong Vincent of the Eighty-Third replaced Col. Stockton in the command of the brigade. Lieut. J. M. Brown, the efficient adjutant of the Twentieth, was promoted to Captain and A. A. G. The Second Maine Regiment having been mustered out, one hundred and twenty-five men, who had enlisted for three years, were transferred to the Twentieth, and joined the regiment at this camp on the 23rd. These men expected to be discharged with their regiment and at first refused duty, but finally accepted the situation and became a valuable acquisition to the command.

May 28th the brigade was ordered to guard the fords of the Rappahannock, the position of the Twentieth being at United States Ford. June 5th another move was made to Ellis Ford. In a few days it became known that the army of Lee was moving north, and the Army of the Potomac entered upon those movements which culminated in the Battle of Gettysburg. At dark on the 13th the Twentieth broke camp and joined the brigade at Morrisville, marching the next day to Catlett's Station. The day following, you will remember as one of the hottest days of your experience. The regiment marched to Manassas Junction. Sunstrokes were frequent, and the men were weary, thirsty and footsore when they bivouacked that night

June 17th the column marched to Gum Springs, and on the 19th to Aldie, where the cavalry had fought and driven back the rebels under Hampton and Stewart. The Third Brigade, having been selected to support the cavalry in a further advance, was put in motion at 3 o'clock on the morning of the 21st and marched to Middleburg, where the cavalry was already advancing. The force of the enemy was two brigades of cavalry supported artillery, which the Third brigade was mainly instrumental in driving from one position to another, behind stone walls and creeks for some six miles.

During this running fight of ten hours duration, the Twentieth lost one man killed, and one officer and seven men wounded. The next day the brigade returned to its former camp at Aldie. During this movement the Twentieth was commanded by Lieut. Col. Connor of the Forty-Fourth New York, Colonel Chamberlain being sick from a partial sunstroke.

The Twentieth remained at Aldie until June 25th, when it marched through Leesburg to the Potomac and crossed at Edwards' Ferry. Continuing the march on the following day, it forded the Monocacy River and camped within two miles of Frederick for two days. At this time Gen. Meade was made commander of the Army of the Potomac, and Gen. Sykes succeeded to the command of the Fifth Corps. On the 29th the march was resumed through Frederick to Unionville.

On the last day of June, a movement was made by a portion of the Fifth Corps to intercept the enemy or ascertain his position. The

Third Brigade took the advance, and marched with skirmishers in front during the afternoon, and camped that night about three miles from the Pennsylvania line. On the 1st of July, having crossed the state line amid great enthusiasm, the column pressed on and late that afternoon reached Hanover. Halting two hours, the march was continued by moonlight, the music of the bands mingling with the cheers of the soldiers. At midnight the exhausted troops went into camp, after a march of thirty-two miles.

At daylight on the morning of the 2nd the troops were again in motion, and at an early hour arrived within supporting distance of the forces engaged at Gettysburg. At four o'clock in the afternoon the Third Brigade was hurried a mile or more to the left under a heavy artillery fire, and the Twentieth, moving "on the right by file into line," took position in the woods on the crest of a small hill, now known as "Little Round Top." the position held by the Twentieth was the extreme left of the Union line, and of great importance.

Company B. was sent forward as skirmishers, but had not deployed when brisk firing commenced on the right, and a large force of the enemy was soon seen marching rapidly to the left through the ravine in our front. So rapid were their movements that the skirmishers were cut off, and were obliged to secrete themselves behind a stone wall. To avoid being flanked, Colonel Chamberlain moved his left wing to the left and rear, making nearly a right angle at the collars. This disposition had scarcely been made when the enemy fell upon the left with great fury.

The struggle was desperate, now one party and now the other holding the ground. The ammunition of the Twentieth was nearly expended when the enemy gave way. The men had scarcely time to collect cartridges from the boxes of the dead and wounded before the assault was renewed apparently by fresh troops. The Twentieth had now lost nearly half its number and began to waver. At this moment Col. Chamberlain ordered the charge. Advancing on the run the Twentieth completely routed the enemy and at the opportune moment the skirmishers arose from behind the stone wall and gave them a volley. Thinking themselves surrounded large numbers threw down their arms and surrendered.

After driving the enemy nearly half a mile the regiment returned to its old position. Having received a supply of ammunition the Twentieth supported by two regiments of Pennsylvania reserves, advanced up the steep and rocky sides of Big Round Top and secured a position which they held during the night with the aid of the Eighty-Third which came up later. The Twentieth went into the fight with 358 muskets and captured 308 prisoners. The regiment lost 32 killed, 97 wounded and 6 taken prisoners on the skirmish line in the night. Detachment's sent out to bury the dead counted in front of the position occupied by the Twentieth on Little Round Top fifty rebel dead and it is estimated that the regiment killed and wounded at least 300 of the enemy. (*Two Views of Little Round Top: a Pivotal Engagement During the Battle of Gettysburg, July 1st-3rd, 1863 During the American Civil War* by Boyd Vincent & Oliver W Norton is also published by Leonaur).

The colours of the regiment were carried by Sergt. Tozier and although exposed on the angle of the line the sergeant and two of the four guards escaped without even a scratch. The splendid fighting qualities developed by the Twentieth Maine on the 2nd day of July, gave it a brilliant reputation throughout the army and gained for Joshua L. Chamberlain the well-deserved title of "Hero of Round Top."

On the morning of the 3rd the brigade was relieved and. moved to the rear of the left centre and lay in reserve during the day. At two o'clock in the afternoon the enemy open upon our lines the most terrific artillery fire ever heard in battle. For two hours the earth trembled and the air was filled with shot and shell.

Then shook the hills, with thunder riven
And louder than the bolts of heaven,
Far flashed the red artillery.

During the night of the 4th Lee's army retreated and towards the close of the next day we were again moving south. Nothing of importance occurred except hard marching through rain and mud till the 10th when Company E. had two men killed and six captured in a skirmish near Fair Play, Maryland. During the night of the 13th the enemy made its escape across the Potomac and the expected battle did not occur. The next day the Fifth corps moved to Williamsport and on the 15th crossed the Potomac at Berlin and encamped at Lovettsville eight miles south of the river.

The march was continued down the valley to the 23rd when our division relieved the Third corps at Manassas Gap. The next morning the whole division was drawn up in line of battle and word was passed along the lines that the heights in front were to be taken at all hazards. Wapping Heights proved to be the most difficult place over which troops ever advanced in line of battle. Up the almost perpendicular hill, through woods and tangled underbrush, the men toiled—and picked blackberries—expecting the enemy to open fire at every step.

The summit was finally reached but the enemy had fled. The magnificent view of the Shenandoah valley obtained from the heights partially repaid the men for the ascent. The "recall" was sounded and the line faced about and marched two miles to the rear. On the 25th the march was resumed, and on the 7th of August the regiment arrived at Beverly Ford, which the brigade guarded till the 16th of September. The command of the brigade having devolved upon Col. Chamberlain by the promotion of Col. Rice, Lieut. Col. Gilmore assumed command of the Twentieth.

September 16th the army advanced to Culpepper where it remained in camp till October 10th, when the Fifth Corps moved to Raccoon Ford on the Rapidan, out finding no enemy returned to camp at night. The next day the enemy having threatened our right flank, the army began to fall back to preserve its line of communication. That night we camped at Beverly Ford. In the morning we retraced our steps, crossed the river, advanced nearly to Brandy Station and bivouacked for the night. It was now ascertained that Lee was moving rapidly around our right and at one o'clock on the morning of the 13th the race for Centreville began.

That night we camped at Catlett's Station having marched twenty-five miles. The bugle sounded "reveille" at an early hour the next morning and the march was resumed. Near Bristoe Station the division halted an hour for coffee and "hard tack" which had hardly been disposed of when a rebel battery opened upon us from the woods. The division pulled out hurriedly and the march from this point to Manassas was rapid and the files were well closed up.

Arriving at Manassas, the corps was formed in line of battle with batteries in position and remained till late in the afternoon listening to the roar of battle some two miles south where the Second corps under Warren was engaged—and all the while we were wondering why we had hurried away from them. About the time that Warren had whipped Hill the Fifth corps was started on the double quick to his assistance. At nine o'clock the corps moved towards Bull Run which we crossed at half past two the next morning, having been on foot twenty-four hours and marched thirty-two miles.

From the 15th to the 20th the regiment oscillated between Centreville and Fairfax. The enemy in the meantime had destroyed the Orange and Alexandria Railroad and begun to fall back to his old quarters across the Rapidan. As fast as the road could be repaired the Army of the Potomac followed. On the morning of Nov. 7th, the Twentieth, now under the command of Major Ellis Spear, was in camp at Three Mile Station. The Rappahannock River at Rappahannock Station was held by the rebel brigades of Hoke and Hayes which it was now determined to attack.

Eighty men under Capt. Morrill were detailed from the Twentieth for the skirmish line which in the advance had gained a position behind the railroad embankment, when the Sixth Corps moved to the attack on the right. Seeing the gallant advance of the line in that direction Capt. Morrill's party dashed forward with the Sixth Maine Regiment and entered the works simultaneously with them. The Twentieth lost in this brilliant affair one man killed and seven wounded.

The next day the regiment crossed the Rappahannock at Kelly's Fold and encamped two miles from the river where occurred the "hard tack" drill. Towards evening on the ninth we recrossed the river and passed a cold and uncomfortable night near the ford.

About this time Col. Hayes of the 18th Massachusetts took command of the brigade. On the 10th we crossed the river again and at sunrise on the 26th marched to the Rapidan which was crossed and the march continued with frequent halts till eight o'clock at night. On the 29th our advance was made to Mine Run where the brigade took a position under a brisk fire from the enemy's lines which were not more than three hundred yards distant. We remained before the works of the enemy until the night of Dec. 2nd when we folded our tents like the Arabs and silently stole away, the Third Brigade forming the rear guard.

Dec. 4th the Twentieth went into camp at Rappahannock Station for the purpose of guarding the railroad bridge during the winter. The rifle pits which had been captured a month before and which had become the last ditch for many rebel dead, were graded off and comfortable quarters erected thereon. The officers, lucky souls, sent to Maine for their wives and the rank and file contented themselves with an occasional furlough. Here was spent the gayest winter in the history of the Twentieth.

This old battle flag in which we naturally feel so much pride, had now become tattered and torn and a new set of colours were procured. The old flag was presented to General Ames and delivered to him in Rockland while on leave of absence that winter. You remember, comrades, how you stood by that flag at Antietam and Shepherdstown;

how you planted it on Little Round Top and defended it through the fierce assaults of that memorable day; and you remember too how:

> *In the brilliant glare of the summer air,*
> *With a brisk breeze around it creeping.*
> *Newly bright through the glistening light.*
> *The flag went grandly sweeping:*
> *Gleaming and bold were its braids of gold.*
> *And flashed in the sun-ray's kissing;*
> *Red, white, and blue were of deepest hue,*
> *And none of the stars were missing.*

Previous to the opening of the campaign of 1864 a reorganisation of the army took place. The old First Brigade of our division was broken up and the Hundred-and-Eighteenth Pennsylvania and the Eighteenth Massachusetts joined the Third Brigade. Gen. Warren was placed in command of the Fifth Corps, Gen. Griffin retained the First Division and Gen. Bartlett took the Third Brigade. On the first day of May the winter quarters of the Twentieth at Rappahannock were broken up and the brigade marched across the river to a camp east of Brandy Station, where the Fifth Corps, now composed of thirty thousand men, was concentrating.

On the morning of the 4th the regiment with about three hundred rifles, under command of Major Spear, crossed the Rapidan at Germania Ford, and entered upon those movements known as the battles of the "Wilderness," the memory of which appears to those who took part in those sanguinary conflicts, more like a dreadful nightmare than a reality. That night the brigade bivouacked on the Orange and Fredericksburg turnpike near the old Wilderness Tavern. On the morning of the 5th, the army was extended along the roads in the densest portion of the Wilderness and the enemy were soon found to be rapidly advancing for the purpose of crushing our line before it could be concentrated.

Upon our division devolved the duty of engaging the attention of the enemy until the rest of the army could get into position. The Third Brigade which occupied the centre, was formed in two lines, the Twentieth being in the second line. When the order was given to advance all three brigades started on the double-quick with a yell, driving the enemy in confusion back upon his reserves. Finding the Sixth Corps had failed to connect on the right, the First Brigade fell back while the Third continued to advance. The enemy quickly took advantage of this and opened a murderous fire on our right from across the road.

At the same time the Second Brigade on the left was being driven back by a heavy force. The Third Brigade was now alone with both flanks exposed. In the confusion each commander acted on his own judgment and a large part of the brigade broke for the rear on the run. At length the order was given to retire. The Twentieth was the last to leave the field bringing off with them a large squad of prisoners and in the retreat, was obliged to make a detour to the left to avoid a force of the enemy which held the open field across which the line had first charged. The breast works built in the morning were finally reached and the line re-established.

The contest was short but the regiment lost about ninety men killed wounded and missing, among them Capt. Morrill of Company B. severely wounded in the face. Nearly all the prisoners were wounded and taken by the skirmish line in our rear. At dawn of the 6th the regiment moved out to the open field where it fought the day before and on the right of the road, and established a skirmish line in the opening with the main part of the regiment in the edge of the woods, sheltered by the brow of a hill, where it lay all day under fire, losing two men killed and ten wounded. Towards night an attack upon the Sixth Corps swept it back until the tiring appeared to be in the rear and there begun to be quite a panic among the regiments of our division but the Twentieth stood firm until the fighting was over when the brigade was ordered back into breastworks.

At nine o'clock the next morning the Twentieth and Hundred-and-Eighteenth were ordered to charge into the woods in front and develop the enemy's strength. The skirmishers were driven in at a run until the line came in sight of the enemy's old position when he opened with a battery which a larger force could have carried, but with two regiments it was impossible. It was evident, however, the main body of the enemy had withdrawn and our force retired a short distance where a skirmish line was deployed and the Twentieth placed in support. In this movement the regiment lost thirteen killed and wounded.

All were brought off except Lieut. F. W. Lane, Company B. who was struck in the head by a piece of shell and taken prisoner. He died in a rebel hospital a few days later. Lieut. J. M. Sherwood was severely wounded and died that night. At dark the army began to move towards Spotsylvania and the Twentieth and Hundred-and-Eighteenth remained on the line where they had spent the day as a part of the rear guard of the corps. At midnight they silently withdrew and followed the corps.

Towards noon of the 8th as they approached Spotsylvania there was cannonading at the front and they then heard of the morning's battle in which the Third Brigade had suffered so terribly. The regiment had halted for breakfast when they were ordered to the front and placed temporarily in Crawford's division, supporting a skirmish line in front of the enemy's position at Laurel Hill. The regiment changed positions several times and during the afternoon was subjected to a severe shelling but had only one man wounded. At four o'clock the Twentieth was allowed to go a short distance to the rear to cook hard tack and make coffee—the first coffee the men had had for three days.

At half past six they went to the front again and were placed in the third line for an attack on the enemy's position. The third line advanced up the hill and lay down until support should be needed. At dark the enemy charged. The lines in front of the Twentieth divided and fell back to right and left and the enemy came suddenly upon the third line, causing the regiment on the left to retreat in confusion and forcing the Twentieth back about two rods. Then ensued a desperate hand-to-hand tight in the darkness. Friend could hardly be distinguished from foe; men fought single combats; revolvers came into play and officers found their swords for once useful.

The regiment took about eighty prisoners and lost six killed, fifteen wounded and two missing. Capt. W. W. Morrill was killed while cheering on his men and Lieutenants Melcher and Prince were wounded. Fighting ceased about nine o'clock but the regiment remained in the same position till morning when it rejoined the brigade. During the night troops in the rear threw out pickets and refused to believe that any Union force was so far to the front. The conduct of the officers and men of the Twentieth on this occasion was worthy of all praise.

During the 9th the regiment obtained rest for the first time since crossing the Rapidan. About five o'clock in the afternoon the brigade supported an attack in which the enemy were driven back. Towards the evening of the 10th the First and Third Brigades went to the front and prepared to charge in three lines upon the enemy's works, but to the great relief of all concerned the movement was abandoned. This was a lucky day for the Twentieth. During the 11th the brigade lay in reserve, exposed to the fire of artillery and musketry from the front. On the 12th the command went to the left and prepared for another charge but Gen. Griffin revoked the order.

The Twentieth moved to the left at ten o'clock on the evening of the 13th and arrived in front of the enemy at Spotsylvania Court House at five o'clock the next morning, having marched all night in mud, rain and darkness. The Twentieth remained in front of Spotsylvania from the 14th to the 20th, losing four men killed. On the 21st another left flank movement began and the next day the brigade was engaged in a skirmish with the enemy. On the 23rd our division reached the North Anna River at Jericho Ford and at once commenced crossing. The Twentieth forded the stream with the brigade and at six o'clock that afternoon assisted in the repulse of the sudden attack on Sweitzer's Brigade.

In this action Major Spear, commanding the regiment, was slightly wounded. The night was spent in throwing up breast works behind which the regiment lay till five p.m. The next day when it moved to the right and front about a mile and bivouacked near the Virginia Central Railroad. On the 25th the column moved down the railroad and found the enemy strongly posted at Noell's Station. Breast works were thrown up for self-protection and for two days a portion of the division was engaged in tearing up the railroad. During the heavy picket firing on the 26th the Twentieth had three men wounded.

At dark the division withdrew from the front and marched with short intervals of rest till six o'clock the next afternoon. It was a hard march through a finely cultivated country which had never before been visited by the desolation of war. That night for the first time in more than three weeks the men slept without an apprehension of danger from any quarter. For twenty-two days the regiment had been almost constantly under fire, and the men who had survived the terrible ordeal wondered how they escaped unscathed.

The Pemunkey River was crossed at Hanover Ferry and the march continued without interruption until the 30th, when still advancing heavy skirmishing occurred and the line of entrenchments covering the approaches to Richmond was reached. On the first day of June the enemy charged our line and was driven back. On the 3rd the Twentieth participated in the fight at Bethesda church, losing two men killed, one officer, Adjutant Donnell, and twenty-three men wounded. The brigade remained in this position till the night of the 5th when it was relieved by the Ninth Corps and the Fifth Corps lay in reserve till the 12th.

The regiment moved on the night of the 12th and crossed the

Chickahominy early the next morning. At nine o'clock on the morning of the 16th the Twentieth crossed the James River on a steam transport and halted a mile from the river, the Fifth Corps still being in reserve and the last to cross over. On the morning of the 18th the Fifth Corps moved to the front and was received with a heavy fire. The Third Brigade being in the centre of the division was somewhat concealed by woods through which they advanced to an open field where they halted and commenced throwing up breast works.

In the meantime, the Second Brigade had gained a position close up to the enemy's lines and the First Brigade lead by our Colonel Chamberlain had made a charge in which its commander fell severely wounded. For gallant conduct on this occasion Colonel Chamberlain was made a Brigadier General on the field by Gen. Grant—the only instance of the kind in the history of the war.

From this time till the 15th of August, the Twentieth occupied works in front of Petersburg in close proximity to the enemy and generally under fire. These works were gradually strengthened and completed, bomb-proofs were constructed and vast covered passages were excavated in every direction. Every means were taken to provide protection from the mortar batteries and sharpshooters of the enemy but without success. On the 22nd of June Capt. Samuel T. Keene was killed by a sharpshooter, and the regiment lost three men killed and several wounded during their occupation of the works. July 30th the Twentieth from their position had a fine view of the grand explosion of the mine and the grand failure which followed.

Early on the morning of Aug. 15th the brigade was relieved by other troops and encamped in the rear. On the 18th marched to the Weldon Railroad which was struck about six miles from Petersburg and possession taken without opposition. That afternoon the enemy made an attack which was repulsed by the Second and Third Divisions. The next day another attack in full force was made and the Third Brigade went up to the right on the double-quick but were not needed. Sunday the 21st, in the morning while the regiment was packing up for a move, the picket line was driven in followed by the rebels charging in several lines, supported by vigorous shelling from their batteries.

The assault extended some distance to the right but their whole line was repulsed with heavy loss, our division capturing 38 officers, 300 men and four battle flags. The Twentieth held a splendid position, their fire enfilading the enemy completely. It was a smart fight and the victory though signal was a bloodless one for the Twentieth.

Sept. 30th the division moved from the Weldon Railroad with the Third Brigade in advance, and found the enemy entrenched at Peeble's Farm. The works consisted of a small square fort flanked by strong lines of breast works. After some skirmishing the brigade charged across the open field in the face of a terrible fire of musketry and canister and captured the works with one piece of artillery and seventy-one prisoners. The gun, limber, six horses and two prisoners were secured by Lieut. A. E. Fernald of the Twentieth and an officer of the 32nd Massachusetts while the rebels were trying to run it off.

A division of the Ninth Corps then took the advance and being attacked just before dark were driven back in confusion. Our division was ordered to the front to check the enemy and after one of the fiercest fights of the campaign they were repulsed and Griffin's Division, and in particular the old Third Brigade, again covered themselves with glory. The Twentieth lost during the day one officer, Capt. Weston H. Keene, and six men killed and Capt. H. F. Sidelinger, Lieut. Alden Miller and fifty men wounded. The brigade commander being injured just before the assault. Major Spear, the only field officer in the brigade, took command, and the Twentieth passed into the hands of Capt. A. W. Clark of Company E.

On the 2nd of October the Twentieth moved to the front and threw up earth works where they remained until the 20th when the regiment took part in a reconnoisance to Hatcher's Run. The next day the troops returned to the works, the Twentieth acting as rear guard and losing one man killed and two wounded. Nov. 8th, Lieut. Col. Gilmore returned and took command and on the 5th of December the corps was relieved and moved to the rear on the Jerusalem Plank Road. The next day the corps moved out for a raid on the Weldon Railroad which continued to be used by the rebels as far as Stony Creek Station. About twenty miles of the road was destroyed and the corps returned to camp on the Plank Road Dec. 12th. This expedition you will all remember as the time when the Fifth Corps got gloriously drunk on "apple jack."

The regiment now supposed that winter quarters had been reached and both officers and men worked like beavers in the erection of comfortable huts many of which were quite elaborate. Major Spear and eight men went to Maine on recruiting service Jan. 15th 1865. Feb. 5th the regiment moved with the corps to Hatcher's Run and participated the next day in a second fight in the vicinity of that historic stream with slight loss. After the engagement the Twentieth went into camp at that place.

March 13th, Lieut. Col. Gilmore having resigned. Major Ellis Spear was commissioned Colonel, Capt. Walter G. Morrill, Lieut. Colonel and Capt. Atherton W. Clark, Major. About the same time a special order from the War Department made Charles D. Gilmore full Colonel and in consequence Maj. Spear could not be mustered. Lieut. Col. Morrill assumed command of the regiment and Major Spear was ordered on duty at Corps Headquarters.

The final campaign of the war was now about to open. On the 29th of March the Twentieth moved across the run and supported Chamberlain's brigade in the action on the Quaker Road. The skirmish the next day resulted in the possession of the Boydton Road. On the 31st the regiment had a hand in the action at Gravelly Run having several wounded, among the m Lieut. J. H. Stanwood, commanding Company E.

April 1st the Fifth Corps was ordered to report to Gen. Sheridan and acted as a sort of foot cavalry, if I may be permitted to use the expression, during the remainder of the campaign. On that day the Twentieth joined in the second attack on Five Forks and were among the first to gain the works, capturing one battle flag and a large number of prisoners.

Then followed the evacuation of Richmond and the pursuit in which the cavalry and the Fifth Corps by their rapid movements sealed the fate of Lee's army and when, on the 9th of April, the white flag of truce came over the field it was to the division bearing the red Maltese cross that it came. When the terms of surrender had been arranged Gen. J. L. Chamberlain, who received his first baptism of fire while an officer of the Twentieth Maine, was designated to command the parade before which the troops stacked their arras and colours and on the 12th the same grand old division was drawn up with our Third Brigade in the main line to witness the last movement of the Confederate Army of Northern Virginia.

The regiment arrived at Arlington Heights May 12th and participated in the great review on the 23rd. Col. Gilmore resigned on the 29th and Major Spear was mustered as Colonel and Capt. A. W. Clark as Major. Col. Spear remained on detached duty. On the 4th of June 1865, the veterans of the Twentieth were mustered out of the service and started for Maine the day following under the command of Lieut. Col. Morrill, arriving in Portland on the 8th

When the regiment left Washington the recruits of the Twentieth were consolidated with those of the Sixteenth and First Sharpshooters. This organisation was known as the Twentieth Maine and remained in the service till July 16th.

ALSO FROM LEONAUR
AVAILABLE IN SOFTCOVER OR HARDCOVER WITH DUST JACKET

THE 9TH—THE KING'S (LIVERPOOL REGIMENT) IN THE GREAT WAR 1914 - 1918 by Enos H. G. Roberts—Mersey to mud—war and Liverpool men.

THE GAMBARDIER by Mark Severn—The experiences of a battery of Heavy artillery on the Western Front during the First World War.

FROM MESSINES TO THIRD YPRES by Thomas Floyd—A personal account of the First World War on the Western front by a 2/5th Lancashire Fusilier.

THE IRISH GUARDS IN THE GREAT WAR - VOLUME 1 by Rudyard Kipling—Edited and Compiled from Their Diaries and Papers—The First Battalion.

THE IRISH GUARDS IN THE GREAT WAR - VOLUME 1 by Rudyard Kipling—Edited and Compiled from Their Diaries and Papers—The Second Battalion.

ARMOURED CARS IN EDEN by K. Roosevelt—An American President's son serving in Rolls Royce armoured cars with the British in Mesopatamia & with the American Artillery in France during the First World War.

CHASSEUR OF 1914 by Marcel Dupont—Experiences of the twilight of the French Light Cavalry by a young officer during the early battles of the great war in Europe.

TROOP HORSE & TRENCH by R.A. Lloyd—The experiences of a British Lifeguardsman of the household cavalry fighting on the western front during the First World War 1914-18.

THE EAST AFRICAN MOUNTED RIFLES by C.J. Wilson—Experiences of the campaign in the East African bush during the First World War.

THE LONG PATROL by George Berrie—A Novel of Light Horsemen from Gallipoli to the Palestine campaign of the First World War.

THE FIGHTING CAMELIERS by Frank Reid—The exploits of the Imperial Camel Corps in the desert and Palestine campaigns of the First World War.

STEEL CHARIOTS IN THE DESERT by S. C. Rolls—The first world war experiences of a Rolls Royce armoured car driver with the Duke of Westminster in Libya and in Arabia with T.E. Lawrence.

WITH THE IMPERIAL CAMEL CORPS IN THE GREAT WAR by Geoffrey Inchbald—The story of a serving officer with the British 2nd battalion against the Senussi and during the Palestine campaign.

AVAILABLE ONLINE AT **www.leonaur.com**
AND FROM ALL GOOD BOOK STORES

ALSO FROM LEONAUR
AVAILABLE IN SOFTCOVER OR HARDCOVER WITH DUST JACKET

ZULU:1879 *by D.C.F. Moodie & the Leonaur Editors*—The Anglo-Zulu War of 1879 from contemporary sources: First Hand Accounts, Interviews, Dispatches, Official Documents & Newspaper Reports.

THE RED DRAGOON *by W.J. Adams*—With the 7th Dragoon Guards in the Cape of Good Hope against the Boers & the Kaffir tribes during the 'war of the axe' 1843-48'.

THE RECOLLECTIONS OF SKINNER OF SKINNER'S HORSE *by James Skinner*—James Skinner and his 'Yellow Boys' Irregular cavalry in the wars of India between the British, Mahratta, Rajput, Mogul, Sikh & Pindarree Forces.

A CAVALRY OFFICER DURING THE SEPOY REVOLT *by A. R. D. Mackenzie*—Experiences with the 3rd Bengal Light Cavalry, the Guides and Sikh Irregular Cavalry from the outbreak to Delhi and Lucknow.

A NORFOLK SOLDIER IN THE FIRST SIKH WAR *by J W Baldwin*—Experiences of a private of H.M. 9th Regiment of Foot in the battles for the Punjab, India 1845-6.

TOMMY ATKINS' WAR STORIES: 14 FIRST HAND ACCOUNTS—Fourteen first hand accounts from the ranks of the British Army during Queen Victoria's Empire.

THE WATERLOO LETTERS *by H. T. Siborne*—Accounts of the Battle by British Officers for its Foremost Historian.

NEY: GENERAL OF CAVALRY VOLUME 1—1769-1799 *by Antoine Bulos*—The Early Career of a Marshal of the First Empire.

NEY: MARSHAL OF FRANCE VOLUME 2—1799-1805 *by Antoine Bulos*—The Early Career of a Marshal of the First Empire.

AIDE-DE-CAMP TO NAPOLEON *by Philippe-Paul de Ségur*—For anyone interested in the Napoleonic Wars this book, written by one who was intimate with the strategies and machinations of the Emperor, will be essential reading.

TWILIGHT OF EMPIRE *by Sir Thomas Ussher & Sir George Cockburn*—Two accounts of Napoleon's Journeys in Exile to Elba and St. Helena: Narrative of Events by Sir Thomas Ussher & Napoleon's Last Voyage: Extract of a diary by Sir George Cockburn.

PRIVATE WHEELER *by William Wheeler*—The letters of a soldier of the 51st Light Infantry during the Peninsular War & at Waterloo.

AVAILABLE ONLINE AT www.leonaur.com
AND FROM ALL GOOD BOOK STORES

www.ingramcontent.com/pod-product-compliance
Lightning Source LLC
Chambersburg PA
CBHW031625160426
43196CB00006B/282